Theorizing Feminism

Theorizing Feminism

A Cross-Cultural Exploration

Chandrakala Padia

RAWAT PUBLICATIONS

Jaipur • New Delhi • Bangalore • Guwahati • Kolkata

ISBN 978-81-316-0430-4

Reprinted, 2018

Published by
Prem Rawat for **Rawat Publications**
Satyam Apts., Sector 3, Jawahar Nagar, Jaipur 302 004 (India)
Phone: 0141 265 1748/7006 Fax: 0141 265 1748
E-mail: info@rawatbooks.com
Website: www.rawatbooks.com

New Delhi Office
4858/24, Ansari Road, Daryaganj, New Delhi 110 002
Phone: 011 2326 3290

Also at *Bangalore, Guwahati* and *Kolkata*

Typeset by Rawat Computers, Jaipur
Printed at Nice Printing Press, New Delhi

To my son,
Abhishek
for his unfailing love and support
amidst all the turmoils in my life.

Contents

Acknowledgement

The present work is the result of my concern and involvement with women's issues for more than three decades. I have been perplexed to see how the entire academic fraternity is fraught with gender biases deeply entrenched in patriarchal values and logocentrism. Feminism has contributed a lot in liberating academia from such gendered notions and theories, and thereby providing legitimacy and authenticity to the disciplines of humanities and social sciences. The present work is a modest attempt to highlight the contribution of all those feminist thinkers who have enriched these disciplines by their penetrating and humanist interventions. I would like to acknowledge and thank all those who have helped me in the completion of this task. Among them I would, in particular, like to thank my *Guru* Padma Bhushan Prof. S.K. Saxena, former Professor of Philosophy at Delhi University, for nurturing my life all along and for sparing his valuable time to read the entire manuscript with utmost care and providing me quite a few suggestions of value. I am at loss of words to express my gratitude to my parents, Smt. Savitri Ginodia and Shri. R.P. Ginodia, for their selfless love, co-operation and encouragement and without whose blessings, I could not have completed this work. I am also beholden to Professor Nalini Pant, former Head, Department of Political Science, Banaras Hindu University, who nurtured my interest in theoretical issues.

My deepest gratitude is for Ms. Snehi Chouhan, who has been associated with this project as junior research fellow and worked very hard to collect all the material and arrange them systematically. Without her untiring efforts and zeal, this work could not have been possible. I owe special thanks to my daughter-in-law Dr. Vinita Chandra, a brilliant scholar and presently Assistant Professor in Banaras Hindu University, for meticulously reading the proofs of this book and also for extending her generous support as and when I needed it. And I have dedicated this book to my son Dr. Abhishek Chandra who stood by me amidst all the turmoil in my life and whose impeccable sense of values has made my life worth living. I am also indebted to my second son, Dr. Abhinav, for his unfailing support and intense love; and to my daughter-in-law Sapna, for her loving and selfless care which would often bedew my eyes with tears of gratitude. I gratefully acknowledge the academic and moral support I received from Dr. Priti Singh, Assistant Professor in Political Science, Vasanta College, Rajghat, in the completion of this work. I owe immense gratitude to Dr. Anuradha Banerjee, Associate Professor in English in Vasant Kanya Mahavidyalaya, Kamachha Varanasi, whose divine presence in my life has enriched my existence in manifold ways.

I would also like to acknowledge that I have been immensely benefitted by the writings of a few scholars: Prof. Jean Bethke Elshtain, Chicago University, U.S.A., Prof. Fred Dallmayr, Nortradom University, U.S.A., Prof. Charles Taylor, McGill University, Canada, and Prof. Bhikhu Parekh, University of Hull, England. My personal acquaintances with all four of them have provided me with some precious opportunities to discuss and get insight into some of the complex theoretical issues.

I also thank the University Grants Commission for providing me with a major grant for carrying out this work. I would be failing in my duty if I do not thank my personal assistant Shri. Rajesh Chaturvedi who bore the brunt of compiling this book working at odd hours with great dedication. It was indeed a pleasure to work with Rawat Publications; without their meticulous editing and untiring efforts, the book would not have been published in the present form and in scheduled time.

Preface

Sciences, which deal with our life and existence in society, are called social sciences. Pre-eminent in this group are sociology, political science, economics, social psychology and history. Unfortunately, it is precisely in these areas of study that the male voice has determined, overbearingly, the modes, values and parameters of our social life. The voice of woman has hardly ever been heard. She has been regarded, all along, as a mere means to help male interests, and her own value and views have been utterly ignored. This prolonged emasculation of her role in a male-dominated society has tended to lower woman in her own eyes and made her internalize demeaning images of her own role in both family and society taken generally. Hers is indeed a very long tale of woe, of quiet resignation to male domination, and to the misery it has engulfed her in. It was only in the twentieth century that some courageous women threw a definite challenge to masculine tyranny, not only in the family but in society at large. The historians among these valiant crusaders tried to rewrite history, quite without distorting facts, yet with meticulous attention to how women would prefer to look at them in the light of their own plight through the ages. This was at once a protest against the very concept of history. Why should historical writing, they agued, highlight only the conquests of kings and emperors and utterly ignore the miserable plight of women under the tyranny of men of lesser rank, the humdrum husbands and the in-laws who far outnumber the royalty and inflict more cruelty on women than the ravages of an average war. The focus of these valiant female historians, in general, was on purging historical writing of its male-centric and ethnocentric bias.

In a similar vein, some political theorists, quite as valiant as their parallels in the field of history, sought to rescue woman from her age-old plight by insisting on a due widening of the very concepts of equality and liberty. How are these concepts warranted if women are obdurately kept out of their range? Nor did the psychologists and economists lag behind in this crusade for improving the lot of women. The former protested against the prevailing tendency to put man above woman, simply because the former's actions are (allegedly) determined only by reason, and the latter's entirely by emotion. Working for the same cause, some select economists emphasized the need for attaching as much value to women's labour at home and in the agricultural sector as to men in white-collar jobs.

A similar resurgence of radical thinking emerged in the field of sociology too. Here, a basic and powerful protest was that no value had so far been put on woman's role of nurturing children in the family which is so vital for producing right-minded individuals who alone can make for a better society. Nor did the realm of philosophy remain untouched by this advocacy of the value of woman. Philosophy is admittedly a search for knowledge and certainty; but is it not a fact that intuition, in which the female heart abounds, is also at times a deliverer of unerring knowledge? Sudden flashes of insight are just as vital for the advance of knowledge as reasoned conclusions. Thus, the feminist scholars we have referred to above may be said to have aimed at modifying the very range and viewpoint of concern of their individual disciplines with the one laudable purpose of ameliorating the lot of women. It is precisely this that the present study seeks to bring out at some length, and with due reason.

The task has naturally required us to survey, in brief, a good deal of available literature relating to the subject. We had naturally to begin by mentioning those works first that have dealt with almost all the main subjects in humanities and social sciences, that is, works like the following: Dale Spender's *Men's Studies Modified: The Impact of Feminism on Academic Disciplines* (London, Pergamon Press, 1981); Abigail J. Stewart and Anne C. Herrmann (eds.), *Theorizing Feminism: Parallel Trends in Humanities and Social Sciences* (Boulder, Westview Press, 1994); Sue Rosenberg Zalk and Janice Gordon Kelter, *Revolutions in Knowledge: Feminism in the Social Sciences* (Boulder, Westview

Press, 2002); Michael Paludi and Gertrude Steuernagel (eds.), *Foundations for a Feminist Restructuring of Academic Disciplines* (New York and London, 1990); Elizabeth Langland and Walter Gove (eds.), *A Feminist Perspective in the Academy: The Difference it Marks* (Chicago, 1982); and Myra Marx Ferree and Beth B. Hess, *Analyzing Gender* (London and New Delhi, Sage, 1987).

Of course, all these works are not equally comprehensive, but what is common to them is the reasoned belief that, so far, knowledge has been cumulatively interpreted by men alone; that woman has been totally ignored, both as an object of, and contributor to the corpus of, knowledge; and that, what is utterly regrettable, such a lopsided advance or rather random accumulation of knowledge has been found satisfactory. Besides the above-mentioned works, there are those that have chosen to focus on a single discipline. Two of these, which are essentially major works on philosophy, may be listed as follows: Ann Gary and Marilyn Pearsall, *Women, Knowledge and Reality* (New York, Routledge, 1992); and Miranda Fricker and Jennifer Hornsby (eds.), *Feminism in Philosophy* (Cambridge, Cambridge University Press, 2000). Both these works generally protest against the lamentable tendency of philosophers to attach more value to sheer intellect than to other aspects of human life and personality. All intense thinking is *felt* as attunement; and where it proceeds as desired, it is also felt as very satisfying. So thought cannot be wholly split up from feeling. Nor is mind ever quite unrelated to the body. A sudden flash of insight at once enlivens the body too. So woman's sensuous needs cannot be ignored in a philosophical concern with human life and personality. As for the alleged overall superiority of men over women, the idea is positively ruinous, because it requires us to believe that the maternal functions of nurturing and caring are intrinsically inferior to outdoor work – a belief which has done very great harm to our attitude to women.

In respect of challenging the realm of history so far, it is difficult to think of a better work than Gerda Lerner's, *The Majority Finds Its Past*, (New York, Oxford University Press, 1979). She argues at length how history comes to us refracted through the male eye alone and as determined by values which consider man (as against woman) as the sole measure of all things. Most sources and collectors of historical material, she adds, were male, and so the selection of historical material relating to women was determined by an exclusively male view of historical significance. Naturally, women's contributions to history were incidentally totally ignored and buried in oblivion for ever. In the field of sociology a work of signal value is *Feminism and*

Social Theory edited by Ruth A. Wallace. She complains of four major lacunae in traditional sociological writings: (a) underrepresentation or wholesale omission of women as subjects of study; (b) exclusive focus on topics and problems that relate only to men; (c) distortion of women's concern with the paradigms, models and methods of sociology; and (d) overmuch reliance on male experience as the norm in all sociological thinking.

Nor has the field of psychology remained indifferent to feminine awakening, and mention may at once be made here of the following works: Corrine Squire, *Significant Differences: Feminism in Psychology* (London and New York, Routledge, 1989) and Erica Burman (ed.), *Feminists and Psychological Practice* (London, Sage, 1990). Both have highlighted how subjects which relate to women have been researched using predominately male samples; how hierarchy in sex is maintained by building on unreliable and even patently invalid evidences; and how the uniqueness of woman's psychological make up, needs, and problems has been utterly ignored.

To turn now to economics, one cannot fail to be struck by *Gender in Economics* edited by Maitreyi Krishnaraj and Joy Deshmukh (Ajanta Press, Delhi, 1993). This significant book points out five dominant defects in the existing economic theories: (a) extensive neglect of those segments of economy where women have been traditionally dominant; (b) indifference to the role of family in determining economic matters; (c) sustained undervaluing of the role of women's labour in both family and fields; (d) clustering of women in unduly restricted occupations, thereby presenting a distorted picture of occupational segregation; and (e) continued discrimination against women in the labour market.

In the field of political science and law, the following works are important: Carole Pateman, *Disorder of Women* (Stanford, Stanford University Press, 1989), Jean B. Elshtain, *Public Man Private Woman* (Princeton, Princeton University Press, 1981), Susan Moller Okin, *Women in Western Political Thought* (Princeton, Princeton University Press, 1979) and Diana H. Coole, *Women in Political Theory* (Sussex, Wheatsheaf Books, 1988). These well-thought-out books have posed formidable challenges to such basic concepts and categories of traditional political thought as equality, liberty and justice. Their basic contention is that the allegedly sex equal laws have simply been blind to what is demanded by sex differences; that men alone have been given the right to exercise the various liberties; and that in being interpreted as sheer uniformity of concern for one and all, justice has simply been indifferent to women's unique and quite different needs and aspirations.

Women sociologists of today have challenged the early socialization theory, which holds that personality is formed once for all in early childhood itself. They build their protest on the hard evidence of facts. The fact indeed is that the possibility of change and growth is ever therein human personality. Given some encouragement and good working conditions, even a diffident, timorous lady can develop into a confident achiever. Is it not a patent fact that in almost every walk of life, and in both the West and India, suitably placed women are doing quite as well as men?

Female psychologists contend, with due reason, that in almost all psychological theories, essentially masculine traits have received more positive evaluation than the typically feminine ones. To illustrate, the gentility of caring has been given much less attention than physical assertiveness. This inequity of regard makes for undervaluation of woman not only in the family, but in society at large. The fact is outrageous. Attitudes that prevail in private life cannot be prevented from influencing our public conduct.

So far, it is clear, our references to works by Indian authors have been few and far between. This defect has to be remedied, essentially because the third world perspective on the subject in question cannot be ignored. Here, what at once comes to the mind is Uma Narayan's *Dislocating Cultures* (New York, Routledge, 1997). It explains at length how scholars from the third world have criticized the prevalent understanding of 'culture' and 'tradition' as being predominantly western, and have, incidentally, provided a distorted representation of the third world woman. Another important work, *Feminism, Post-modernity and Development* (London, Routledge, 1995), edited by Marianne H. Marchand and Jane L. Parpart, also refers to this defect and suggests the ways and means by which the 'white-dominated' theories could be so transformed as to provide for the experiences, knowledge and political mobilizations of the 'third world' women and 'women of colour'.

Besides the books referred to above, articles from various important journals have also been consulted, the more important of them being the following: *Indian Journal of Gender Studies, Signs, Feminist Studies, Feminist Review; Social Problems, Annual Review of Sociology, Economic and Political Weekly, Feminist Economics, Sociological Bulletin, Social Problems, Political Theory* and *Atlantis*.

All these sources can be divided into two categories: one that deals with the Western feminist criticism of the social sciences; and, the other which discusses the third world critique of both Western feminism and contemporary social sciences. There is no doubt that all the above books have added an important gender dimension to the study of social sciences. Yet, none of them presents a comprehensive picture of all the challenges posed by feminists to social sciences as they have so far been. Many of the works referred to are an independent study of just one particular discipline. Further, most of the works have presented a critique of dominant models from the Western perspective only and that too in a predominantly liberal context. They utterly ignore voices from the third world and its indigenous perspectives.

The present work is a modest attempt to fill this gap, and it is precisely with this end in view that I have divided the study into nine chapters. The first chapter, *Historical Background: The Development of Feminist Theory in the West* tries to map the history of women in the West and to show how, from the classical era to the modern period, women have always had a subordinate position in society – a fact that paved the way to the emergence of feminist theory in the West, ranging from the views of Mary Wollstonecraft to those of Simone de Beauvoir. It also describes how the movement underwent a shift in the very nature of women's demands from those for equal rights, as seen in the first wave liberal feminism, to a pressure for recognition of the distinctiveness of feminine needs during the second wave feminism; and then, finally, to the theoretical construction of an independent feminine subjectivity – covering not only woman's characteristic needs and aspirations, but her potential for various achievements – an emphasis, I may add, which distinguishes the postmodern writings.

The second chapter, *Contesting Meanings: Feminist Explorations in the Realm of Philosophy* tries to show how the discipline of philosophy too suffers from a male bias. It refers to the works of various feminist scholars like Suneja Gunew, Alison M. Jaggar, Iris Marion Young, Genevieve Lloyd and Marilyn Frye, who contend, with due reason, that all the major concerns of philosophy – methodology, epistemology and ontology – take into account only the male ways of thinking, feeling and behaving, and utterly neglect these aspects of human psyche as they relate to woman's life and personality. Incidentally, they also make pointed references to the misogyny that disfigures the work of great philosophers like Plato, Aristotle, Rousseau and Hegel. The chapter further projects how a distinctively feminist philosophy can remedy such defects.

The third chapter, *Unearthing Androcentrism: Feminist Excavations in the Realm of History* builds on the contributions of some of very eminent historians like Gerda Lerner, Mary Beard, Joan Kelly

Gadol and Sheila Rowbotham. It reveals how these feminist historians have uncovered a running male bias in history writing. Even liberal, socialist and Marxist history writing is shown to suffer from an androcentric approach. The very periodization of history is shown to suffer from this bias. The periods which have been acclaimed as the most enlightened ones are precisely those in which the abjectness of women's condition was at its worst. Only male progress was taken into account.

The fourth chapter, *Resisting Logocentrism: Feminist Challenges in Sociology* tries to show how the discipline of sociology also suffers from androcentrism. Even the founding fathers of sociology – like Karl Marx, Max Weber, Emile Durkheim and Georg Simmel – appear to have discriminated against women. They studied only the world of man, his values and perceptions, pushing women to the periphery. Further, the chapter gives a detailed account of the protests of feminist sociologists against the long established theories of stratification and socialization etc.

The fifth chapter, *Rupturing the 'Masculine': Restoring the 'Feminine' in Psychology* unearths the hidden subconscious male chauvinism permeating psychological writings through all the ages. The reference, here, is to the significant contributions made by feminist scholars like Corrine Squire, Nancy Chodorow, Jean Baker Miller, Carol Gilligan and Janet Sayers. Further, an attempt has also been made to show how the discipline of psychology discriminates against women by taking male as the norm for the whole human race, thus distorting both theory and practice of psychology.

The sixth chapter, *Dismantling Metanarratives: Feminist Interventions in Economics* projects the androcentric approach as it has prevailed in all the main concerns of economics, namely, theoretical formulations, empirical investigations and public policy making. To this end, some thought has also been given here to the inadequacy of the neo-classical or Marxist framework within which economics is generally studied; and also to how empirical investigations have so far tended to leave out women altogether, resulting in formulation of policies that are beneficial to men alone. Further, the chapter highlights the contributions made by feminist theory to the discipline of economics by adding gender as a category of economic analysis.

The seventh chapter, *Bridging the Public and Private Gap: Feminist Voices in Political Science* describes how contemporary feminist theory has challenged all the categories of traditional political thought, which project men as superior to women. So far, the male has always been portrayed as productive, political, public and rational; and the female, as non-political, non-productive, private and merely emotional. Generally, this chapter highlights the contributions of feminist theorists to the dismantling to all such sexist assumptions and unveils the fallacies underlying biased concepts and misconstrued values that have ruled the discipline all along.

The eighth chapter, *Deconstructing Western Feminist Theory: Authorizing Third World Women's Voices* dwells on this particular perspective in feminist theory, and shows how it differs from the Western perspective. Though the feminists of the third world accept some of the criticisms of social science by the Western feminists, they strongly disagree with the latter's essentialist, universalist, and monolithic constructions of the third world. The chapter also projects the contributions of eminent feminists like Anzaldua, Trinh-ti-Minh-ha, bell hooks and others in bringing the third world perspective to the mainstream feminist discourse.

The final chapter, *Conclusion,* summarizes all the challenges posed by feminist scholars to the various disciplines of humanities and social sciences, and discusses various feminist alternatives towards making these disciplines gender-sensitive.

The methodology adopted in this work is not merely historical but also analytical.

1

Historical Background

Development of Feminist Theory in the West

Women have remained a 'silent' population throughout the world. Forms of gender discrimination have been almost universal. As opposed to males who have always been projected as 'productive', 'political', 'public' and 'rational', women have been generally dubbed as 'non-political', 'non-productive', 'private' and 'emotional'. Lamentably, all socio-political structures and institutions – the state, market, organizations of civil society and cultural institutions – have been instrumental in reinforcing gender inequality.

The present chapter, however, is specific in this concern. It confines itself to a discussion of women's position in the West since the Greek period. Such a survey is essential to understand what follows as a legitimate reaction, namely, the times, tenor and language of the emergence of feminist consciousness in Western history. What was the reason for women's revolt against the current practices of period in which they lived? What was denied to them so stubbornly and callously that they had to seek the path of rebellion? What is the cultural context against which they have raised their voice of freedom? And, what was the world view of the times that kept them confined to a subordinate position? A brief review of their social condition, as well as of the writings of some of the key philosophers of those times, would pave the way to the subsequent course of this study. However, as we look at the past, the purpose is not to delve deep into the details of history as a whole, but only to determine the precise reasons because of which the feminist voice was so very feeble, or even utterly quiet in those ages.

Women's Position in the West Through Ages: Some Reflections

History in the West has generally been quiet in respect of women. What is more, there was a time when the writing of women's history would have seemed a rather tame venture, for motherhood and homemaking were not treated as significant activities; and, to speak generally, women were regarded as making an inert, passive world of their own. As a result, their manifold contributions to, and suffering in a male-dominated world, were simply not recorded; and whatever little traces of feminine history are available now are hardly truthful, for the recording has been done by males who alone held the reins of power, determined official concerns, and controlled public archives. The private sphere of family life never became one of their major interests. Women were regarded as utterly incapable of doing anything spectacular and therefore just undeserving of a place in history. This bias, unfortunately, has prevailed throughout the course of history. In respect of Greek history the point can be supported by looking at Greek literature which is replete with references to matriarchal societies of the Amazons. Over a period of time, a matrilineal system, based on judging descent from the female line, was replaced by a patrilineal system. What is more, except in respect of the sphere of religions, the Greek world view regarded women as inferior to men in every sphere – be it political, social or legal. To illustrate, in the Homeric saga, the male was the leitmotiv of Greek ethics, and a woman's contribution was limited to just inspiring men to heroic deeds, abiding by marital faithfulness and beautifying her body for the sake of male pleasure. In the Pandora myth[1], the great poet Hesiod reflects a highly misogynic view of female sex when he depicts woman as the root of all evil and a source of human misery – a view that came to prevail in quite a good deal of classical Greek literature. Hesiod put it thus:

> For of old the tribes of men lived on the earth apart from evil and grievous toil and sore diseases that bring the fates of death to men. For in the day of evil men speedily wax old. But the woman took off the great lid of the jar with her hands and made a scattering thereof and devised baleful sorrows for men.[2]

How, apart from her contact with man, a woman can be the source of all moral evil and proneness to diseases is quite beyond comprehension. Yet, unquestionably, the bias has prevailed from the very dawn of history. The Biblical Eve, the Greek Pandora, Aristotle's view of females as nothing but only incomplete males, are just a few glaring examples to show how the feminine part of humanity was degraded in Greek society. *A woman was all along portrayed as a defective, incomplete, lower grade of male that just lacked something.* Thomas Browne puts it all very pointedly: "Man is the whole world, and the breath of God, woman the Rib and crooked piece of man."[3]

In Greek culture, indeed, woman's status went on declining. From Herodotus to Thycydides, woman gradually became a mere prisoner of the home. Even during the age of Pericles, which saw the very pinnacle of Greek cultural achievements, women were downgraded. Pericles himself pleaded for the seclusion of women; and his famous funeral speech a part of which runs as follows clearly regarded woman as inferior to man: "If I must also speak a word to all those who are in widowhood on the powers and duties of women, I will cast all my advice in one brief sentence. Great will be your glory if you do not lower the nature which is within you – hers most of all whose praise or blame is least bruited on the lips of men."

There is plenty of evidence to show that Greek women had very limited freedom outside their home. They could of course attend weddings, funerals, some religious festivals, and were also allowed to pay brief visits to female neighbours, but their main concern was to be house making and bearing children.[4] Wives and daughters were not allowed even to watch the Olympic games, simply because the participating athletes did not wear clothes. Chariot racing was the only game in which women could participate.

Excepting Sparta, Greek girls in most city-states stayed at home until they got married. Marriages mostly took place during the teenage, and before marriage, the girls learnt to read in school or at home. They also learnt important household skills like spinning, weaving, sewing, cooking and other household jobs. What is more, worshipping the (female) goddesses was fairly common. Goddess Athena, for instance, was revered as the goddess of wisdom, war and crafts. The coins of Athens even bore a picture of hers. On the other hand, however, the generality of women enjoyed very few rights. They could not own property or cast their votes. They had no say in the functioning of the state, though, as a part of their public duties, they were surely expected to play an important role at funerals. There were three main classes of women in ancient Greece. Wives generally stayed at home and kept themselves busy in activities like weaving. As a rule, they were not allowed to go anywhere except to the venue of religious ceremonies. There was yet another class – of concubines – who were poor women comprising widows, slaves, such girls as were left to die in their very infancy by their parents, and prostitutes. The third one was the class of hetaera who were educated and were therefore allowed to accompany men to intellectual and social gatherings.[5] The number of such women was quite small. A wide disparity existed between the rich and the poor. Daughters and wives of rich citizens received a lot of protection, whereas the prostitutes were subjected to all forms of sexual exploitation.

A close look at history reveals that women's position in Athens was no better than that of chattel, that is, just a kind of moveable property. Even a wife's child bearing responsibilities could be taken over by concubines without any social protest.[6] Athenian society never tolerated women at public places, except at funerals and all-female festivals. In his *Politics,* Aristotle explicitly states that a husband should keep not only his children but his wife under unrelenting control. The implicit, underrunning argument was that just as slaves are naturally meant to be ruled by free men, so women are meant to be ruled by men, and that, otherwise, the 'natural' order would be violated:

> Man is full in movement, creative in politics, business and culture. Woman, on the other hand, is passive. She stays at home, as is her nature. She is matter, waiting to be formed by the active male principle ... Man consequently plays a major part in reproduction; the woman is merely the passive incubator of his seed.[7]

Aristotle thus believed that women's souls were impotent and needed the active assistance of man.

The emancipated woman was a rarity even in Roman times. Roman society was a brutal, slave-based society where a ruthless dominator model of male control over woman and domination of 'inferior men' by 'superior men' regulated life at all levels – be it personal, familial, national or international.[8] In comparison to any free male in Rome even the most assertive, independent and visible woman was always in bondage to men.

When, with the collapse of Rome, the middle age started and Christianity gained a firm grip on Europe, women's position deteriorated further. The Church and Christian missionaries simply acquiesced in the traditional view of woman which imposed many restrictions on her. She was excluded from the covenant community.[9] This was done essentially on the basis of Biblical interpretations which supported inferiority of women by placing all the blame squarely on Eve for the 'fall' of humanity. Rules were hardened in respect of marriage and divorce. Differently from classical society, marriages now could not be dissolved. A woman was forced to stay with her husband even if he was not good. As for the late middle ages, they may well be regarded as one of the most brutal periods of history for women. This period not only tolerated, but promoted misogyny, and in cases of sexual impropriety it was always the woman who was blamed. What is worse, if she remained unmarried, or married but could not become a mother, she was treated as a witch.[10] Her denigrated status is thus clearly reflected in the brutal customs prevalent in this period.

In the feudal system of this period, war was always a possibility. Serfs and their families were protected by lords who in turn expected them to fight when called upon to do so. The lords were even allowed to test the virginity of the serf's new bride on the wedding night. Thus, the young bride had to feel humiliated and dishonoured on the very first night of her married life.[11]

At marriage, the bride would be given in exchange for a dowry of money or jewellery; and, at some places, the prevailing custom required her to kneel down in front of her husband – a practice that symbolized his absolute power over her.[12] Further, as her husband was himself controlled by the lord of the estate, she too became subjugated not only to her husband, but to his lord too. The last 300 years of medieval Europe, which included the periods of Renaissance and Reformation, were years of ferment and change extending into realms which included women. Yet, theological statements of the time still echoed the theme of man's superiority over woman. A few others of similar import are put by Carmody as follows: woman is subordinate to man because she bears greater responsibility for the curse that came with the original sin; women are simply to provide procreation and companionship to men; the natural order assigns women only those functions that correspond to her sexual and procreative organs; and adulterous women should be stoned to death, but unfaithful husbands are not subject to any punishment.[13] Thus, even within the days of Reformation no perceptible improvement took place in the lot of women.

Similarly, the Renaissance, which surely marked a break from medieval thought, reverted to the classical Greco-Roman ways of thinking, which emphasized the supremacy of the rational, scientific attitude and is (supposedly) accessible to man alone, and thus further cemented the supremacy of the male over the fame. Thus, broadly speaking, all through these ages, misogyny continued to govern Europe. Women venturing outside the prescribed gender roles were consistently looked down upon. It may be added, in passing, that from antiquity to the present, the absence of concrete, detailed information about woman in actual life stands in sharp contrast to the profusion of discourse and imagery relating to her in art and literature. To illustrate, whereas Olympus is filled with gods and *goddesses*, Greek city-states had no female *citizens*. The Virgin reigns above altars at which (male) priests officiate but they have no female priests. Marianne is the incarnation of the French Republic, the most virile of regimes. The Attic vases of 5th and 6th centuries BC transcribe everyday life. It is only by analysing the way in which images on such vases change over time that we can get some idea of the prevailing attitude in respect of gender. Marriage rites signify only the physical transfer of the bride from one place to another, and a getting ensnared in a series of acts that symbolize mere separation from one end and subjugation to the other, not any significant raise to a new life-stage of felicity and responsibility.

To turn again to the vases, where a *virtuous* woman is portrayed as a spinner of yarn, though the society of which she is a part is indifferent to the value of labour, her actual feminine beauty is represented in terms of mere ornaments, and the figure as such is kept quite vague or hidden from view. Thus, we here get a very clear hint as to the uncertain, self-divided character of the prevailing attitude towards the female sex. Even literary images of women were so visualized that they tended to mask their actual figural charm. The 'lady' of 'refined love' of whom Guillaume de Poitiers sang so zestfully in the 12th century may well appear to rule men's hearts, but one must always bear in mind that such poetic representations show woman not as she was, but only as some clever men imagined her to be simply with a view to promote a new sexual strategy. Much the same thing can be said of the sophistication of romantic love. Balzac said: "Woman is a slave that one must learn to place upon a throne by showering her with fragrances. Men celebrate the Muse and exult in the inaccessible Madonna and Angel".

Philosophers, theologians, jurists, doctors, moralists and educators have been tireless in their efforts to fix the norms relating to the true functions and proper behaviour of women. But mostly they have been male, and they speak from a spurious height of assumed superiority. This explains why misogyny is very well reflected in the works of political philosophers like Plato, Aristotle, Rosseau and Hegel.[14]

In the middle ages, Bishop Gilbert of Limerick observed that "women [who] marry [are only expected to] serve those who pray, work and fight". This conception of woman's role as merely subservient was reared on a queer idea of social utility, and quite without regard to their willingness or otherwise to leave the home. It required them to extend the benefits of maternity to society at *large*. Demands of religion and morality were both subordinated to the whims of man. Be it Pagan or Christian in ideology, Rome insisted that young women remain *virgins* and serve as models of feminine modesty and chastity. Women had to wear veils, for it was believed that in a respectable woman, as Horace said, "one sees only the [overall] figure", instead of being captivated by any particular organ or limb. Horace's sentiments were echoed by Saint Paul, and nineteen centuries later, by Barbey'd 'Aurevilly. Decent women remained shut up in their gynaecium or Victorian homes. Later on, these physical barriers were replaced by more sophisticated systems of education aimed at the internalization of discriminatory social norms, so that instead of having to be imposed from outside, restrictions put by men could become ingrained in woman's own nature.

Thus, say the feminists, the history of women has always been the tale of a silent, subjugated and powerless part of humanity. To bring women's voices into the mainstream history, it was necessary to grant them freedom to express their own independent views directly, in place of male representations of how the females they thought and what they felt and aspired for. They had to be provided direct access to the main presentational means of expression, namely, gesture, speech and writing. At this point, however, fairness demands a little qualifier. Women were given the freedom to write for *private* consumption. In this context, the earliest texts we have (by women) are the Pythagorean letters. Religious writing was another form of expression open to women. This is evident from *Hortus Deliciarum*, a work by Hildegard of Bingen and Herrard of Lansberg. But, from the areas of writing on science, history and philosophy, women were totally excluded. Luckily, however, some committed thinkers and reformers emerged on the scene and raised their voices against such a suppression of women. This select band of thinkers, to which we now turn, bestirred the feminist movement throughout the world.

History of Western Feminist Movement

The origins of the Western feminist movement can be traced back to medieval times. From the 15th century itself women's voices were beginning to be heard, and the first woman to write about the rights and duties of women was the French woman Christine de Pisan (1364–1430). Her writing centred around debates on women's roles in society. It did not yet constitute any analysis of power relations between men and women. Yet, influenced by these debates, a significant number of women challenged accepted ideas about the role of women in 17th century England. Of these, Aphra Benn and Mary Astell have been outstanding. Unlike the earliest debates, the discussions that occurred at this time stemmed from the challenges being posed to women's traditional roles as a consequence of the emerging capitalist course of development. The old system of family-based domestic industry was gradually declining, creating a sharp distinction between the public world of employment and the private world of homely occupations. This distinction between the public and the private involved a gradual exodus of women from the former and a concomitant devaluation of work in the family; and it is at this turn of events that the feminists question the legitimacy of such a lowering of the value of those who preferred to keep themselves confined to the welfare of the family. Self-effacing and devoted wives and mothers ceased to command the respect that they deserved.

By the early 18th century, feminist consciousness grew even bolder, as many more women were dissatisfied with their subordinate position in the society. However, during this period, we do not find any direct challenge to women's inferior social and economic positions or to the discriminatory sexual division of labour. Nor do we see, here, any coherent political programme demanding that the rights of male citizens be extended to women too. Feminists of these times believed that women could be made independent of men only through education and exercise of reason. This was the period when more emphasis was laid on women's rationality and its full utilization. The upsurge was quite natural as this century was fully dominated by two revolutions – American (1776) and French (1789) – which advocated the principles of liberty, equality and fraternity, and were inspired by a deep faith in man's independent power of reason.

However, this period also suffered from a deep paradox. On the one hand, as we have already said, the two great revolutions referred to above expressed their faith in man's ability to think and act rationally and pleaded for liberty, equality and fraternity; on the other hand, they failed to press the same measures for women. Even, there was a widespread consensus among the philosophers that the Enlightenment principle of rational individualism could not be extended to women, who, were by their very nature, (allegedly) incapable of being generally or essentially rational. This preconception permeated the writings of Voltaire, Diderot, Montesquieu and, above all, Rosseau. They maintained that women are essentially creatures of emotion and passion, and therefore they have an important role to play as wives and mothers; they are biologically unsuited to work in the public sphere.

All these ideas came to be challenged by the end of the 18th century. Quite a few attempts were made to show that the liberal ideas of Enlightenment could be successfully applied to women as well. Of those who took the lead in this venture the most prominent was Mary Wollstonecraft. In one of her well-known works, she argued that, as commonly understood, femininity was just a contrived social *construct* that distorted rather than reflected women's true nature, needs and potential. Woman is not a mere plaything for titillating male senses but is an independent being, who is both capable of and entitled to every kind of training and discipline. If she is given the right kind of education and due access to the sources of knowledge, she too can become capable of making rational choices of surpassing significance. This eminent feminist was pained to see that a man's wife was seen as merely a subsidiary aid to his success and not an active partner in his trials and decision-making. She never acquiesced in, and even protested against the dichotomy which is generally made between the public and the private, and argued that, in so far as a happy home life was directly conducive to man's effective involvement in public life, domestic duties were to be put on a par with public responsibilities.[15]

The ideas of Wollstonecraft and other liberal feminists faced severe criticism from the Utopian socialists who claimed that this feminist approach failed to give any thought to the *non*-sexual forms of oppression that existed in society. They argued that within a competitive capitalist society, the mere acquisition of equal rights, as advocated by the feminists in question, would not suffice; and that the emphasis should rather be on the abolition of private property, which would automatically provide for economic and legal independence to women. The best known of these early socialists are Frenchmen St. Simon (1760–1850) and Fourier (1772–1837) and the British thinker, Robert Owen (1772–1837). Now, the ideas of the Utopian socialists had a great impact on intellectuals in both England and America. For example, William Thompson (1775–1844) wrote an appeald entitled, 'Appeal on Behalf of Women' (1825) became very popular at this time. A leading follower of Robert Owen and himself a prominent economist, Thompson went beyond Wollstonecraft's ideas on representation. While strongly supporting the idea of full political rights to women in affairs of the state, he emphatically added that the actual getting of such equal rights would be possible only when common ownership and cooperatives replaced private property and competition as bases of social organization.[16] However, the ideas of Utopian socialists did not get much support from people in general, and it was the liberal ideas which dominated the feminist movement for the coming decades. It was these ideas that quickened the first wave of feminism, that is, liberal feminism, and if we have to pick the one person who gave the most powerful upthrust to this wave, we cannot choose any one but John Stuart Mill, the father of contemporary liberalism. His epoch-making work, *The Subjection of Women* (1869), written with Hariet Taylor, proved to be a watershed in liberal feminist history. This work served as the Bible for all those who strove to fight against male domination and to secure justice for women. Mill's is indeed categorical in his pleading for equity:

> The principle which regulates the existing social relations between the two sexes – the legal subordination of one sex to other-is wrong in itself, and now one of the chief hindrances to human improvement; and ... it ought to be replaced by a principle of perfect equality, admitting no power or privileges on the one side, nor [any] disability on the other.[17]

In the USA the most powerful push to the American feminist movement was provided by Elizabeth Cady Stanton who, however, developed her ideas essentially in the context of some specific moral reforms for women. Here, the demands of feminists included a plea for reform of the divorce and child custody laws, and for education, employment opportunities and due legal protection for women etc. It was as a sequel to her efforts, along with those of Lucretia Mott, that the first ever women's rights convention – that is, the Seneca Falls Convention – was held in 1848. It was an event of momentous significance, for it was signed by as many as 68 women and 32 men, and because it boldly declared: "All men and women are created equal." Eleven resolutions were passed, including some for equality in education, employment, and one favouring the law which provided for suffrage to women. Hereby, to be sure, a singular feminist consciousness received the mightiest push.

As a result of this awakening, most of the demands of earlier feminists were met by the end of 19th century. In the fields of education, employment and legal affairs etc., ample facilities were provided to women in both England and America. Yet, the truly significant goal was not yet attained and it is easy to explain why we say so. The education which was being imparted to women served only to reinforce the traditional roles of mothers and wives by stressing domestic skills as their main qualification – an emphasis which naturally made for low wages to women. In other words, the equality granted to women was only formal. Nevertheless, it is also true that these reforms had made women more autonomous and independent in many ways. In both Britain and America, they began serving on school boards, and in working class movements and in administering poor laws etc. Through these new engagements, they became skilled in campaigning for and organizing movements, as also in fund raising and public speaking. Yet they continued to suffer from two major disabilities. First, as we have already hinted, the educational structure was geared more to the needs of men than to those of women, as they were being educated only in traditional skills; and secondly, they were still not given the right to vote. As a revolt against this background, suffrage campaigns began to take shape in the 20th century, and by 1945 many countries had granted women the right to vote. The first country in the world to do this (in 1894) was New Zealand. This was shortly followed by Australia. In Europe, Finland and Norway both enfranchised women before 1914, and most other countries did so shortly after the First World War. In Britain, however, it was only in 1928 that women were granted the right in question, and in America it was only after the passing of the 19th constitutional amendment in 1920 that all adult American women became enfranchised. This victory of suffrage campaign became an inspiring symbol of the feminist movement. Yet it was just one step in the direction of securing all legitimate rights for women. Most of them realized that, in spite of having secured suffrage, they continued to receive discriminatory treatment in many other ways. Therefore, they continued to struggle for amelioration of their lot in various directions and in different parts of the world. In 1960s the feminist movement received a quite new momentum primarily as an after-effect of the publication of Simone De Beauvoir's *Second Sex* in 1949. The women's movement now entered a new era, which may be called the 'second wave of feminism'. Simone de Beauvoir was one of those fiery feminist thinkers who revolted for long and with due reason against the existing male-centric norms and values. She fiercely attacked those age-old customs and traditions which kept women in continued slavery and as mere captives of men. To quote her words:

> The masculine and feminine are used symmetrically only as a matter of form, as on legal papers. In actuality the relation of the two sexes is not

> quite like that of two electrical poles, for man represents both the positive and the neutral, as is indicated by the common use of man to designate human beings in general, whereas woman represents only the negative, defined by limiting criteria, without reciprocity ... A man is in the right in being a man; it is the woman who is in the wrong. It amounts to this: Just as for the ancients there was an absolute vertical with reference to which oblique was defined, so there is an absolute human type, the masculine.[18]

It was from this era, distinguished by the missionary zeal of Simone de Beauvoir, that regular and impassioned dialogues and debates began taking place on the major directions of women's emancipation. Critique and counter-critiques, cultural and cross-cultural interaction, and modern vs postmodern currents of thought – all began emerging on the feminist landscape, and in rapid succession. A clear understanding of these various currents of thought can be had only by dwelling on the conceptual history of feminist thought to which we now turn.

Conceptual History of Feminism: From Liberal Feminism to Postmodern Feminism

For a proper understanding of the political orientation of feminism Alison M. Jaggar has recommended four distinct approaches: Liberal Feminism, Marxist/Socialist Feminism, Radical Feminism and Postmodern Feminism. All these approaches see women and their existential situation as central to social progress, and focus on the following select questions: Why is it that in virtually all historically recorded societies men appear to have absolute power over women, and how can this state of affairs be changed? How can the gathering and dissemination of knowledge be so regulated that women may be effectively helped in their political conduct and secure release from the clutches of age-old slavery and bondage? Now, as we shall presently see, different answers are given to these questions by the approaches we have distinguished, so that one cannot truly speak of a single, unified body of feminist thought.

Liberal Feminism

Liberal feminism is based on the simple premise that both man and woman are born equal and are gifted with the same rational faculties, and that, therefore, women should not be denied equality of opportunity for pursuit of all those activities which are open to men. It further believes that every individual is capable of independent self-determination, and that his (or her) progress lies simply in exercising this capacity ever better. What here receives special emphasis may be listed thus: legal and political rights, education, employment, political participation and full legal equality for women. The most famous expression of liberal feminism is found in John Stuart Mill's *The Subjection of Women* (1869). Here, in this epoch-making work, he declares that what is now called the nature of women is but a spurious concept arising out of forced oppression in some directions and unnatural stimulation in others. He adds that had women been granted the same kind of rights and freedom as men, their nature would have been construed quite differently. In America this particular thought has found eloquent expression in Betty Friedan's work, *The Feminine Mystique* (1963). She points out that during the Second World War, just because women in America were made to believe that their only fulfilment lay in domesticity, they were willy-nilly pushed into a life of unrelieved passivity and despair. So, Friedan insisted that women be freed from the 'feminine mystique' (of woman's lot as mere domesticity); that the most pressing need of the moment was to make women see that (and how exactly) they could make a mark even outside the four walls of their homes. This end, she maintained, could be attained only by means of the right kind of education.

In spite of its obvious fairness, liberal feminism was subjected to vigorous criticism by many other feminist thinkers. They argued that the feminism in question concentrated only on rights in public sphere and utterly neglected the need for equity of freedom and regard also in home life. Further, liberal feminism was accused of being ambivalent, for whereas, on the one hand, it agreed to state intervention for protecting individual rights, on the other hand, it pleaded for maximum individual autonomy. Criticism also revolved around the hidden risk that though such feminism may decrease woman's dependence on men, it could also increase her dependence on the patriarchal state limitlessly. The dissident scholars are seen to allege also that the idea of full legal equality as propounded by the liberal feminists is questionable in may many ways. It ignores not only the current differences in social roles of the sexes, but also their innate biological differences. For some select critics, the problem goes even deeper. They allege that liberalism is based on an incomplete understanding of human nature and motivation, and is marred by utter indifference to and even devaluation of women's experiences and of society's reproductive needs. Further, they contend that the liberal idea of human nature is virtually a kind of 'political solipsism'.

Jaggar levels this charge against liberatism on the ground that it regards each individual as rational, independent, competitive and autonomous, and so incidentally ignores the attitudes of nurturing, cooperation and mutual support that are essential bases for the welfare of human society, and have also been the typically dignifying traits of women's lives.[19] Critics have also attacked the liberal concept of reason on four main grounds: (1) its view that the working of reason is universally objective is based on a view of humanity which is patently limited, for it ignores the fact that men often reason in biased ways; (2) it neglects the sensuous side of feminine nature because it insists only on the value of mind over the body, not at all vice versa; (3) it ignores or devalues other forms of knowledge and modes of activity such as intuitive knowledge and impulsive activity; and hence (4) it fails to understand the limits of reason and its inappropriateness in many areas of life.

Further, it is contended that the liberal feminists continue to believe in a sharp public-private dichotomy, which is detrimental to their own cause, and that they do not understand how this dichotomy creates problems in private spheres like the family, say, by allowing greater power (in the family) to those of its members who also work in the public sphere. It is further contended that even modified liberal principles cannot be a fruitful guideline to understand the reasons of, and remedy for women's subjugation.[20] The equal rights theory can, no doubt, provide a starting-point for future struggles, but it fails to provide insights into society's complex power structures and public-private relationship.

This manifold critique of liberal feminism paved the way to the emergence of many other kinds of feminist theories, of which the Marxist theory is importantly one.

Marxist Feminism

This approach believes that the inferior position of women is due essentially to the class structure of society. The argument is that in the present industrial civilization society is divided into two clear classes, viz., the bourgeois and the proletariat; that the bourgeois class coerces the proletariat necessarily; and that in such a class-based society most women and men will inevitably remain oppressed until the capitalist economic system is replaced by a classless society.

According to Frederick Engels, one of the best known Marxists, the control of property by men of wealth naturally strengthened their position within the family. In his words, "the overthrow of mother right was the world historical defeat of the female sex. The man took command in the home also; the woman was degraded and reduced to servitude; she became the slave of his lust and a mere instrument for the production of his children". Arguing further, Engels said that acquisition of private property by men naturally tended to make them dominate woman in the family, because she becomes economically dependent upon men, as a result of which "within the family he is the bourgeoisie, and the wife represents the proletariat". Thus, both Marx and Engels insist that the exploitation of women would come to an end only with the abolition of private property.

This kind of Marxist feminism found an eloquent expression in the works of many thinkers of 19th and 20th centuries. For example, August Bebel, Clara Zetkin (1857–1933) and Lily Braun (1865–1916) of Germany took the lead in propagating the ideas of Marxist feminism. According to them, it is only a communist society woman would be freed from domestic toil; and the very severance of working class from ownership of property, coupled with the entry of proletarian women in industry, would naturally remove the economic determinants of gender imbalances. All questions relating to the lot of women have to be looked at against the background of the evils that are perpetrated by the very continuance of a bourgeoisie society and its vicious basis, namely, private property. In Russia, we may note, two feminist thinkers actually tried to apply orthodox Marxism to the lot of their women. One of these, Nadezhda Krupskaya, was Lenin's wife and the other was Alexandra Kollontai (1873–1952). In her pamphlet, *The Woman Worker*, Krupskaya argued that though women's participation in the labour force was showing signs of good progress, their ultimate liberation could come about only through participation in the class struggle. Kollontai did not lag behind. She campaigned vigorously against the bourgeoisie women's movement and demanded that this be replaced by the rival solidarity of proletarian men and women. She was also the first to attack the male-dominated party hierarchy and demanded that separate women's organizations be established within the party itself.

However, this particular Marxist approach was itself subjected to severe criticism. Some of its opponents argued that Marxism involves a crude reductionism, overly simplifying the situation into a matter of direct and necessary relation between economic organization and the situation of women; that it gives no importance to the role of reproduction; and that, to speak generally, Marxist philosophy is based on an exclusively male view of the world which simply gives no thought to women's needs and experiences. Some other contentions in this context are that the concept of 'productive labour' is entirely based on a paradigm of male activity which merely ignores the domestic work performed by women; that the whole view of history as a process through which men increase their mastery over nature reflects an essentially male view, which is responsible for our current ecological crisis; and that the drive to subdue or conquer nature is quite unprofitably preferred to what may be called the typically feminine way of working with and understanding nature.

Socialist Feminism

Marxism provided ideological assistance to quite a few socialists. Yet, they also differed from Marxism in the following ways:

1. they refuse to attribute every ill to the class structure of society; and therefore
2. they favour gradual and piecemeal social reforms, instead of a revolutionary attempt to do away with the class structure in one radical sweep.

One of the leading socialist thinkers of America, Charlotte Perkins Gilman (1860–1935), was categorical in her opposition to both the theory and method of social change as advanced by the followers of Marx. She contended that human freedom would come about not through class conflict and revolution, but through the regulated and peaceful furtherance of tendencies that are already present in modern society; that the granting of economic independence to women would automatically transform the existing oppressive family structure; and that it would attenuate the trials of motherhood by enabling women to secure paid nursing assistance, and also put the child-parent relations on an even keel by preventing the father from appearing as the exclusive controller of family affairs.

Another most prominent anarchist-socialist feminist of America was Emma Goldman. She laid emphasis on the values of human individuality, trust, freedom and cooperation; struggled to strike a balance between equality and individuality; and declared that "peace or harmony between the sexes and individuals does not necessarily depend on a superficial equalization of human beings, nor does it call for the elimination of individual traits and peculiarities". According to her, the problem that confronts us today is "how to be one's [own individual] self and yet [remain] in oneness with others, to feel deeply with all human beings and still retain one's own characteristic qualities."[21] Emancipation [she believed] should make it possible for woman to be human in the truest sense. Goldman sought the emancipation of woman not through class struggle or political concessions but through attainment of autonomy by discovering her own true self. This American feminist does not see any conflict between self-discovery and selfless service. In this context, her following eloquent words are worth quoting; "To give off one's self boundlessly, in order to find one's self richer, deeper, better … [this] alone can fill the emptiness, and transform the tragedy of woman's emancipation into joy, limitless joy."[22]

However, this new wave of socialist feminism was also criticized on two main grounds:

1. it could not liberate itself from the rigidity of economic determinism and that; and
2. its methodology and world view were both determined by a male-centred approach.

Radical Feminism

Quite differently from the three main strands of feminism, namely, liberalism, Marxism and socialism, there emerged yet another stream of thought: radical feminism. It argued that the Marxist and liberal positions both ignored the ubiquity of male power. This new school of thought rejected the liberal claim that the cause of women's oppression lay only in their being bereft of political or civil rights, and also the classical Marxist belief that women were oppressed essentially because of a class-cleft society. Instead, it explained the many forms of social tyranny in terms of the basic evil of sexual oppression. For these radical feminists, the play of masculine power is not just confined to the public world of economic and political activity but also operates in the domain of relationships between the sexes. They hold that "the personal is political" in the sense of being as much the scene of male domination as the political sphere, and that the distinguishing character of women's oppression is their oppression as women, not as an (allegedly) inferior social class. For them, the real explanation of women's oppression lies in sexual oppression, i.e., their dependence on men for fulfilment of sexual desires.[23] To such oppression all women are alike subject, and this very fact of shared oppression may be taken to turn women into a kind of sisterhood. In this context, Johnson remarks: "[One] of the basic tenets of Radical Feminism is that any woman … has more in common with any other woman – regardless of class, race, age, ethnic group, nationality – than any woman has with any man."[24] Others like him claim that by virtue of their very natural functions and capacities of reproduction, peacemaking, nurturing and sharing, women are superior to men who are competitive and aggressive by nature. These ideas found detailed expression in quite a few works that came out in 1970s. Some of these may be listed thus: Kate Millett's *Sexual Politics,* Shulamith Firestone's *The Dialectic of Sex* and Germaine Greer's *The Female Eunuch* etc. All these authors attacked the state, the present state of the family, the economic system and the various patriarchal structures also in the realm of culture, religion, language and knowledge – a phenomenon which induced women, if unknowingly, to accept and get imbued with male-centric perceptions. This particular approach is visible in the writings of Dale Spender, Andrea Dworkin, Robin Morgan, Mary Daly, Eisenstein etc., though all of them have worked it out differently.

This specific view of power and politics has also been vigorously criticized by quite a few feminist scholars, and the criticisms turn around four interrelated points: (i) The view in question fails to explain the complex origin of male power. It sees patriarchy either as an autonomous form of oppression or as the cause of other forms of oppression. Being unable to explain how exactly the male power has originated, it naturally fails to provide an adequate strategy for ending male domination. (ii) Radical feminists are a bit too categorical in their claim when they view man only as the enemy of woman. All men, the critics argue, are not in a position to dominate women but may even be subordinate to them; and despite the general imbalance of power, loving and non-exploitative relationships between men and women still exist in our society. The extreme anti-man, separatist ideas promoted by radical feminists would lead only to lesbian separatism which will only harm the legitimate sensuous interests of women. (iii) In their over-enthusiasm to project the wrongs done by men over the centuries, the radical feminists have erred in projecting women as passive victims in every case of man-woman conflict. Such an exaggeration of male-female disharmony is likely to prevent women from entering the social scene as co-makers of history or as agents of change in the future.[25] The truth indeed is that the radical feminists have erred in talking of the universal domination of womanhood, as if oppression of women were an identical phenomenon everywhere. The fact, on the other hand, is that reproductive rights mean something very different in different societies. For example, whereas the Romanian woman is forced to bear at least six children, the Chinese woman is compelled by the 'one child' policy to abort her second pregnancy. Similarly, whereas the white American career woman does not incur any censure if her contraception has failed, the Puerto Rican woman is sterilized against her will.[26] What is more, the radical feminists' monolithic conception of feminine oppression is not really as comprehensive as it claims to be. It covers only the experiences of white middle-class women and not at all the very different problems faced by the working class and the third world women. The needed attention to these ignored women comes to the fore only with the emergence of postmodern feminism.

Postmodern Feminism

The Postmodern Feminist School challenged the basic premises of all the three strands of thought we have so far dealt with – the liberal, Marxist and radical feminists – on the ground that they have all based themselves on meta-narratives which were more a matter of hearsay than a true picture of the actual state of things. This school of thought rejected the simplistic, overly general definitions of social phenomena, which simply missed the complexity of life as lived experience. The postmodern feminists, on the other hand, focused on local and specific facts and on historically accurate analysis, and with due regard to the varying spatio-temporal and cultural contexts of situations and happenings. In general, they called for the recognition and celebration of difference(s), and stressed the importance of renewed attention to dissident voices that have been silenced forcibly.[27]

To put it briefly, the postmodernists have questioned all the basic assumptions of modern age, particularly the belief that rational thought alone can guarantee progress and enlightenment to humanity, and that society can be ordered only in accordance with the demands of reason, knowledge and justice. They further argue that because our understanding of reality is mediated by language and experience, it is bound to appear differently to each one of us; that, therefore, there can be no impersonal, objective or "God's eye view"; and that we have to be content with individual subjectivities. Concepts which claim to cover every aspect of life and experience have to be studiously avoided. Three popular exponents of this school of thought are Julia Kristeva, Helence Cixous and Luce Irigray. They all alike emphasize the need to explore the intricate relationships between language, sexuality and power and to develop 'non-phallocentric' ways of thinking.[28]

The postmodernist emphasis on subjectivity has been vigorously criticized by quite a few feminist scholars.[29] They contend that so much emphasis on subjectivity is likely to harm the very possibility of collective political action and to make it impossible to speak of women's trouble in general. Are we to determine every individual woman's lot before planning any ameliorative measures for them?

Various other critics allege that postmodernism is essentially a conservative theory which turns feminism from a revolutionary social movement into an inward-looking elite activity; that by virtue of its overemphasis on subjectivity it discounts the very possibility of general measures for collective welfare; and that by denying all validity to such concept words as right, justice and reason, postmodernism denies legitimacy to feminist attempts to change the present condition of society. In this context, Weedon warns "We cannot afford to abandon reason entirely to the interests of patriarchy. Reason, like experience, requires both deconstruction and reconstruction in the interests of feminism."[30]

This historical survey has presented us with a clear picture of development of feminist theory in the West. It should now be obvious that by 1970s feminist theory had emerged as a strong interdisciplinary subject which posed a major challenge to all the traditional categories of thought employed in the various disciplines of humanities and social sciences. What has been the rationale behind these challenges, and how they can be met with, will be explored in the forthcoming chapters on Philosophy, History, Sociology, Psychology, Economics and Political Science. We propose to begin with the discipline of Philosophy.

Notes

1. This myth holds that God Zeus was mightily angered by the fact that Prometheus had stolen the sacred fire from heaven, so he decided to punish the mortal man. He ordered Hephaestus to mould a woman out of earth, a woman of such entrancing charm and beauty as would bring misery upon the human race. Thus was Pandora, the "all gifted" first woman created. Aphrodite gave her beauty, Hermes speech, boldness and cunning. Prometheu's brother Epimetheus made her his wife, ignoring Prometheu's advice never to accept any gift from the gods; ignoring also Prometheu's specific instructions not to open a mysterious box which he had left with Epimetheu's safekeeping. Pandora, consumed with curiosity, lifted the lid, releasing all the ten thousand ills that have been plaguing mankind ever since.
2. J. Hastings (ed.), *Encyclopedia of Religion and Ethics*, Vol. 6, Edinburgh: T.T. Clark, 1908–1921, p. 670. Here, quoted from Amaury De Riencourt's *Woman and Power in History*, New Delhi: Sterling Publishers, 1989, pp. 96–97.
3. See C.W. Eliot (ed.), *Harvard Classics*, Vol. 3, New York: P.F. Collier & Son, 1937, p. 323.

4. However, it must be pointed out here that most of the Greek women did not do their housework themselves, rather they got it done by the female slaves.
5. Hetairai were influential women of some social standing. Many of them like Aspasia, Clepydra, Thargelia etc., made a mark in the fields of Greek history and literature.
6. See Marilyn B. Arthur, "Early Greece: The Origins of Western Attitude towards Women", in John Peradotto and J.P. Sullivan (eds.), *Women in the Ancient World: The Arethusa Papers*, Albany: Suny, 1984.
7. Cited in Rusalined Miles, *The Women's History of the World*, Topstield, MA: Salem House, 1989, p. 47. Here, quoted from Linda. L. Lindsey's *Gender Roles: A Sociological Perspective*, New Jersey: Prentice Hall, 1997, p. 96.
8. R. Eisler, David Loye and Kari Norgaard, *Women, Men and Quality of Life*, Pacific Grove, CA: Centre for Partnership Studies, 1995, p. 123.
9. Gerda Lerner, "A New Angle of Vision", in Shiela Ruth's *Issues in Feminism: An Introduction to Women's Studies*, Mountain View, CA: Mayfield, 1995.
10. Rhoda Unger and Mary Crawford, *Woman and Gender: A Feminist Psychology*, New York: McGraw Hill, 1992, p. 503.
11. See M. Angela Lucas, *Women in Middle Ages: Religion, Marriage and Letters*, New York: St. Martin's, 1983, p. 85.
12. Ibid., p. 87.
13. See Denise Lardner Carmody, *Women and Religions*, Englewood Cliffs, New Jersey: Prentice Hall, 1989, pp. 175–76.
14. Their views have been dealt with in great detail in the forthcoming chapter on Philosophy.
15. Mary Wollstonecraft, *Vindication of the Rights of Women*, Harmondsworth: Penguin, 1978, p. 263.
16. Quoted from Valerie Bryson, *Feminist Political Theory*, London: Macmillan, 1992, p. 33.
17. John Stuart Mill, *The Subjection of Women*, London: Virago, 1983.
18. Simone de Beauvoir, *The Second Sex*, London: Vintage, 1997, p. 15.
19. See Alison Jaggar, *Feminist Politics and Human Nature*, Brighton: Harvester, 1983.
20. See Carole Pateman, "Feminist Critiques of Public Private Dichotomy", in A. Philips (ed.), *Feminism and Equality*, Oxford: Basil Blackwell, 1987. Also see S.M. Okin, *Justice, Gender and the Family*, New York: Basic Books, 1990.
21. Emma Goldman, "The Tragedy of Woman's Emancipation", in Alice S. Rossi (ed.), *The Feminist Papers*, New York: Columbia University Press, 1974, p. 509.
22. Ibid., p. 516.

23. R. Rowland and R. Klein, "Radical Feminism: Critique and Construct", in Suneja Gunew (ed.), *Feminist Knowledge: Critique and Construct*, London and New York: Routledge, 1990, pp. 272–75 and p. 282.
24. See L. Johnson, "Socialist Feminism", in Suneja Gunew (ed.), *Feminist Knowledge: Critique and Construct*, London and New York: Routledge, 1990, p. 310.
25. See L. Segal, *Is the Future Female: Troubled Thoughts on Contemporary Feminism*, London: Virago, 1987, p. xi.
26. Valerie Bryson, *Feminist Political Theory: An Introduction*, London: MacMillan, 1992, p. 191.
27. See Marianne H. Marchand and Jane L. Parpat, *Feminism, Post Modernism, Development*, London: Routledge, 1995.
28. Rosemary Tong, *Feminist Thought: A Comprehensive Introduction*, London: Unwin Hyman, 1989, p. 233.
29. See Valerie Bryson, *Feminist Political Theory: An Introduction*, London: MacMillan, 1992, p. 229.
30. Chris Weedon, *Feminist Practice and Poststructuralist Theory*, Oxford: Basil Blackwell, 1987, p. 10.

2

Contesting Meanings
Feminist Explorations in the Realm of Philosophy

Philosophy has all along been regarded as such a search for truth and knowledge concerning the universe, human existence, perception and behaviour as is pursued by means of reflection, reasoning and argument. Western philosophy is said to have began from wonder, or from our feeling curious in respect of what is so far unknown but in some sense significant. Indian philosophy, on the other hand, is thought to have arisen out of our natural desire to avoid or overcome suffering. Taken together, the two approaches require us to be watchful in respect of what is there and, at the same time, to be as much sensitive to the suffering of others as to our own.

Has traditional philosophy been true to these requirements? Feminist explorations in the discipline suggest a negative answer. They have convincingly revealed the prevalence of a male bias all along. They allege:

> Women have either been concealed in the history of philosophy, i.e., rendered invisible, or quite literally abused; or at best … [presented] as less than 'rational' sex … and therefore less 'human' than men and relegated to the realm of 'nature' rather than 'culture' and so on and so forth.[1]

Challenging this attitude, feminist theorists call for an insertion of the 'feminist world view' within the discipline of philosophy so that human life may be studied as a whole, and the subject may come to acquire the comprehensiveness it aims at, as opposed to the special sciences which are all limited in their concern. It is therefore necessary for feminists to enter the areas of theory and research in philosophy to get it rid of its androcentricity. Sheila Ruth believes that, because of its professed aim at comprehensiveness, the discipline of philosophy is most suitable to address feminist questions as well:

> Philosophy, after all, is really a natural place to explore the essential issues of feminism. Where else, if not in ethics or political philosophy, would one consider the principles involved in abortion, ERA, male/female/human relationships, subordination, freedom, etc.? Where else, if not in epistemology or language philosophy, would one explore sexist rhetorical devices, words and naming, male/female or masculist/feminist consciousness? Where if not in metaphysics would one explore matriarchal religion, the implications of female/male divinities, and so on?[2]

Ruth also presses a point of obvious contemporary relevance. To the traditional problems of philosophy, a new one has been added in the 20th century, namely, the problem of meaning, and it is of unquestionable value. Indeed, how can any question be sensibly addressed, much less answered, unless what the question means is properly understood? Following this emphasis, Ruth wonders how the word human can be taken to mean just male? How is it proper to use the two words interchangeably?

> The construction of a universe where man (male) and human were coextensive was not problematic [but was quietly accepted] in a belief system that deemed women not quite human if it deemed them at all. Women did not function for the male conceptually, because they did not function politically, economically, or, for that matter, intellectually.[3]

The feminist complaint is indeed loud and clear. Women have been taken to be virtually non-existent. Their experiences and perspectives have not been taken note of. They have not been taken to make any contribution to philosophic speculation, nor even to the range and modes of philosophy's concern and articulation. Feminist scholars also challenge the underlying male-centric metaphysical and epistemological assumptions. They insist, with due reason, that traditional philosophy has not only devalued women's intellectual efforts but also ignored their specifically feminine moral concerns, such as security and undisturbed privacy of life for single women and widows. Alison Jaggar contends that all major concepts and theories of traditional philosophy reveal "a distinctly masculine way of approaching the world"[4]; and Ruth readily agrees:

> Male voices, perspectives, interests, ideas, and modes dominate all thinking. For all intents and purposes, official intellection and male intellection have become co-existensive. In the realm of thought, the male is universalized. As a result, the categories of relevance have been appropriated by the male frame of reference: If Male=human, universal primacy, then: That which is of importance is [what the male perceive as important]; that which is holy is [what the male perceives as holy]; that which can persuade is [what the male perceive as persuasive]; the way one reaches conclusions is [the way men reach conclusions], and so on.[5]

Feminists in general contend that it is because of such a biased approach (as referred to above) that traditional philosophers have treated the private realm of family as a realm mired in the concrete, particular, and merely subjective, and so not worthy of serious philosophic concern. Philosophers have mostly used 'value hierarchical thinking' and 'normative dualism'. To illustrate, they give greater value to what is seen by the male as higher – say, sheer intellect, cold reasoning and overt marks of culture – than to the subtler forms of refinement such as uncomplaining fortitude, wholly selfless helpfulness, or to the emotive-intuitive sources of knowledge and behaviour which are distinctive of the being and life of women. Such value hierarchical thinking and normative dualism are patently biased. Caren J. Warren roundly condemns it all as the 'logic of domination' – an attempt to justify the subordination of the allegedly lower (i.e., woman) by the supposedly higher[6] (i.e., man).

Challenging this androcentric approach, feminist philosophers have tried to isolate and explain the limitations and biases of specific philosophies and their proponents, instead of making vague, general accusations. Generally, of course, they

(a) highlight the misogyny in the work of political philosophers;
(b) seek to determine and reinstate the work of unduly ignored women philosophers; and
(c) challenge the very methodology, epistemology and ontology of some of the most eminent names in the field of philosophy.

Quite generally, the feminist scholars highlight the male bias in the works of traditional philosophers. They have demonstrated that the history of philosophy has been sexist and has done horrible damage to women. Further, the broad contention is that

> Verification of misogynist beliefs in the 'learned' writings legitimated sexist ideas and practices in religion, medicine and social institutions and reinforced the worst kinds of oppression, from witch-burning to clitoridectomy[7] [that is, the surgical removal of that highly sensitive

> organ located in front of the opening of the vagina which, like the penis in males, becomes erect when sexually stimulated]; and that feminist philosophy is a response to this misogyny. It is an attempt to 'right the balance' and to serve as a 'corrective' to this bias in the discipline.[8]

This response, we may note, is directed not at anything vague, but at specific instances of biassed thinking in the works of poets and philosophers.

Bias in Philosophers' Views on Women: Plato, Aristotle, Rousseau and Hegel

Thus, in his *Works and Days and Theogony*, Hesiod declares that all evil is traceable to the world's first woman, and so advises us never to trust her.[9] The great epic poet Homer seems to share this nefarious view.[10] Further, in the *Republic*[11] and the *Laws*[12], even Plato regards woman as inferior to man in quite a few ways. Thus, while determining the norms of education for the guardians to be, Socrates, whose views are hardly ever questioned by Plato, is seen to declare that in theatrical performances it is only *men* of virtue, not *women*, who are to be allowed to participate. Plato objects even to the representation of women in the staging of plays:

> We must adhere to our original principle: Those who are to become guardians .... They should neither do nor imitate other things. If they must imitate, let them imitate what is appropriate to their vocation. From childhood on, let them pattern themselves after men who are – among other things – courageous, temperate, reverent, and free (395, pp. 92–93)....
>
> Then those who are educating to become good men ought not – since they are men – to play the parts of women, young or old. They should not imitate a woman quarrelling with her husband, blaspheming against heaven, boasting and swollen in her own conceit, or grieving and wailing over misfortunes, still less should they impersonate a woman who is sick or who is in live or [in] labor (395E, p. 93).[13]

In the *Laws* Plato goes to the extent of saying that a woman is "secretive and crafty by nature", and that her "natural potential for virtue is inferior to a man's, so she is potentially a greater danger, perhaps even twice as great".[14] Plato indeed viewed woman as weaker than man, though he does not specify what sort of failing this weakness is – emotional or merely physical. If a woman's weakness is to be taken as physical, it would not necessarily mean that she is 'secretive' and 'crafty,' because she will need male protection and so will have to be candid with those men whom she expects to protect her. As for Plato's list of cardinal virtues – justice, wisdom, courage and temperance – is it not clearly defective because it just does not include the highly prized virtue of selfless service of which woman is eminently capable? Is not this virtue indispensable for the cohesion and welfare of a family which is the basic unit of an integrated society, as distinguished from a mere multitude of human beings.

As for Aristotle, he outdoes even Plato in denigrating woman. The following excerpt from Diana Coole, a leading feminist scholar, is worth quoting.

> A comparison of the *Politics* with the *Republic* seems at first sight to suggest that Aristotle [only] reverted to, and reinforced gender distinctions that had been transcended by Plato ... [A closer look at Aristotle's work, however, shows that] while the Platonic method favours radical change, its Aristotelian successor offers a conservative argument predicated upon naturalist and *functionalist* premises.[15]

The point may be clarified thus, following Aristotle's general view of reality. According to him, reality is dynamic. But growth and development are nowhere random. Be it an animal or a plant, each individual's growth is determined by its final cause, that is, by what it is to become ultimately. A seed necessarily tends to develop into a tree and a child into a grown-up human being. Likewise, a girl realizes her full significance as a female in becoming a mother, that is, by participating in the function of reproduction. But, in so doing (according to Aristotle), she is only a passive participant; she only provides matter to the process of reproduction, and the father provides the imprint of human personality (or the human form) on this matter: Man is thus the active agent and so may be regarded as superior to woman.[16] Here are some of his own sayings.

> Since "the form, is *better* and more divine in its nature than the matter, it is *better* also that the superior one should be separate from the inferior one. That is why whenever possible and so far as possible the male is separate from the female" (*Generation of Animals,* II, 932a, cf. 1, 727b and II 738b). Woman is "as it were an infertile male", and even in regard to reproduction, "a male is male in virtue of a particular ability, and a female in virtue of a particular inability (*Generation of Animals,* I, 729a, 731a).[17]

Now, Aristotle's reasoning here is clearly suspect. First, though it may well be regarded as one of the important functions of woman, reproduction is not all that a woman does for the family. Her role is here rich and many-sided. She may well be a daughter, a sister, a mother, as freely as a devoted wife. But being a wife does not only mean being a passive participant in the sexual act. If a man gets sexually excited by her looks and by the very curvaceous tenderness of her figure, should not this seductive impact of sheer femininity be said to precede, and so be regarded as the effective cause of stimulating the male sexually who may therefore be said to merely receive the stimulating impact, and so to be simply passive so far, before actively exercising the sexual function? What is more, in all her various capacities, a female lends to the family a touch of sweetness, and often also of solace, whenever necessary. It is this embracive aroma of love and gentleness and her wifely/motherly role of caring and sharing which may be regarded as a woman's essential contribution to the family and so also to society, if indirectly. She may indeed be regarded as a check on man's tendency to be harsh and aggressive; and in that sense as superior to man, because regulative of his proneness to wrong behaviour. Further, would it be fair to deny that, as a mother, woman is an active and powerful, if silent determinant of a growing child's character? Apart from all this, the latest scientific researches tend to suggest that in respect of intuitive power, woman is superior to man.[18]

In Aristotle's writings there is a good deal said about women, which is patently questionable. See, for instance, his following overtly categorical remark:

> Virtues and actions are nobler, when they proceed from those who are naturally worthier, for instance, from a man rather than from a woman.[19]

How is man naturally worthier than woman? Is superior physical power necessarily an index of moral superiority? Does not the very self-conscious sense of being physically stronger often compel a husband to maltreat his wife physically? And, is physical power by itself enough to keep one steadfast in adverse situations? Consider again the following quote from Aristotle's *Politics*:

> They must all share in (moral goodness), but not in the same way – each sharing only to the extent required for the discharge of his or her function. The ruler, accordingly, must possess moral goodness in its *full* or *perfect* form because his function ... demands a master – artificer, and reason is such a *master artificer*, but *all other* persons need only possess moral goodness *to the extent* required of them. It is thus clear that ... temperance – and similarly fortitude and justice – are *not*, as

> Socrates held, the *same* in a woman as they are in a man. Fortitude in the one, for example, is shown in connection with ruling; in the other, it is shown in connection with serving; and the same is true of the other forms of goodness .... To speak in general terms, and to maintain that goodness consists in "a good condition of the soul" or in "right action" or in anything of the kind, is to be guilty of self-deception. Far better than such general definitions is the method of simple enumeration of the different forms of goodness ...[20]

Now, in spite of his acknowledged eminence as a philosopher, the chinks in Aristotle's argument here are easy to see. True, it does not help our thinking much if we speak of goodness in general. We must distinguish its various forms. But, is the fortitude seen in governing people unquestionably superior to the same quality as seen in quietly nurturing a whole family in moments of financial stringency, or in bringing up children as a widow? Is what is publicly observable necessarily superior to what works and sustains one quietly and without wilting? Does not a great work of art or a masterly technological innovation owe its origin to invisible creative processes in the hidden regions of an intensely focussed mind?

Unfortunately, even Rousseau's attitude to woman is just as uncharitable, which is surprising, because he places a great deal of emphasis on equality. He too defines woman's nature in terms of her function, that is, her sexual and procreative role in life. On the other hand, men are acclaimed by him for their limitless potential for rational thought and creativity, suggesting thereby that women are utterly lacking in these qualities. Consider, in this context, Rousseau's own following words:

> ... It is not enough that a woman should be faithful; her husband, along with his friends and neighbours, must *believe* in her fidelity .... Nature herself has decreed that woman, both for herself and her children, should be *at the mercy of man's judgement* ... worth alone will not suffice, a woman must be *thought [to be] worthy*; nor [is her] beauty, [enough;] she must be *admired*; nor [mere] virtue [will do;] she must be *respected* ... "What will people think" is the grave of a man's virtue and the throne of a woman's.[21]

Now, it is easy to see how Rousseau's thinking here is quite questionable. It is too sweeping to say that a woman's fidelity will suffice as a virtue only when it is recognized as such by people around her. There are cases where the husband is unduly suspicious (may be because he himself is having some extra-marital affairs) and where his friends and neighbours quietly go by his judgement. In such cases, it would be clearly unfair to suspect a woman's faithfulness. Even, generally, it is wrong to make the value of an individual's virtue dependent on public opinion. A virtue is an excellence which a person/man grows up into; it is rooted in his (or her) character; it may not be easily perceived from the outside. It is also too much to say that woman can claim to be truly beautiful only if her beauty is acknowledged as such by others. A simple example is enough to expose the falsity of this view. Suppose, an Englishman marries a black beauty and takes her to his country. There, precisely because of her colour, the wife may not be regarded as beautiful by the (white) people in general. But will this in any way detract from her beauty as her own countrymen regard it? Here, however, Rousseau may hasten to point out that in so arguing we only subscribe to his view, if unknowingly; for, we still do not cease to regard the beauty in question as dependent on the opinion of others, it being immaterial whether these 'others' are white or black. To this out ready be rejoinder would be that the positive reaction of others to an individual's beauty is relevant only when they belong to that individual's own cultural environment, and that Rousseau fails to specify this. We could also give a quite different rejoinder. One has to see the difference between the beauty of a living feminine figure and the beauty of the same figure as represented in a portrait. The latter will be an object simply of admiring contemplation; the former, on the other hand, is very likely to kindle in us a desire to possess the figure for intimate fellowship. As Plato said, beauty evokes love. This means that the essential value of beauty lies in bringing and keeping people together. Their mere acknowledgment of an individual's beauty is not enough.

Unfortunately, even a great philosopher like Hegel is not able to see the possibility of exceptional qualities in women. On the other hand, in a rather circuitous way, he too argues for the inferiority of woman as against man. The following statement from his *The Philosophy of Right* is worth noting in this regard:

> The difference in the physical characteristics of the two sexes has a rational basis and consequently acquires an intellectual and ethical significance. This significance is determined by the difference into which the ethical substantiveness as the concept, internally sunders itself in order that its vitality may become a concrete unity consequent upon this difference. Thus one sex is mind in its self-diremption into explicit personal self-subsistence and the knowledge and volition of free universality, i.e., the self-consciousness of conceptual thought and

> the volition of the objective final end. The other sex is mind maintaining itself in unity, as knowledge and volition of the substantive, but knowledge and volition in the form of concrete individuality and feeling. In relation to externality, *the former is powerful and active, the latter is passive and subjective.*[22]

Following the above line of thinking Hegel develops his views thus:

> "Man is naturally capable of performing many activities that are ordinarily beyond the power of woman. The more important of these activities are: struggle for existence; abstract thinking, such as we find in theoretical science and philosophy; and pursuit of impersonal ends. In other words, man is more dynamic, reflective, and capable of doing steadfast and selfless endeavour. Woman, on the other hand, is rather passive and generally confined to the pursuit of more or less personal ends. Further, whereas the distinctive capacities of man flower in state management which requires him not only to learn and labour but also to discipline himself in order to lead and control vast masses of men, woman attains her destiny as a person by exercising and cultivating her native capacity for service and sacrifice in looking after the family and keeping it as one. Apart from this, it is only in a limited number of disciplines that woman can be educated with profit. Subjects which do not suit her native capacities are those that require the use of abstract reasoning and creative imagination in abundant measure, such as advanced science, philosophy, and certain forms of artistic production. At the same time, the fair sex excels in respect of intuition and feeling, as against logical thinking and art activity. Finally, whereas a grown-up man is to a great extent capable of regulating his own development, a young woman, because of her very vulnerability, has to depend on, and be guided by male care and counsel. A woman grows best in the quest of love; a man discovers himself in the heat and turmoil of toil and struggle. So it follows that man has his actual *substantive* life in the state, in learning, and so forth, as well as in labour and struggle not only with the external world but also with himself. In the family, he only lives a subjective ethical life on the plane of feeling. Woman, on the other hand, has her substantive destiny in the family, and to be imbued with family piety is her ethical frame of mind. Women are not incapable of being educated, and they may even hit upon some fruitful ideas, besides excelling in matters of taste, and looking elegant, but they cannot attain to the ideal. They are not made for activities which demand a universal faculty such as the more advanced sciences, philosophy, and certain forms of artistic production. The difference between men and women is similar to that which obtains between animals and plants. Men correspond to animals, while women correspond to plants, because their

> development is more placid and the principle that underlies it is a rather vague unity of feeling. When women hold the helm of government, the state is at once in jeopardy, because they regulate their actions not by the demands of universality but by arbitrary inclinations and opinions.[23]

Now, as outlined above, Hegel's views and the arguments which are made to prop them up cannot bear scrutiny. To begin with, it is not true to say that women are incapable of abstract reasoning. So far, there is absolutely no empirical evidence to suggest that women students do not perform well as their male classmates in the study of subjects like science and philosophy. Even if the inferiority in question were a fact, it would not follow that women, on the whole, are inferior to men. For, if we press the point (as Hegel does) that woman is deficient in the capacity for *abstract* reasoning, the implication would be that she is well equipped in respect of *concrete* reasoning; and such reasoning, it is easy to see, is at least as important for the conduct of life as abstract reasoning is for a fair part of science and philosophy. It may here be noted in passing that at least two significant turns in philosophizing today, namely, phenomenology and existentialism, do not attach much importance to abstract reasoning. And, to turn to traditional Indian philosophy, it attaches at least as much importance to regulative principles of conduct as to the laws of logic. Further, it is also difficult to accept Hegel's view that woman is inferior to man on account of her being governed by feeling instead of reason. Here, however, everything depends on what Hegel may be taken to mean exactly by the word 'feeling'. He himself does not specify it; so we have to determine the meaning ourselves. Now, going by how the word is actually used, there are at least three main meanings of 'feeling': feeling *for* others or sympathy; emotion, as when we say that in dealing with an adversary our attitude should be governed by cool thinking, not by the feeling or emotion of anger; and the ability to see the difference between two seemingly similar objects, as when we say, "she has a feeling for colour," which means that the individual in question can see the difference between two close shades of the same colour. Now, if we take 'feeling' in the first sense – that is, as concern for the needy – it would not appear to be any less important than reason in dealing with others in everyday life. And if we take 'feeling' as emotion, would it be possible for Hegel to deny that the sustained pursuit of any ideal is impossible without having intense love, obviously an emotion, for the ideal in question? Further, so far as the maintenance of interpersonal relations is concerned, love is at least as important as reason. Here, reason *is* needed to see whether the other's attitude towards us is right or wrong and the feeling or emotion of love is needed as making for immediate patience with his (or her) wrong attitude, say, out of love of humanity in general, and so making for tolerance of weaknesses that are common to us. Finally, if we take feeling as the ability to discriminate, say, two adjacent shades of colour, or of a musical note, it would be fair to assume that since she is (according to Hegel) governed essentially by feeling, woman can also do well in the region of arts like painting and music.

What we have just said can be supported by an additional argument. Any form of art activity is the manipulation of some given material. So reasoning, as involved in choosing the right way to handle the material, may be said to be *concrete*. The presence of such reasoning may be said to be adequate in women upon Hegel's own view; for when he emphasizes the lack of *abstract* reasoning in women, the implication obviously is that she is not deficient in *concrete* reasoning. Further, this too is untrue to hold, quite generally, that a woman grows in the passive way of a plant, and that she does not actively regulate her own development. The fact of the matter is that the growth of a woman's personality as a wife, or as a mother, proceeds not only by just assimilating, so to say, the love and affection of her family's other members, but also by actively sharing – and steadfastly and courageously wrestling with – their problems.

Be that as it may, out of the four thinkers we have picked for attention, neither the idealists, Plato and Hegel, nor Aristotle and Rousseau who are commonly thought to be more alive to the claims of empirical reality, have been able to do justice to the value of woman as an individual or as a member of the human family. This defective attitude is also evident in the views of Descartes, Spinoza, and others whose views will be referred to later in this chapter.

Against this misogyny of traditional philosophers, various feminist scholars have alleged that women have made distinct contributions to philosophy. In this regard, they have cited the prevalence of various women philosophers who have hitherto received no mention in books on history of philosophy. The earliest attempt in this direction was made by Gilles Menage, who published *A History of Women*

Philosophers in Latin in 1690. He has refuted the long standing claim that there have been no or very few women philosophers in the past. Further, he classifies women philosophers according to their respective school of thought and cites the name of about twenty Greek women thinkers who lived between the 12th century BCE and the death of Aristotle (322 BCE) or shortly afterwards.[24]

Following this work, several feminist philosophers have recently examined those sources critically that have been handed down to us. They claim that these sources have 'distorted', 'trivialized', or ignored women's participation in philosophical pursuits. They have also exposed and provided a corrective to the sexist and other biases of many of the traditional non-feminist scholars and commentators of the past century. Simultaneously, they have drawn our pointed attention to the uncongenial circumstances of an average woman's daily life which prevented women from making mentionable contribution to Greek thought.

Sr. Prudence Allen[25] has mentioned in her work quite a few creative women authors. She discusses, among others, the poet Sapphio, the rhetorician Aspasia of Miletus, Diotima of Plato's *Symposium,* and a number of women adhering to the Pythagorean school and to the later Neo-Pythagorean tradition, whose letters and fragments have been preserved. Allen also discusses a passage in which Diogenes Laertuis lists by name a number of women in Plato's Academy and includes in this list two well-known women – Lastheneia (Lasthenia) of Mantinea and Axisthea of Philuis (Phliasia).

Another significant work on similar lines is by Mary Ellen Waite[26] which covers the period from 600 BCE to 500 CE. It includes translations of texts attributed to women thinkers as well as biographical, interpretative and critical analytical writings. It contains a discussion by Aspasia of Miletus, revisiting the controversial passage in Plato's dialogue, *Menexenus* in which Plato's Socrates recites a funeral oration in which he says, "Aspasia taught him". Waite also devotes a chapter to Diotima. She rejects the arguments purporting to establish that the Diotima of Plato's *Symposium* is a fictitious character. She even argues for the thesis that the views ascribed to her in Plato's dialogue are in fact Diotima's own views.

Further, in her essay published in the journal *Hypatia* (1986), Kathleen Wider argues that it was in no way exceptional to find a woman seriously engaged in philosophical inquiry; and she does a great deal more. She emphasizes the importance of situating the work of women thinkers in the context of their lives; determines the sexist bias in some of the very sources that give information about women thinkers in ancient Greece; examines the arguments supporting interpretations of some 20th century scholars, e.g., concerning Aspasia and Diotima; and urges that arguments for maintaining that Diotima is a fictitious character come to look especially weak when the underlying sexist biases are revealed.

It is not that women do not find any mention in Plato's dialogue. In *Meno*, for example, we find the following words:

> The speakers were among the priests and priestesses whose care it is to be able to give an account of their practices.

But, apart from such stray references, few women were given personal recognition in their own time for making significant contributions to philosophy or, for that matter, in any area of cultural pursuits. This is, however, not to deny the occurrence of exceptional cases. One woman, who is often cited, Aspasia of Miletus, was prosecuted in Athens for impiety, like Ana-agoras, Socrates, and others. Ultimately, Aspasia was acquitted, but the notable point is that the court system in Athens thought it necessary to prosecute a woman on a charge which was, so to say, reserved chiefly for those who were engaged in the study of nature and for teachers and other foreigners labelled as Sophists. It may however be added that Aspasia was not an ordinary woman. She was then the mistress of Pericles, if not his wife. Moreover, she was from Miletus and not, at the time, a citizen of Athens. Any way, it is only the feminist historians who recall with honour the contributions made by her.[27]

So far, however, we have been talking of philosophers and of their anti-woman bias generally. Let us now turn to the task of indicating how the male bias is present in at least three distinct domains of philosophy, namely, methodology, epistemology and ontology.

Methodology

Methodology occupies a very significant place in every intellectual discipline. It means the rationally determined and time-tested ways by which our sciences and philosophies arrive at their posited truths concerning the world and its content. Quite generally and in brief, it may be said to be a study of method and procedure. Now, in the field of philosophy, feminist explorations have revealed that here even methodology suffers from a male bias, and that it is grounded in male-centric assumptions, to the utter neglect of female perspectives. Feminists therefore press for questioning the very methods that philosophy has traditionally employed, and allege that such a methodology needs to be interrogated on the ground that it does not cover women as objects of and contributors to philosophic activity. In this context, Mary Daly has done some very significant work. Quite generally, her protest runs as follows:

> The tyranny of Methodology hinders new discoveries. It prevents us from raising questions never asked before and from being illumined by ideas that do not fit into pre-established boxes and forms. The worshippers of method have an effective way of handling data that does not fit into the Respectable Categories of Questions and Answers. They simply classify it as non-data, thereby rendering it invisible.[28]

How and where the methodology of philosophy errs is a question of detail. Yet such questions arise from the very way in which methodology is regarded generally. Consider, for instance, the view of Rosenberg who defines methodology as "the application of reason to its own operations, the rational study of rational practices."[29] But has methodology paid enough attention to the limits of reason and to the heuristic potency of intuition? One can hardly say, yes; and this is probably why Genevieve Llyod is driven to say that the female philosophers we find in the history of philosophy "have been philosophers despite, rather than because of, their femaleness; [and that] there has been no [recorded] input of femaleness into the formation of ideals of Reason."[30]

The Greeks believed in rationalism, which posited logic as the final test of truth. In the 17th and 18th centuries, empiricism regarded sense-perception as the sole source of valid human knowledge. Hegelian dialectics proceeds on the assumption that thought progresses by isolating and reconciling contradictions in ever wider syntheses. Karl Marx believed in dialectical materialism, according to which not only knowledge in general, but even stray individual ideas of value are determined by material conditions. Quite differently, the philosophy of mysticism holds that knowledge is communicable, if at all, only in terms of poetic imagery and metaphor. The feminist complaint here is that all this talk of the rise, operation and progress of reflection and knowledge utterly ignores the personal, concrete and the specific. Even Descartes who claimed that his method would be suitable "even for women" (a method of pure thought, moving impersonally from universals to particulars by the pure activity of the mind) assumed that philosophical activity demands total concentration free from all practical concerns. Now, one may here put up some protests at once. Is it not a well-known fact that the eight-fold path prescribed by Lord Buddha is a well reasoned and so eminently philosophical attempt to meet the most pressing practical problem of overcoming suffering? And, the *yamas* and *niyamas* of Patanjali – are they not meant to make for attainment of the supreme goal of philosophic endeavour, that is, spiritual emancipation?

Be that as it may, feminist methodology challenges all the aforementioned philosophies, specially in so far as they relate to our collective life, and directs us to look for the political significance of personal experience. Mitchell makes the point as follows:

> The Politics of Experience is a method of generating creatively new political insights from an analysis of *personal experience*. It is the heart and process of consciousness, raising a group effort to speak the up spoken, bring to conscious awareness what is far from consciousness.[31]

The truth that the above quote seems to suggest may be brought out by referring to the way India has won its political independence. The struggle was essentially non-violent, under Gandhiji's leadership. But what exactly was that which made him think of non-violence as a method of political protest? It was simply the fact that his heart bled for the downtrodden masses of India. The experience that was here at the root of the matter was surely not the humdrum experience that comes from sense-perception or from one's skill in dealing with the world for making a successful living, but from the intensely personal experience of an ethico-religious character; and it is this appeal to the compassionateness that is embedded in every human heart that crystallized the need for a collective revolt and so, as the quote says, brought 'to conscious awareness' what was earlier far from consciousness, or was just simmering in the sub-conscious minds of people at large.

In this way, by appealing to personal experience feminist methodology presses for a "distinct way of doing philosophy". It does not profess to be "objective, abstract or universal", and insists that women's experience must be taken into account. Does not a mother's experience of nurturing children selflessly deliver the philosophic (or basic) truth that the very continuance of humanity depends as much on self-sacrifice as on the intake of material nourishment? The evidence of personal experience is indeed as potent a source of philosophic wisdom as logical reasoning.

Led by such like thinking, the feminists try to create a new methodology which emphasizes gender as a basic fact of social life. It does not deny or discount the value of objective experience, but only seeks to validate the importance of the private, emotional, interiorized, intimate world.[32] It contends that much of what is regarded as sociological knowledge about human behaviour is in fact knowledge about male behaviour only, and that what passes by the name of academic discourse is, in reality, an exclusively male discourse that just arrogates to itself the labels of science, rationality and scholarship. Consider, for instance, Aristotle's definition of virtue only as the mean between two extremes. Is any amount of caring for her young ones an extreme for a devoted mother? Is martyrdom is a choice between caring too much and too little for one's own life?

Further, feminist methodology is not so much a matter of garnering knowledge as of raising women's awareness in respect of their present lot and the ways to ameliorate it. In the words of Catherine A. Mackinnon, "for feminism the personal is epistemologically the political and its epistemology is its politics". It means that, according to feminism, personal experience is a determinant of needed political action, and the knowledge of (women's) personal lot is alone that epistemology which is to decide how (women's) political life is to be conducted. Feminism presents Judy Grahn's 'Common Woman' as speaking the "common language" of Adrienne Rich; and what 'consciousness raising' means is not only "to know different things as politics ... [but] to know them in a different way. Women's experience of politics, of life as [determined by sex] gives rise to its own method of appropriating that reality: feminist method."[33]

Such a methodology, feminists claim, is a 'first order' methodology because it begins by focusing on the concrete and the specific and deferring resort to abstraction and generalization to a later stage. Consciousness raising involves "collective critical constitution of the meaning of women's social experience, as women live through it". Where philosophers take recourse to abstract generalization, feminists try to debunk it, so to say, by opposing it to the personal. Similarly, whereas philosophers seek objective truth, feminists consider it important to look at the individual's actual point of view; and where philosophers tend to suggest that emotion and personal feeling are impediments to truth, feminists press the claims of direct, personal experience as an important source and verifier of truth.[34] The emphasis, we may note, is warranted by the very sensible distinction that Bertrand Russell has drawn between knowledge by description and knowledge by acquaintance.

What is more, feminist philosophers believe in adopting an interdisciplinary approach? They have argued that they are constrained in their work by the more or less rigid limits drawn by tradition in the established frameworks of existing disciplines. They therefore rely on an eclectic methodology which draws on various disciplines. Nor is this penchant unjustified. Take, for instance, matters relating to sex. Do they fall only within the province of psychology, and are not also the concern of ethics and sociology and of politics which, in our country, is yet to deal satisfactorily with the question of women's empowerment?

Epistemology

Closer attention to the fair sex, we may note, is also demanded by some lacunae in epistemology as it has so far been in the field of philosophy. Here, rationalism and empiricism are the two dominant theories. According to the proponents of the rationalism theory, an individual's actions and beliefs should be based on reason rather than on intuition or the teachings of others. Empiricism, on the other hand, believes that knowledge can only be gained through experiment and observation. Now, to turn first to rationalism. Questioning its emphasis on reason in traditional philosophy feminists say that reason is undoubtedly of pre-eminent value in the getting and progression of knowledge. But how is it fair, as being true to fact, to hold that women are deficient in respect of the ability to reason? And yet this is what Aristotle has done. He holds that it is "through a certain incapacity that the female is female,"[35] that this intrinsic female incapacity ... [signifies] a lack in the "principle of soul"[36] and that it is this which makes women's ability to use reason inferior to that of men. Here, one can only wonder if reason is necessary only for a professional philosopher, and has no place at all in a mother's decision to teach her children more by means of exemplary conduct than by merely verbal instruction. Unfortunately, even Plato appears to regard women as creatures of sheer passion. This is evident not only in his reflections on the ideal state in *Republic* but in his other dialogues, such as *Symposium* and *Timaeus* also. In respect of *Republic* we may here cite the following words of Jane Flax: "The imagery of the cave in the *Republic;* the world of shadows ... [and] *the unconscious and ... [and] the womb which the light of reason cannot penetrate or dispel,* reveals the fear of regression to that *preverbal* state where feelings, the needs of the body and women [as mothers] rule."[37]

See, next, the views of St. Augustine who does not deny rationality to woman but yet regards her inferior to man:

> "[We] see man, made in your [God's] image .... And [who] resembles you, ... because he has the power of reason and understanding. And

> just as in man's soul there are two forces; one which is dominant because it deliberates and one which obeys ... in the same way in the physical sense *woman has been made for man. In her mind and her rational intelligence she has a nature the equal of man's but in sex she is physically subject to him in the same way as our natural impulses need to be subjected to the reasoning power of mind,* in order that the actions to which they lead may be inspired by the principles of good conduct ... ."[38] Then you took man's mind which is subject to none but you and needs to imitate no human authority, and renewed it in your own image and likeness. You made rational action subject to the rule of the intellect, *as woman is subject to man.*[39]

Now, turning to the modern age, one discovers the same kind of thought in Descartes who makes a desperate attempt to escape from the body, sexuality and the wiles of the unconscious. For him, the self needs "no place and depends on no material thing". It is completely self-constituting and self-sustaining. This view of the self entails complete indifference to the body and to its interaction with self. Now, because of this excessive emphasis on the independence of self, the manifest plurality of (embodied) individuals is naturally lost sight of; social relations become adventitious; and the question of securing knowledge of woman's life and problems just does not arise. Spinoza's devaluation of woman, though indirect, is quite as definite as has been done by any other male philosophers. This is evident from his following statements: A strong man is one who is a man of reason, and who "rightly realizes that all things follow from the necessity of the divine nature, and come to pass in accordance with the eternal law and rules of nature; [he] will not find anything [deserving] of hatred ... nor will he bestow pity on anything,"[40] for pity is "womanish."[41] It is indeed evident here that the ideal of Spinoza is a purely masculine one. The ultimate degradation for his "Man of Reason" is to be "womanish", which is equated with being under the sway of passions utterly unrelieved by reason.

Quite rightly, therefore, the renowned feminist scholar Alison M. Jaggar decries such Western epistemology as the mere "myth of dispassionate investigation". In such a philosophy of knowledge emotion is all along viewed with suspicion, and sometimes even with hostility. Jaggar alleges:

> Not only has *reason* been contrasted with emotion, but it has also been associated with the mental, the cultural, the universal, the public *and the male,* whereas emotion has been associated with the irrational, the physical, the natural, the particular, the private, *and of course, the female.*[42] Such a derogatory western attitude towards emotion, like the

> earlier western contempt for sensory observation, fails to recognize that emotion, like sensory perception, is necessary to human survival. Emotions prompt us to act appropriately .... Without emotion, human life would be unthinkable. Moreover, *emotions have an intrinsic as well as an instrumental value.*[43]

Such writing is no mere rhetoric. It speaks for truth. Take, for instance, the emotion of joy. Can anyone deny that this emotion is intrinsically likeable. Can any question be more senseless than: "Why do you want to be happy?" And, can anyone doubt that joy in one's appointed work is conducive to both mental health and greater, better output?

Hence, the feminists argue, such a theory of knowledge is urgently needed which will focus on understanding all that determines human behaviour rather than only on reason which presses for "justification, verification and control". Their attempt is many-sided; it seeks to recontract philosophy in such a manner that its methods and subject matter may both attach due value to women's experiences. The 1980s have indeed seen the evolution of a new feminist epistemology, and its architects all begin from the common ground that the activities of "knowing itself and thinking about knowing" are alike embedded in the complex networks of power and politics. The eminent (male) scholars occupy seats of power, and it is political influence that determines who will be allowed or denied access to the citadels of informational material. The feminists protest with one voice that the dominant theories of knowledge in the Western philosophical tradition have so far focused only on that kind of information which is accessible to the select few – information which Lorraine Code has rightly characterized as "a commodity of privilege".[44] Several feminist writings have revealed this academic elitism in the field of professional philosophy.[45]

From 1983 onwards there has indeed been a proliferation of epistemological projects. Feminists have moved on from arguing for the epistemological significance of the sex of the knower[46] to exposing the androcentricity of epistemological projects in most of their Anglo-American forms. Mapping out how feminist interventions have been reshaping epistemological inquiry, Sandra Harding has discerned three principal strands within it: feminist empiricism, standpoint theory and postmodernism.[47] Each one of them calls for some remarks by way of clarification.

Feminist empiricism takes as its starting point the contention that, like any other potential knower, feminists too have to base their knowledge on empirical evidence if they are to move capably about the physical world and engage effectively with the social, political and 'natural' realities that constitute their environment and inform their experiences. Its main proponents maintain that prospects for a better philosophical understanding of human existence and the factors that determine its character and development will improve as large numbers of women enter the domains in which 'received knowledge' is sifted and made serviceable. These domains are mainly universities, laboratories, publishing houses, journals, editorial boards and funding agencies.

Some feminist philosophers have further argued that a somewhat more radical approach than that of simple feminist empiricism is required for a feminist epistemology. They plead for a radically new standpoint for looking at matters relating to epistemology. This they characterize as the feminist standpoint, and in so doing they refer to parallels in history. Just as the viewpoint of capitalist ideology represented proletarian subordination to the bourgeoisie as natural, so the viewpoint of patriarchal ideology represented the subordination of women to men as quite natural. Further, from their own chosen viewpoint, the Marxists too base their reflections on the material circumstances of proletarian lives. So, there is nothing odd in the feminists' decision to start from the material-historical circumstances of female lives.[48]

The third category of postmodernist feminist philosophers[49] is usually more radical than the empiricists or standpoint feminists. Feminists of this category believe, as Cole says:

> Postmodern epistemologies are … essentially critical. They insist that it is only through [a] thoroughgoing deconstruction of our intellectual heritage … [every word of which should be questioned]; [b] abjuring of privileged standpoints and claims to objective truth; and [c] a relentless critique of the relation between knowledge-making and power-guarding can a liberatory feminist thinking and practice proceed [profitably].[50]

Differences of detail are surely there in the views of postmodern epistemologists, but they all agree in maintaining that the three main objectives of feminist epistemology are:

(a) To highlight and reform the relationship between knowledge-making and power-holding in different cultures.
(b) To open the doors of the institutions which create and process received knowledge to those who have been so far been kept out.

(c) To gain, through such endeavours, social justice for women, and to provide a more impartial and comprehensive body of "knowledge for everyone".

Ontology

The way is now paved to speak of ontology as the feminists would like it to be. Ontology, incidentally, is that branch of metaphysics which deals with the nature and essence of things or of existence. It is no doubt a necessary discipline, but the irony is that the knowledge what essentially has come to women is mediated through male experience. Take, for instance, the ontological argument for God's existence, namely, the argument that the concept of God is necessarily the concept of a being who cannot but exist. One may accept the argument as valid, but what is the warrant for surreptitiously interpreting this necessary existent as exclusively male, a movement of thought which is clearly implicit in speaking of God and God's (attributes) as *He* and *His*. It is left for practising men of religion like Ramakrishna Paramhansa to emphasize that it is more helpful for the growth of faith to think of God as the Mother.

What is worse, as Simone de Beauvoir points out, women have just not been expected to "trouble ... [their] heads about" questions such as, 'what is reality' or 'of what is the world constituted'? Marilyn Frye shows that since women have been left out of the patriarchal concept of reality, reality comes to appear only as what male philosophers take it to be essentially:

> The exclusion of women from the phallocratic scheme is impressive, frightening, and often fatal, but it is not simple and absolute. Women's existence is both absolutely necessary to and irresolvable problematic for the dominant reality and those committed to it, for [though] our existence is *presupposed* by phallocratic reality, ... it is not and cannot be encompassed by or countenanced by that reality. Women's existence is a background against which phallocratic reality is a foreground.[51]

What we have just cited is by no means pellucid. So, it needs to be clarified. A phallocratic scheme (or plan of reflecting on what is there) is dominated by male attitudes (or biases). So it may be said to exclude women. This exclusion, however, is not – nay, it cannot be – absolute. The existence of women has got to be admitted; otherwise what men will be said to lord over, as they in fact do, according to the scheme in question. So, the exclusion here spoken of cannot be taken literally. It only means that women receive very little attention, and so remain an uncomprehended something (or 'irresolvable problematic') for the 'dominant reality', that is, the male world with its anti-woman attitudes. So, in a nutshell, this reality occupies the foreground of philosophic thought and feminine existence just lurks in the background, waiting to be given due attention by resurgent feminism. In such a warped view of reality the even-keel vision of woman as a complementary half of humanity just cannot arise.

The dichotomies envisaged in such an ontology are thus only the following: self-other, mind-body and active-passive. The male-female dichotomy does not – and cannot – figure, in the way it should, in such a stunted scheme of things. In the last sentence of the above para the words we have put in italics serve a definite purpose. They are meant to suggest not that man-woman dichotomy does not figure at all in traditional philosophy, but only that it does not figure there in the way it should. The truth indeed is that Western culture has all along identified woman with the natural, the physical, or the merely bodily attributes. Nature is personified as a female, "a mother". Women are portrayed as more closely linked to nature, and so less integral to civilization and the cultural order than men. Men are regarded as 'rational agents', 'makers of order and measure', 'controllers of history'; and women, on the other hand, as simply 'emotional vessels', 'subjects of orders and measures' and 'passive observers of history'. This ill-conceived power play within conceptual dichotomy surely underpins, if not quite directly, the dominance of man over woman. So, one of the main tasks of the feminist mission is to undo all such dichotomies as exaggerate distinctions into divisions, namely, culture-nature, transcendence-immanence, universal-particular, mind-body, reason-emotion, public-private, and male-female etc.

Now, it is easy to show that dichotomies such as these are not true to fact. Take, for instance, the one that opposes immanence to transcendence. If by word transcendent we mean "in a surpassing degree" cannot God be said to be immanent in or within us in a surpassing degree? This indeed is the repeated verdict of saints that God is our innermost essence, and that if we are to attain to Him we have therefore to do most intense soul-searching for excavating, so to say, the very seeds of evil in us. As surpassingness, therefore, transcendence here becomes a quality of God's immanence in us, as also of our introspective search for uprooting evil. How then can we posit a relation of mere opposition between immanence and transcendence? Take, again, the case of man-woman distinction. The difference is obvious. Yet, if femininity is taken to signify tenderness and passivity, is not the average man often seen to become softened as pulp in calamity and steadied anew by wifely support? It is here that the old Indian concept of *ardhnāriśwar* appears quite valid. There is a tender vein in every man and a core of steal in every woman. Try to attack a mother's child in her presence and see how tigerish she readily becomes. Love, like sheer endurance, can be easily a mix of flint and steel.

What, however, is lamentable is the practical consequence of the dichotomy we have been talking of. Just by assimilating her to the order of nature, woman has been ranked lower than man in respect of culture, because culture is regarded as a refining of what we naturally are. Just as regrettable is the fact that even Aristotle's writings are not free from such defects. Right from his early thinking as recorded in *Physics* to his later work, *Generation of Animals*, Aristotle took the dualistic opposition between the male and the female as his starting point, and he used it as the model for the relation of form to matter, which is at the core of his entire ontology.[52] Form, in his view, is rational and active, and matter is irrational and passive. It is, in this context, noteworthy that far from being just an aberration in Aristotle's thought the male-female dualistic opposition runs through his entire ontology. It is his explicit view that the free adult male – or rather only the Athenian citizen – qualifies as a full person, because only he is possessed of a properly functioning and rational capacity; that to be born as a female is the most common kind of deformity;[53] and that the free male adult's relations with others, say, female non-slaves, children, are largely determined by his obligation to behave reasonably on their behalf. At this point, however, it is necessary to add that Aristotle ranks women higher than slaves. Accordingly, he holds that whereas wives are to be managed and not rigidly controlled, slaves and children are to be ruled over firmly. Allied to this view is his argument that because of a woman's natural attraction for man, a wife does not need that thoroughgoing control as a slave or barbarian does.

Aristotle, however, is not alone in ranking man higher than woman. Hegel too may be said to do this in his version of patriarchy. Nor is Sartre's individualism in his well-known work, *Being and Nothingness*, free from this bias, which looms large also in the works of Hobbes, Locke and Nozick. It is as a result of being pained at by this running bias of philosophers against women that the feminist Catherine Mackinnon reacts as follows:

> Gender here is a matter of dominance, not [merely of] difference. Feminists have noticed that [though] women and men are [equal in respect of individual differences [they are] not equally powerful. Explaining the subordination of women to men, [Catherine says that] a *political* condition has nothing to do with difference in any fundamental sense, [and that it is rather the very] ideology of difference [which has been conspicuous] in its enforcement, [and hence the real cause of] male dominance ... [intrinsically or naturally] men are not ... supreme and [nor are] women subordinate by nature ... the fact that [they are yet] socially [inferior is just a wilful and biased exaggeration of the] *difference* [which of course] is gender-based.[54]

A great deal of recent feminist work has been a reaction against the unduly heightened opposition not only between body and mind, but between emotion and reason too. What lends a definite edge to this reaction is the painful awareness that whereas the mind's capacity to reason has been regarded as inseparable from masculinity, being feminine has been dubbed as simply a matter of bodily and emotional existence. What is more, an extra acuteness is lent to the anti-woman attitude by positing a virtual disjunction between the mind (with its capacity to think) and the body. The following excerpt from Descartes is worth quoting here.

> I thereby conclude that I was a substance, of which the whole essence or nature consists in thinking ... so that this 'I', that is to say, the mind by which I am what I am, is entirely distinct from the body.[55]

The disjunction in question is visible in the works of Plato as well. As we say so, we have in mind his views like the following:

> ... [When] the soul uses the instrumentality of the body for any inquiry, whether through sight or hearing or any other sense – because using the body implies using the senses – it is drawn away by the body into the realm of the variable, and loses its way and becomes confused and dizzy, as though it were fuddled, through contact with things of a similar nature .... But when it investigates by itself, it passes into the realm of the pure and everlasting and immortal and changeless ...[56]

Here, the body is (so to say) cast in the role of a bad companion of the soul – a companion that impedes the souls effective functioning. Here, it may be added that whereas for Descartes the mind or soul is just the locus of certainty, for Plato soul is 'pure' and 'divine' and, therefore, the body is to be subordinated in to and by the soul or mind.

Now, feminists have not been to slow to draw pointed attention to this tendency to exaggerate the importance of mind as against the body. Susan Bordo, for instance, does this in a way which is balanced and truthful:

> Not all historical conceptions view the [inhibitive pull of the] body as equally 'inescapable' .... But what remains the constant element throughout historical variations is the *construction* of body as something apart from true self (whether conceived as soul, mind, will, creativity, freedom ...) and a sundermining the best efforts of that self. That which is not-body is the highest, the best, the noblest the closest to God; that which is body is the albatross, [that is, an oppressive and inescapable fact] the heavy drag on self realization.[57]

Bordo adds that throughout the history of Western philosophy, the female body has been devalued in a variety of ways; that women have been all along depicted as incapacitated for right thinking and conduct by the 'unbearable weight' of the body; and that man, on the other hand, has been idolized "like a pure idea, the one, the All, the Absolute Spirit".

The feminist philosophers' argument in this context is that a preferable starting point for understanding the contents of human consciousness would be not the rational self as such, but as enlarged and enriched by its connectedness with others;[58] and that the concept of a radically isolated subject as the seat of consciousness is not only vacuous but impossible. Surely, we begin to think and speak not in solitude, but always in concert with our culture and with its specific representatives in whose care we find ourselves. We form ourselves through an integrative process that is ongoing; our thoughts are never entirely our own; and intersubjectivity is a basic fact, whereas merely individual subjectivity is simply an abstraction. Here, we may note, the feminist view is supported by quite a few insights of psychoanalysis and postmodernist thought which lend credence to the view that instead of being isolated and self-complete, ourselves are embodied (so open to environmental influences), malleable and socially constructed.[59]

It is important to see what the concept of self's being embodied essentially implies. It means not only that the self acquires its filling of knowledge through the senses, but also that it is the fact of embodiment which makes selves appear as distinct individuals and provides for the possibility of healthy interpersonal relations which alone can make for the individual's self-improvement and moral advancement. Building on their national intellectual tradition, French feminist philosophers have not only placed the phenomenology of lived experience at centre stage, but have also made exciting progress in constructing the basis for an emancipatory philosophy of the body. They have also pointed out that the dominant tradition in Western philosophy has made women's bodies problematic in two contradictory ways. First, woman and body are equated as essentially physical, with the result that woman's entire personality comes to appear as a merely sexual object. Secondly, the sexualized woman is yet either ignored in philosophy, by just subsuming her under the rubric Nature, or if she is dealt with philosophically, it is only from the viewpoint of how she appears to man. Even her sexuality is contoured as an invitation to male indulgence rather than as a source of potential for such activities as call for tenderness, such as upbringing of children and nursing. She is thus obscured as a subject or agent of helpful activity and discussed only as an object.

The truth indeed is that, as Iris Marion Young has ably pointed out, a woman's specific embodiment as such generates experiences that are just not available to men and so have not been touched on in traditional philosophy. Some of these experiences may be listed thus: the feeling of having breasts, the experience of pregnancy, and, above all, of delivering children. How exactly it feels to nourish a life directly with something which is an exudation from one's own being, and how the labour that makes for the birth of a child is at once and happily cancelled at the very sight of the issue – does the male philosopher have any idea of such experiences of intimate self-giving and electric displacement of pain by bliss? Merely to say that human lives make a chain or that pain and joys make a necessary *dvandva* is one thing; to see it happen in one's own life, and in a way which is not open to view, is quite another. Some of the innermost recesses of personal experience are for ever beyond the ken of masculine intelligence. If, as quite a few philosophers in this day and age insist, our subjective experience is as much of value for philosophic reflection as the experience that impinges on our senses, the male philosophers must be said to suffer from an inherent handicap, and they need, necessarily, the aid of feminist philosophers. In the experiences we have listed, are not the distinctions of self and the other, and of giving and possessing quite heavily bedimmed, if not utterly effaced?[60] To be sure, the *self* does not emerge out of the exclusion, or subjection of the 'other', as it is freely to do in post structuralist philosophy. Instead, it is from a primordial intersubjectivity that both 'self' and the 'other' emerge.

It is just as important to see the frivolousness of the view that "emotions ... [are] passions which constitute confused and therefore potentially misleading modes of perceiving reality", a view which is surprisingly present in the writings of both Bacon and Descartes.

> Even generally, "... in western thought ... emotions have tended to be dismissed as private, 'irrational', inner sensations, which have been tied, historically, to women's 'dangerous desires' and 'hysterical bodies' ... the dominant view ... seems to have been that emotions need to be 'tamed', 'harnessed' or 'driven out' by the steady (male) hand of reason ...".[61]

Even Spinoza subscribes to the view that emotions only tend to obscure right knowledge. Kant too remarks that "women's philosophy is to feel, not to reason".

Now, feminist philosophy seeks to undo these dualisms in order to end gender injustice – a form of injustice which traditional philosophy has just been oblivious of. They feel specially piqued by such unfair and untrue remarks as the following from Kant:

> Women will avoid the wicked not because it is not upright but only because it is ugly .... Nothing of duty, nothing of compulsion, nothing of obligation! They do something' only because it pleases them .... I hardly believe that the fair sex [sic] is capable of principles. Her philosophy is not to reason but to sense. All the other merits of a woman should nite to enhance the character of the beautiful which is the proper reference point ... all education and instruction should have [this] before its eyes .... A woman who has a head full of Greek, like Mme Dacier, or carries on fundamental controversies about mechanics, might as well have a beard.[62]

Now, it is easy to see that the second and third sentences in the above quote harbor a ruinous dichotomy. Is the doing of duty necessarily opposed to doing what pleases one? Cannot the feeling of constraint in doing one's duty utterly dissolve in the loving discharge of one's natural obligations, such as that of a mother in relation to her children?

Towards a Feminist Philosophy

So a truthful and balanced feminist philosophy is indeed a need of the day, and it is rightly being developed along the following lines of thought: All thought processes must be grounded in social and historic reality, and 'reality' is not one and the same for all. Differences of race, class, gender and sexuality etc. – all are determinants of our view of reality, and so also of thought processes. For example, if social and political feminist philosophy is done only from the Western point of view, the needs, aspirations and contributions of black women will be ignored and find no place in the field of philosophy. Further, philosophy should base itself on the fact of intersubjectivity instead of beginning with the isolated, if a thinking 'I' our reference here to Descartes' 'I think, therefore I am'. The feminist protest would here run thus: If I think I necessarily think of something, therefore, the fact of my thinking should be taken to imply not merely my existence but of myself and the object thought of. Indeed, the subject and object of knowledge cannot be separated; they can only be distinguished. Where, in the act of thinking, the subjective ends and the objective begins cannot be demarcated. Cannot an act of thinking about something at once be self-conscious too? The search for truth should aim not only at what is there, as merely objective; it has to be such a form of strategy as runs as a kind of growing into the realization of truth. Theory itself has to be a form of practice so, instead of opposing reason to what is an other to it, a feminist philosophy expands the concept of reason; and avoiding dominant models of knowledge, it recognizes its status also as material, textual and institutional.

It would however be wrong to think that the feminist challenge is confined to just two fields of philosophy, that is, ontology and epistemology. It extends to the philosophy of art and religion as well. On the one hand, it questions the propriety of regarding the traditional creative skills of women as mere craftsmanship; and, on the other hand, it protests against the philosophers' tendency to think of God essentially in male terms. Many objects of craft are beautiful to look at and invite disinterested attention, besides being practically useful. How then can we draw a sharp dividing line between art and craft? And, to turn to religion, what is the warrant for overemphasizing the male attribute of omnipotence and self-existence at the expense of, say, maternal solicitude? And why is it that, by way of verifying the truths of religion, only the experience of male saints is taken into account? What is worse, the male bias is present in the field of biomedical ethics too. Women's health issues have surely not been given as meticulous attention as those of men. Some feminist medical ethicists advocate a revision of the entire concept of medical care for women. They want it to be more holistic than it presently is. Quite a few of women's menstrual problems are due to sheer stress, and this stress is not a little due to husbands' aggressive attitude and leaving the task of looking after children entirely to wives. Spot diagnosis is by no means enough. bell hooks is therefore justified in speaking as follows:

> That aspect of feminist revolution ... [which] calls women to love womanness, that calls men to resist dehumanizing concepts of *masculinity* [such as the one which equates this attribute with just ruling over woman] is an essential part of our struggle. It is the process by which we move from seeing ourselves as objects to acting as subjects. When women and men understand that working to eradicate patriarchal domination is a struggle rooted in the longing to make a world where everyone can live fully and freely, then we know our work to be a gesture of love. Let us draw upon that love to heighten our awareness, deepen our compassion, intensify our courage, and strengthen our commitment.[63]

Even the discipline of history requires a proper estimation of the value of women. Why we say so will be brought out in the chapter to follow.

Notes

1. Angela Miles and Geraldine Finn (eds.), *Feminism: From Pressure to Politics*, Jaipur and New Delhi: Rawat Publications, 2002, p. 206.
2. Sheila Ruth, "Methodocracy, Misogyny and Bad Faith: The Response of Philosophy", in Dale Spender (ed.), *Men's Studies Modified*, London: Pergamon Press, 1981, p. 52.
3. Ibid., p. 45.
4. Alison M. Jaggar, "How can Philosophy be Feminist?" *American Philosophical Association Newsletter on Feminism and Philosophy*, April 1988, p. 6.
5. Sheila Ruth, "Methodocracy, Misogyny and Bad Faith: The Response of Philosophy", in Dale Spender (ed.), op. cit., p. 46.
6. Caren. J. Warren, "Critical Thinking and Feminism", *Informal Logic*, 10(1), (Winter 1988).
7. See Henricus Institoris, *Malleus Malificorum* (translated Montague Summers), New York: B. Bloom, 1970. See Ben Barker Benfield, "The Spermatic Economy: A Nineteenth Century View of Sexuality", *Feminist Studies*, Vol. I, No. 1, 1972, pp. 45–74.
8. Florence Howe, *Seven Years Later: Women Studies Program in 1976*, Report of the National Advisory Council on Women's Educational Programs, USA, 1977.
9. Hesiod, *The Works of Hesiod*, Callimachus and Theogonis (trans.), London: J. Banks, 1889. Hesiod, Works; Theogony, p. 585 and cf. p. 57, Works and Days, p. 73 ff.
10. Homer, *The Odyssey*, VII, E.V. Rieu (trans.), London: Harmondsworth, 1946, pp. 50–60.
11. See *The Republic*, Book III, Richard W. Sterling and William C. Scott (trans.), New York: W.W. Norton, 1985, 387e-388a, 395, 431b-c, 605d-e.

12. *The Laws*, 639b.
13. *The Republic*, op. cit., 395E, p. 93 and 395C, pp. 92–93.
14. Plato, *The Laws*, translated with an introduction by Trevor J. Saunders, London: Penguin Books, 1970, pp. 262–63.
15. Diana H. Coole, *Women in Political Theory*, Sussex, Wheatsheaf Books, 1988, pp. 29–35
16. Aristotle, *Generation of Animals*, II A.L. Peck (trans.), London: Loeb Classical Library, 1970.
17. Ibid.
18. The female brain may have an ability to integrate complex material in a way the male brain simply doesn't. Weston H. Agor found, in his study of over 2,000 executives and government leaders, that women score slightly higher than men on a scale designed to measure their intuitive ability. See Mark Bricklin, Mark Golin, Deborah Grandinetti and Alexis Lieberman, "Female Intuition: Myth or Fact?" in *Positive Living and Health*, Bombay: Rajendra Publishing House, 1990, p. 477.
19. Aristotle, *The Art of Rhetoric*, 1, 1367a, John Henry (trans.), Harward, Loeb Classical Library.
20. Aristotle, *Politics*, 1, 1260a, Ernest Barker (trans.), London: Oxford University Press, 1946.
21. Emile, B. Foxley (trans.), New York, 1969, p. 325, 328.
22. W.F. Hegel, *Philosophy of Right*, T.M. Knox (trans.), London: Oxford University Press, 1973, p. 144.
23. Ibid., pp. 263–64.
24. Gilles Menage used the texts of Herodolus, Plato, Aristotle, Diogenes, Laertuis, Jamblicus, Clement of Alexandria, Plutarch, Porphyry, Suidas and other sources.
25. *The Concept of Women: The Aristotelian Revolution 750 BC – 1250 AD*, Montreal: Eden Press, 1985.
26. Mary Ellen Waite (ed.), *A History of Women Philosophers*, Vol. 1, Chicago: Chicago University Press, 1987.
27. Alison M. Jaggar and Iris M. Young (eds.), *A Companion to Feminist Philosophy*, Oxford: Blackwell Publishers, 1998, pp. 9–11.
28. Mary Daly, *Beyond God the Father*, Boston: Beacon Press, 1973, p. 11.
29. Jay Rosenberg, *The Practice of Philosophy*, 2nd Edition, Englewood Cliffs: Prentice-Hall, 1984, p. 6.
30. Genevieve Llyod, *The Man of Reason: 'Male' and 'Female' in the Western Culture*, Minneapolis: University of Minnesota Press, 1984, p. 108.
31. Juliet Mitchell, *Women's Estate*, New York: Vintage, 1973.
32. Catherine Mckinnon, "Feminism, Marxism, Method, and the State: An Agenda for Social Theory", *Signs*, 7, 1982, pp. 515–44.
33. Ibid., p. 536.

34. Many psychologists have proved that women tend to prefer social interactive process more than men do. Carol Gilligan has tried to prove it by defining the differences between the two. Men are abstract and universalistic in their approach, whereas women are concrete and relativist in their approach. Men are more power-sharing and enjoy rights, whereas women are more responsibility-sharing and interested in relation building, Carol Gilligan, *In a Different Voice,* Cambridge: Harvard University Press, 1982.
35. Aristotle, *Generation of Animals*, Book 1, Chapter 20, 727a, 15.
36. Ibid., Book II, Ch. 3, 737a, 25.
37. Jane Flax, "Political Philosophy and the Patriarchal Unconscious: A Psychoanalytic Perspective of Epistemology and Metaphysics", in Nancy Tuana and Rosemarie Tong Beulder (eds.), *Feminism and Philosophy,* Boulder, CO: Westview Press, 1995, p. 226. (Here Flax refers to Plato's *Republic,* translated by F.M. Cornford, New York: Oxford University Press, 1947, pp. 227–35.
38. St. Augustine, *The Confessions,* R.S. Pine-Coffin (trans.), Baltimore: Penguin Classics, 1961, p. 344.
39. Ibid., p. 345.
40. Spinoza, *The Ethics,* R.H.M. Elwes (trans.), Mineola, NY: Dover, 1955, 2, Part V, Prop., XLII, p. 270.
41. Ibid., Part V, Prop., III, p. 248.
42. Alison M. Jaggar, "Love and Knowledge: Emotion in Feminist Epistemology", in Ann Garry and Marilyn Pearsall (eds.), *Woman, Knowledge and Reality: Explorations in Feminist Philosophy,* London: Routledge, 1992, p. 124.
43. Ibid., p. 139.
44. See Eve Browning Cole, *Philosophy and Feminist Criticism,* New York: Paragon House, 1992.
45. Sandra Harding and Merrill Hintikka, *Discovering Reality: Feminist Perspectives on Epistemology, Metaphysics, Methodology, and Philosophy of Science,* Dordrecht and Boston: Reidel Publishing Co., 1983.
46. Arguments for the epistemological significance of the sex of the knower have been advanced by the following scholars in particular:
    - Geneviove Lloyd, *The Man of Reason: 'Male' and 'Female' in Western Philosophy,* London: Methuen, 1993.
    - Evelyn Fox Keller, *Reflections on Gender and Science,* New Haven: Yale University Press, 1985.
    - Susan Bordo, *The Flight to Objectivity: Essays on Cartesianism and Culture,* Albany: Suny Press, 1987.
47. Sandra Harding, *The Science Question in Feminism,* Ithaca, New York: Cornell University Press, 1966.

48. The leading articulators of standpoint epistemologies may be listed as follows: Patricia Hill Collins, Nancy Hartsock, Hillary Rose, Dorothy Smith.
49. See Linda Alcoff and Elizabeth Polter, *Feminist Epistemologies*, London: Routledge, 1993.
50. See Eve Browning Cole, op. cit., p. 94.
51. Marilyn Frye, "To See and be Seen: The Politics of Reality", in Ann Garry and Marilyn Pearsall (eds.), *Women, Knowledge and Reality*, New York: Routledge, 1992, pp. 87–88.
52. Aristotle, *Physics*, Book Alpha, 192a.
53. Aristotle, *Generations of Animals*, 728a, 18 and 766b, 20.
54. Catherine A. Mackinnon, *Feminism Unmodified*, Cambridge: Harvard University Press, 1987, p. 51.
55. Descartes, *Discourse on the Method and the Meditations*, translated by F.E. Sutcliffe, Harmondsworth: Penguin, 1968 (originally published in 1631 and 1647).
56. Edith Hamilton and Hintington Caims (eds.), *Plato: The Collected Dialogues*, Princeton, New Jersey: Princeton University Press, 1961, p. 62.
57. Susan Bordo, *Unbearable Weight: Feminism, Western Culture and the Body*, Berkeley, CA: University of California Press, 1993, p. 5.
58. See Lorraine Code, "Second Persons", in *What Can She Know? Feminist Theory and the Construction of Knowledge*, Ithaca, New York: Cornell University Press, 1991, Chapter 3, pp. 71–109. Also see, Caroline Whitebeck, "A Different Reality: Feminist Ontology", in Carol. C. Gould (ed.), *Beyond Domination: New Perspectives on Women and Philosophy*, New Jersey: Rowman and Allanheld, 1983, pp. 69–88.
59. See, for example, Rosi Braidotti, *Nomadic Subjects*, New York: Columbia University Press, 1994; Judith Butler, *Gender Trouble*; Moira Gatens, *Imaginary Bodies*; Grosz, *Volatile Bodies*; Young, *Throwing Like a Girl*.
60. Iris Marion Young, "Pregnant Embodiment: Subjectivity and Alienation", *Journal of Medicine and Philosophy*, 9, 1984, pp. 45–62.
61. S.J. Williams and G. Bendelow (eds.), *Emotions in Social Life*, London: Routledge, 1998, xv. (Introduction).
62. Quoted by Carol Gould, from Kant's Observations on the Beautiful and the Sublime, in her essay, "Philosophy of Liberation and the Liberation of Philosophy", in Carol Gould and M. Martofsky (eds.), *Women and Philosophy: Towards a Theory of Liberation*, New York: G.P. Putman, 1976.
63. bell hooks, "Feminism: A Transformational Politic", in *Talking Back*, Boston: South End Press, 1989, pp. 26–27.

3

Unearthing Androcentrism

Feminist Excavations in the Realm of History

Feminist historians have alleged that the history of humankind has been written as essentially the history of men. Women are generally absent from the pages of history. References to women have been made only when they distinguished themselves in some typically male field of activity such as fighting a battle or leading a revolt. Two cases in point are Joan of Arc and Rani Lakshmi Bai. Such neglect of women in historical accounts has led to serious distortions in understanding the processes of historical change. Karl Marx has rightly remarked: "Anyone who knows anything of history knows that great social changes are impossible without the feminine ferment. Social progress can be measured exactly by the social position of the fair sex."[1]

Feminists contend that history writing reflects a male bias all along. Its focus has always been on those areas of human activity where males played a dominant role, such as politics, diplomacy and wars. The few women that figure in the pages of history are those who could successfully perform some male roles or were loved by eminent men. The experiences of majority of women were quietly ignored. At the most they were portrayed either as a subordinate passive lot, or as those who reacted to male pressures or to restrictions imposed by the patriarchal society. By treating women only as victims of oppression, history placed them in a male-defined conceptual framework.[2]

As Berenice Carroll puts it:

> On the one hand, most of the events, institutions, movements, and written documents of the past which the historians hold to be important have been led or produced or symbolically represented by men, and insofar as women have been active in these endeavour, they are thought to have identified themselves with the leadership and models presented by men. On the other hand, in so far as women have not been active in the ways which historians deem significant, they are conceived to have lived out their lives in a limited number of stereotypic roles, essentially changeless over time and therefore irrelevant to the 'intellectually interesting' questions of historical change.[3]

Feminists allege repeatedly that whereas spectacular, but often destructive, male activity like warring has always been reported in history, woman's quiet, but life enhancing contribution, through child bearing and housekeeping, has been consistently ignored. As for women who posed some kind of challenge to males, references to them were simply avoided because instruments of knowledge were all controlled by men.[4] The very notion of historical significance has been understood in male terms. A female received some mention only when she displayed some male excellence. Woman as such was accorded no respect. In an utterly male-centric world she just got no chance to realize her potential as a sexually distinct being. It is obvious that such "history written primarily from the perspective of the authoritative male subject – the single, triumphant consciousness"[5] – cannot but be biased and incomplete in its representation of the totality of human life and existence.

Contributors to Feminist History

Luckily, such lacunae of traditional history have been duly brought out by feminist historians – both male and female. They point out that indifference to women's contribution to society in the past has led to the same neglect in the present too. So, quite rightly, they have undertaken the dual task of restoring 'women to history' and 'history to women' in three clear ways:

(a) They have redefined the methods and categories of history writing.
(b) They have focused on sex, along with race and class, as an important category of analysis, which has helped them in rejecting stereotyped conceptions of women's nature.
(c) They have further transformed our understanding of social changes, that is, of how domestic and public spheres got

alienated from each other, as a result of which women lost control over production and property and even over their freedom and capacity for self-development by participating in public activity. Some of the better known pioneers in this field have been the following: Mary Beard, Gerda Lerner, Kelly Gadol, Sheila Rowbotham and Caroll Smith-Rosenberg.

Mary Beard

Mary Beard was one of the first feminists to insist that woman had made significant contributions to history.[6] What is more, she developed this emphasis in terms of a regular view of women's history. Beard opposed the view that women had all along been merely an oppressed group, and asserted that throughout the course of history they had made an essential contribution to the building of civilization, though it has remained unrepresented so far. Describing women as a 'force' in history, she outlined, at fair length, their role as rulers, queens, merchants, abbesses, teachers and institution builders. She insisted that a close, comprehensive and unbiased look was needed to determine and evaluate the contribution of women to history, as also their changing condition and status in its different periods.

Gerda Lerner

A similar assertion was made by Gerda Lerner[7] after a close study of the traditional attitude towards women in history. Besides complaining that women had been ignored even in the cultural history of mankind, she suggested that women's past could be reclaimed only if history is written also as an account of life as actually lived by the generality of mankind and not merely as it is found in books which focus only on the spectacular achievements of some men. She outlines an alternative historiography for women which rejects patriarchal methodologies. Lerner's most important contribution to women's history, as well as to feminist theory, is the reasoned protest that in any historical account, racial differences, as well as differences of education and class, must be taken into account.

Kelly Gadol

Another pioneering historian to question the authenticity of 'history', as it has so far been, is Joan Kelly Gadol. Her two main protests are: first, that instead of reflecting the course of events which is in fact continuous, "history is generally arranged into [staccato] periods shaped by wars and revolutions"; and second, that the periods which are regarded as periods of progress – as, for example, the Renaissance – are actually misnomers because these were precisely the times when women, who are as much a part of the living content of history as men, actually lost in terms of power and status.[8] Further, in her essay, 'The Social Relation of the Sexes', written from the Marxist point of view, she argues that in order to understand the full and complex relations of sexuality, class and social organizations over the different ages, historians must explore in an ethnographic manner the way in which the owning or lack of property determines women's role in both public and private spheres. In other words, in order to ensure a faithful recording of historical changes, we must focus on gender and social systems not as separate areas of analysis but as having an interactive and fairly predictable impact on each other.

Caroll Smith-Rosenberg and Sheila Rowbotham

Yet another scholar to question the adequacy of the periodization of history, as it has been done so far, is Carroll Smith-Rosenberg. She points out that though the sensual, emotional and private lives of the 19th century woman "created a woman's culture which most historians know something about ... virtually no one has written about [it]". She names this specific feminine culture as 'domestic feminism', and proposes that by studying it one can understand and write about the ways in which women's friendships provided them with wider, if more or less contingent, identities than those created by their limited family environments.[9] In any case, no understanding of history can be adequate without a due consideration of the aforesaid cultural world of women. As against this emphasis on feminine culture, woman's actual experience in different periods of history becomes the main subject of attention in the work of Sheila Rowbotham. She brings out how exactly the public accounts of the experience in question deviate from its reality. It is with this end in view that, in her well-known book *Hidden From History*[10] she talks at length about the experiences and activities of the working class women. In *Dreams and Dilemmas,* she shows how class divisions could disrupt women's politics, as they actually did, for example, during the suffrage campaign. In yet another significant work, *Women's Consciousness, Man's World*[11] Rowbotham gives an extensive account of women's resistance to, and alternatives to male power. She also contends that no current concept has been able to capture the force of woman's movement and her capacity to offer resistance in the most adverse circumstances. This is why she rejects the term patriarchy, which is obviously unable to convey the history and force of women's resurgence.

There are quite a few other pioneering works in the field by scholars like Dale Spender,[12] Carl N. Degler,[13] Dierdre Beddoe,[14] June Purvis,[15] B.G. Smith,[16] Berenice Caroll,[17] Michael Paludi and Gertrude Stevernagel,[18] Bridenthal S. and C. Koonz[19] and M. Hartmann and L. Banner.[20] We have, however, thought it proper to omit referring to their views, just with a view to avoid repetition of the feminist challenges that we have already spoken of.

Androcentrism in History

Feminist historians have also tried to explain how exactly women have been ignored in traditional history primarily because of the pervasion of our culture and attitudes by patriarchal values. This, they explain, has happened in two ways. First, biological sex differences have been taken as due warrant for the separation of activities for man and woman, and this very division has been taken to justify the dominance of man over woman.

Secondly, simply in virtue of being spectacular and quite open to view, man's activities like "war and politics ... [have been] considered more important and significant than [the quiet and self-effacing activities of] child bearing and child rearing."[21] The very concept of historiography has been given a vicious slant. This should become clear as we proceed.

Historiography

Here, in respect of historiography, the feminist challenge has proceeded as follows. The long standing dichotomies – as against mere distinctions – of nature and culture, work and family, public and private have unjustifiably, if incidentally, have worked as an unholy alliance in just opposing woman to man, ousting her from participation in many important areas of human activity, and so violating the very concept of historiography.[22] Thus, in the early 1970s, the inter-sex relation was understood and discussed as a kind of confrontation between nature and culture, obviously without any regard for the fact that there is a good deal in view human nature – say, our instincts of gregariousness and protective love – that facilitates desirable cultured attitudes. Men and their activities were viewed as synonymous with culture straight off, and so deserving of more regard than women and her activities, which were seen as merely natural, and so undeserving of explicit regard by society and history which, as we have said, was regarded as essentially a recording of the spectacular. Woman thus became unworthy of any scholarly, political or theoretical interest and inquiry.

The division arbitrarily installed between 'work' (as exclusively public) and 'family' was rapidly "recast into the hierarchy of male and female work, paid and unpaid". Childbearing, child rearing, taking care of the family were not considered 'work' *per se,* so not entitled to any payment, and therefore inferior to male activities. What is worse, we repeat, the very concept of historiography got distorted.[23] Gerda Lerner observes that men have regarded only their own experiences as fit material for history and have left out women completely. Carl N. Degloer rightly remarks: "Traditional historiography has excluded women not only inadvertently but sometimes programmatically from 'universal' or 'general' history."[24] Such a view of history is clearly mistaken. It is neither objective (or impartial) nor adequate or comprehensive.

Historical Methods

Feminist historians have drawn our attention not only to the general nature, but to quite a few actual instances of this vitiation of historical sense, writing and periodization.[25] Liberal histories of the 19th century, we are told, confined themselves mainly to the activities of eminent men in political, economic, intellectual, literary and artistic circles. Where women are mentioned in the general histories of this period, it is mainly in the context of their struggle for suffrage, and here, unfortunately, the focus is on the middle class women only, to the utter neglect of working class women. Lerner very aptly explains this neglect as follows:

> As long as historians considered as significant activities mainly the control, exercise and transmission of political and military power, women, who were outside the power structure ... were of necessity ignored. At best their contribution to power was peripheral and could be easily passed over as [only an indirect] 'influence'.[26]

However, with the rise of social history during the 1960s, the experiences of the powerless and the inarticulate began to be taken into account by trained historians. With this development, it was expected that now women's role would be certainly taken into account and her marginalization in history would come to an end. But, disappointingly, the work of social historians still took cognizance only of powerless men and completely overlooked women in similar plight. Even when socialist and labour historians challenged the class bias of history, they totally ignored women. They saw women primarily as mere members of this or that family and seldom as persons in their own right. There is no doubt that, by social historians, the working class leisure patterns was taken to mean attention only to the pub, the working man's club, the football match and the music hall.[27]

In writing labour history too, gender was not considered as a category of historical analysis. Although women cooperated with men in the shoe making, textile, garment, telephone, electrical and meat packaging industries, their contribution was never recorded. As a result, their specific needs and interests were always ignored. Mention was made only of the male labourer, and the male leadership of trade unions under which women had to work. Thereby, women were marginalized more than ever before. This sexual division of labour relegated them to the most insignificant segments of the work force. Labour history till recently has remained concerned with organizational and trade union history, attaching minimal importance to those corners into which women had been pushed willy nilly. Here, their appearance was only marginal[28] in terms of number. What is most humiliating and painful is the fact that historians of labour considered the working men's behaviour alone as the norm and measured women's behaviour in terms of accordance with that norm, callously ignoring the fact that what women lacked in terms of brute physical strength could be more than made up for by greater commitment, watchfulness and nimbleness of fingers. Quite indiscriminately, any deviation from the male standards of output was looked down upon, and the history of female labour came to appear as the 'deviant behaviour' of working women.[29]

Marxist History

Such was also the case with Marxist history. Even the most illustrious of Marxist historians seemed to forget women in their accounts. Karl Marx, who gave a specific meaning to the term 'social class', identified two main classes of capitalist society in his work, *The Communist Manifesto*, the bourgeoisie who own and control the means of production; and the proletariat who own nothing but their own labour which they, so to say, sell to the bourgeoisie in the form of wages. Both these classes, however, are defined in terms of the male sex alone; women are mentioned usually in their family or sexual roles, that is, as wives or mistresses.[30] A similar neglect can be seen in the writings of the great historian E.P. Thompson. In his study, *The Making of the English Working Class,* which covers the period 1780–1832, Thompson defines social class as a relationship that appears "when men, as a result of common experiences ... feel and articulate the identity of their interests as between themselves and as against other men whose interests are different from (and usually opposed to) theirs". His major emphasis is only on the way working class *men* were active in creating the identity of a social class. Of women he hardly makes any mention.[31] Hobsbawrn, too, in his book, *Labouring Men,* included topics relevant only to the male working class in the 19th century.[32] He assumed that within the working class only men went out to work while women stayed at home. In doing so, he ignored the paid and unpaid work that the working class women did for families. This indifference to the lowly, it is clear, hardly squares with how Marxist history professes to proceed, that is, 'from below' or 'from bottom up'.[33]

Unfortunately, the same narrowness vitiates the histories of working class women's education in the 19th century. This education, especially as it related to the working class women, was represented as peripheral to mainstream educational concerns. Most of the histories of 19th century education tend to focus on administration of education and on the educational institutions that boys and men were likely to attend, such as state-aided schools, secondary schools, public schools, technical institutions and universities. Even most historians of working class education paid little attention to women's education.

This neglect, it may be noted, is still allowed to continue. What is more, even 'family history' is deeply fraught with patriarchal biases and assumptions. Women's work in mothering and nurturing children is not seen from their point of view. Historians surely put a great many questions relating to such work, but only from the viewpoint of a patriarch, and unmarried and widowed women are almost excluded from the family history, as if they did not exist. Such neglect looks satanic in monographic studies like those done by Philip Greven where family history confines itself rigidly to father-son relationship and the property matters affecting them, completely ignoring the equally vital father-daughter and mother-child kinships. What is worse, the heart-warming role of daughters in supporting the education of their brothers and in maintaining parents in old age has been nefariously withheld.[34]

A similar callousness is also seen in the history of labour force in industry, where women have been roundly held responsible for most of the evils in industrial society. It is hardly a relief to turn to works like that of Margaret Hewitt's *Wives and Mothers in Victorian Industry.*[35] Here, she seems to oppose the very idea of married women's working outside the family on the ground that the high scale of infant mortality was due simply to the fact that the infants of working mothers were consigned to the vagaries that attend the feeding bottle and the childminder. More recently, Edward Shorter had the audacity to say that working class women became good mothers only when they left the workforce and devoted themselves single-mindedly to their children.[36] Shorter[37] and Demause[38] took a rash step further when they said that those women in the recent past who chose to work outside the home could not be said to love their children. All in all, studies such as these did not quite approve of the impact of women's working on their family life.

Another way in which patriarchal biases are revealed in family history writing has been the use of the concept, domestic power (of women) as a measure of their societal status. Daniel Scott Smith attributed the lower birth rate in 19th century to women's increasing control of over their reproductive lives.[39] The truth however is that it was more the exacting demands of a developing industrial system, rather than women's own desire to minimize the strains of maternity and related problems, that made for a declining both rate. Hence, the term 'domestic feminism' used by Daniel Scott is a misnomer.

Women have also been ignored from demographic histories. However, demographic data regarding fertility fluctuation and sex ratio tell us a lot about the lower status of female in society over a long period of time. Until the late 1970s, demographic history did not take into account the differences in the experiences of women and men. Information regarding the differences in survival rates of men and women was very meagre. Moreover, the study of mortality from a gender perspective was peripheral. Important questions, such as socio-cultural influences on mortality and their repercussions on the status of women, were left out. It is only recently that the demographic history has started focusing on the specifics of each sex. This recovery of sexual differentials through demographic history has provided true understanding of the social and economic situation of women in individual societies.[40] The recovery of such a perspective promises a more comprehensive understanding of the history of sexual division of labour, and perhaps even of a history of complex sexual differences, as distinguished from the blanket difference of mere gender.

The neglect of women's experiences can also be seen in the mainstream studies of ecclesiastical politics or popular religiosity. These studies do not regard women's distinctive religious experiences as a significant analytical category, and so distort the writing of religious history. Oppositely, scholarship relating to modern women's religious history is impressive and continues to flourish.[41] These works have uncovered an abundance of women's roles in Jewish and Christian spiritual traditions as missionaries, fundraisers, preachers, moral reformers and nuns. In her work, *The Creation of Feminist Consciousness*, Gerda Lerner reveals that one could locate instances of female resistance to patriarchal religious authority almost in every historical period.[42] Similar assertions are also made by 19th century American feminists like Sarah Grimke, Matilda Joslyn Gage and Elizabeth Cady Stanton, who produced scathing critiques of patriarchal Biblical religion and its debilitating effect on women's status.

The pervasive omission of women from various histories suggests the need for developing multiple narratives that could document a comprehensive historical vision of the significance of female presence.[43]

Periodization

Now, turning to our next point – that is, biases which vitiate the very periodization of history – we come across several feminist historians who have also challenged this facet of history writing as it has been done traditionally. They have shown how this segmentation of the course of history takes only male experience as the norm for the whole of humanity; and how the periods which are regarded as veritable turning points in history are measured exclusively in terms of male progress. The most victorious period for man has been the darkest period for women. This has been made quite clear by the works of Renate Bredenthal[44] and Joan Kelly Gadol.[45] It is now obvious that the history of women demands a different periodization. So far, this has been done on the basis of wars, conquests, revolutions, and/or vast cultural and religious shifts. Such a procedure naturally omits even the major contributions to history made by women. It is, in this context, instructive to note that recent studies on Renaissance[46] have made it clear that it is precisely in this period of man's unprecedented successes in various fields that women were subjected to greater restrictions than they had experienced earlier.

In their work on the American Revolution, Linda Kerber and Joan Hoff Wilson[47] declare that the American Revolution and the political changes in the age of Jackson affected women quite adversely. Increasing opportunities for education and upward mobility for men coincided with the exclusion of women from such advances. Professionalization of medicine and law also harmed women's interests, for it kept them out of the practice of medicine for almost a century. Similarly, the granting of political rights to large groups of white men, who were earlier excluded from voting and representation, resulted in widening the gap between the opportunities given to men and women in the social sphere.[48]

Likewise, early capitalism in Europe in the 15th and 16th centuries, and in the United States during the late 18th century, led to the opening of various avenues of work for men only.[49] Women could not profit from such opportunities partly because of their time-consuming and debilitating reproductive roles. The situation remained so until some avenues for women's development were provided by modernization, which brought with itself improved medical knowledge and techniques, better distribution of basic services, such as improved sanitation, decrease in infant mortality as also in the risk of death at childbirth. However, these various facilities and improvements did not help all women similarly and simultaneously, but different classes of women at different times, and in uneven measure. The European middle class women benefited in the 18th century; American white middle class women in the 19th; and the lower class and black women in the 20th century.[50]

As for the age called Enlightenment, the very word appears a little suspect. The period it signifies was not as uniformly felicitous as its very meaning required. True, many welcome changes took place in this period. The power of Europe's traditional authorities – namely, the kings, nobles and Church dignitaries – was questioned, if indirectly, by the following words in the United States Declaration of Independence: "All men are equal". This Declaration affirmed that the individual had rights which had to be protected by society; and that the power to elect or reject a leader rested with the generality of people. But the word 'people' was taken to mean only men; and so, here too, women were given a raw deal. Further, just as women were regarded inferior to men in the Western context, the black women were discriminated against as inferior to the white women generally. Thus, the tyranny of the male is reflected throughout in the periodization of history.[51]

Women's History: Challenging Conceptual Frameworks

As already pointed out, traditional historians approach women's history in a male-defined framework. In this context, Gerda Lerner[52] distinguishes two approaches in which such history is written, namely, *compensatory history* and *contributory history.*[53] Both, according to her, are infected with the male bias. Lerner adds that, until very recently, that kind of women's history which has been written in the compensatory manner, is essentially a history of few notable women. It ignores the majority of women and their experiences. It also fails to take notice of the fact that different classes of women have different experiences, and that to comprehend the full complexity of female society at a given stage of its development, it is essential to take into account such experiential differences.

Compensatory history, according to Lerner, fails to take into account the various stages of development in feminine consciousness. It fails to realize that woman does not react to a work imposed by men with their own notion of significant activity in the same way as to a task which is women-oriented,[54] that is, which is suited to their nature as women. As for *contributory history,* it surely describes women's contribution to male-defined society, but this contribution is judged not so much from the viewpoint of its effect on movements or events as from that of norms which are set by and acceptable to men.[55]

Indeed, to speak quite generally, the criteria which are used to measure the extent and character of success or failure are set by men, in utter indifference to the fact that the very femininity of women demands a quite different set of norms. To bolster this particular point[56] Gerda Lerner refers to two woman of substance, namely, Margaret Sanger and Jane Adams, and develops her argument as follows: If, along with contribution to society at large and towards keeping population in check, the release of women from domination by men and provision for their proper education had also been regarded laudable objectives. Margaret Sanger, who is regarded only as the founder of birth control movement, could also be fairly acclaimed as a woman who raised "a revolutionary challenge to the centuries old practice by which the bodies and lives of women are dominated and ruled by man-made laws". Similarly, instead of being lauded only for her contribution to social work as a whole, Jane Adams would have been admired also for evolving a system of "living and working for a new generation of [those] independent, educated women of the late 19th century *who chose not to marry*".

It is noteworthy here that the two approaches to writing history – *compensatory* and *contributory* – are both alike in segregating women's activities from those of men even where the former had added substantially to the reach and effectiveness of the latter. For example, no historical work takes notice of the fact that the anti-slavery movement[57] was very substantially helped by the petitions and campaigns, and fund raising activities conceived and organized by women.

Writing Women's History

It should now be clear that indifference to women in recorded history has been not only ontological, but methodological and epistemological, thus vitiating the discipline as an intellectual enterprise. It is the red-hot awareness of this unrelieved callousness that made the feminist historians see very clearly the need to rewrite history in such a way that one could not only become better aware of the lot of women in the past, but the very concepts and categories used in history writing could be properly amended. This is what explains the dawn of missionary, yet truthful and balanced history writing by women. What they aim at in their writing is not the utter exclusion of references to men but only at projecting the truth, without exaggeration, that women have been essential, not peripheral to the making of history. They maintain that both men and women have to be duly kept in mind, and that only then can history be termed as a 'universal history'.

It would however be wrong to believe that this women's history is significant only because of its balance and comprehensiveness. Its acuity of thought is also remarkable. It has shaken the conceptual foundations of traditional historical concern, namely, its periodization, categories of historical analysis and theories of social change.[58] It further challenges such truths[59] of history, as have so far been accepted thoughtlessly – the age-old belief, for instance, that a woman's true place is only the home. This belief is obviously a sheer dogma. One does not need any extra eye to see the vital rule of women in hospitals as nurses if nowhere else; and only the incorrigibly hidebound can abstain from acclaiming the participation by women today even in such hazardous ventures as manned space flights.

To turn anew to the crop of revolutionary female historians we have been talking of, they have effectively argued that the belief in question is not as deeply rooted in tradition as historians have thought it to be but is a relatively recent phenomenon that took shape in the early 19th century when middle class women were just pushed into the private sphere of home life, and men – relieved of family responsibilities – found themselves free to venture into the public world.[60] As a result of such challenges thrown by women historians gender became a category of historical analysis in the late 20th century. Earlier, gender was hardly given any place in major social theories. Joan W. Scott refers to this lacuna expressly: "Some of those [social] theories built their logic on analogies to the opposition of male and female, others acknowledged [the] woman question; but gender as a way of talking about systems of social or sexual relations does not appear."[61] The recognition of gender as an analytical and cultural category for historians and sociologists has implications for all forms of history as they are actually written. Today, women's history is not simply a search for some specific object which has been neglected in olden days, but is a wholesome attempt to undo the estrangement between cloistered human groups such as widows and nuns on the one hand and humanity in general[62] on the other. In the words of Michelle Zimbalist Rosaldo, "women must be understood ... in terms of relationship – with other women and with men – (not) of difference and apartness".[63] A similar plea for an inclusive view of history is made by Gisela Bock: "History, then, is not only of male, but also of female, experience. It should not be studied only in male or apparently gender-neutral perspectives, but also in female and gender encompassing perspectives."[64] It is obvious that if this emphasis is duly heeded, that is, if gender is considered along with race, class, and ethnicity etc. in the analysis of any given period or event, new dimensions will be added to the traditional idioms of history.

It may, however, be added that this reconstruction of women's history has not been easy, and that the difficulty relates to availability and scantiness of relevant material. As most of the historical sources were written and collected by men, and libraries and archives had organized their material in accordance with the traditional categories of male-oriented history, there were few entries under the caption 'women', and material relating to them was quietly put under the 'male' category.[65]

Recent feminist scholarship has opened up quite a few new avenues of historical research. This follows as a sequel to looking at older sources afresh, from a different perspective and with a new set of questions in mind. In this context two signal attempts may be referred to.[66] Analysing the archaeological evidence from Catal Huyuk, Barstow made it clear how an extremely complex and materially rich culture had evolved and existed for over a thousand years without the emergence of a clear-cut social and political hierarchy. She attributed this to the fact that social organization in Catal Huyuk was probably women-centred, with the cult of goddesses providing a unifying ideology.

Similarly, Rohrlich has re-examined the code of Hammurabi with a view to bring out the connection between the growing subordination of women, the destruction of clan egalitarianism and the emergence of state in Sumer. Further, she argues that Hammurabi's law code, which has often been thought of as a means of guaranteeing the rights of women probably, actually curtailed their opportunities by strictly delimiting the spheres within which they could function.

Besides the reinterpretation of traditional sources and growing emphasis on primary sources like diaries and autobiographies, search for new kinds of sources has also begun. Oral history has proved to be an important method of gathering material for women's history, just as the growing search for women's autobiographical writings has unearthed a large number of such texts as can be of great help in restructuring women's history.

As a result of such efforts, feminists now feel enabled to write a history which will duly acknowledge the value of women's experiences. Such a history, they believe, will promote women's collective consciousness of their rights, duties, and capacity for various achievement. History will then chime with woman's true 'psyche', and become truly representative of women.[67]

Why this has not happened so far will be the subject of our next chapter.

Notes

1. Marx in a letter to a friend, cited in E. Janeway, *Powers of the Weak*, New York: Morrow Quill, 1981, p. 3.
2. See Gerda Lerner, *The Majority Finds Its Past*, New York: Oxford University Press, 1979, p. 146.
3. Berenice Carroll (ed.), *Liberating Women's History: Theoretical and Critical Essays*, Urbana: University of Illinois Press, 1976, p. xi.
4. See Dale Spender's *Women of Ideas and What Men Have Done to Them*, London: Routledge and Kegan Paul, 1982. Similarly, in *Mothers of the Novel*, Spender challenges the received wisdom of the male literary establishment that Jane Austen was the first woman novelist. Before Austen, according to Spender, there were more than a hundred good female writers whose contribution to history of the novel has been ignored.
5. Elizabeth Fox Genovese, "Placing Women's History in History", *New Left Review*, No. 133, May/June, 1982.
6. Mary Beard, *Woman as Force in History*, New York: MacMillan, 1946.
7. See Gerda Lerner, op. cit., 1979.
8. Joan Kelly Gadol, "Did Women Have a Renaissance?" in Renate Briedenthal and Claudia Koonz (eds.), *Becoming Visible: Women in European History*, Boston: Houghton Mifflin, 1977, pp. 137–64. Also see, Joan Kelly

Gadol, "The Social Relation of the Sexes: Methodological Implications of Women's History", *Signs*, Vol. 1, No. 4, (Summer 1976), pp. 809–24.

9. Carroll Smith-Rosenberg, "The Female World of Love and Ritual: Relations between Women in 19th Century America", in E. Abel and E.K. Abel (eds.), *The Signs Reader: Women Gender and Scholarship*, Chicago: University of Chicago Press, 1983.
10. Sheila Rowbotham, *Hidden From History*, London: Pluto Press, 1973.
11. Sheila Rowbotham, *Women's Consciousness, Man's World*, Harmondsworth: Penguin, 1973.
12. Dale Spender, *Men's Studies Modified*, London: Pergamon Press, 1981; *Women of Ideas and What Men Have Done to Them*, London: Routledge and Kegan Paul, 1982.
13. Carl. N. Degler, *Is there a History of Women?* Oxford: Oxford University Press, 1975.
14. Dierdre Beddoe, *Discovering Women's History*, London and New York: Longmans, 1998.
15. June Purvis, *Hard Lessons*, Oxford: Polity Press, 1989.
16. B.G. Smith, *The Gender of History: Men, Women and Historical Practice*, London: Harvard University Press, 1998.
17. Berenice Caroll (ed.), op. cit., 1976.
18. Michael Paludi and Gertrude Steuernagel (eds.), *Foundations for a Feminist Restructuring of Academic Disciplines*, New York and London: Routledge, 1990.
19. R. Bridenthal and C. Koonz (eds.), op. cit., 1977.
20. M. Hartmann and L. Banner (eds.), *Clio's Consciousness Raised: New Perspectives on History of Women*, New York: Harper, 1974.
21. See Gerda Lerner, op. cit., 1979.
22. See Gisela Bock, "Challenging Dichotomies", in Karen Offen et al. (eds.), *Writing Women's History: International Perspective*, London: Macmillan, 1991.
23. See Gerda Lerner, "New Approaches to the Study of Women in History", in *The Majority Finds its Past*, New York: Oxford University Press, 1979.
24. Carl. N. Degler, op. cit., 1975.
25. See June Purvis, op. cit, 1989, p. 13.
26. Gerda Lerner, *Teaching Women's History*, Washington: American Historical Association, 1981, p. 6.
27. Jane Lewis, "Women, Lost and Found: The Impact of Feminism on History", in Dale Spender, op. cit., 1981, pp. 55–56.
28. The only exception is that of the needle trade.
29. Gerda Lerner, op. cit., 1981, p. 20.
30. See June Purvis, "Hidden From History", in *Hard Lessons*, Oxford: Polity Press, 1989.

31. E.P. Thompson, *The Making of English Working Class*, Harmondsworth: Penguin, 1972.
32. E.P. Hobsbawm, *Labouring Men: Studies in the History of Labour*, London: Weidenfeld and Nicolson, 1987.
33. H.J. Kaye, *The British Marxist Historians*, Oxford: Polity Press, 1984.
34. See Philip J. Greven, Jr. *Four Generations: Population, Land and Family in Colonial Andover*, Massachusetts: Ithaca, 1970.
35. Margaret Hewitt, *Wives and Mothers in Victorian Industry*, London: Rockcliff, 1958.
36. Edward Shorter, *The Making of the Modern Family*, New York: Basic books, 1976.
37. Ibid.
38. Llyod Demause, "The Evolution of Childhood", in Llyod Demause (ed.), *The History of Childhood*, New York: Psycho History Press, 1974.
39. Daniel Scott Smith, "Family Limitation, Sexual Control and Domestic Feminism in Victorian America", in M. Hartmann and L. Banner (eds.), op. cit., 1974.
40. See Anne-Lise Head-konig, "Demographic History and its Perception of Women from the Seventeenth to Nineteenth Century", in Karen Offen et al. (eds.), *Women's History: International Perspectives*, London: Macmillan, 1991. In this essay, the author maps the shift of perspective in this important historical field. In examining the demographic history of Western European women between the 17th and 19th centuries, she demonstrates how such sexual differentials can inform our understanding of the social and economic situation of women in a particular society.
41. Rosemary Radford Reuther and Rosemary Keller (eds.), *Women and Religion in America*, San Francisco: Harper and Row, 3 Vols., 1981.

    Gail Malmgreen, *Religion in the Lives of English Women, 1760–1930*, London and Sydney: Croom Helm, 1986.
42. Also see, M.P. Ryan, "A Women's Awakening: Evangelical Religion and the Families of Utica, New York, 1800–1840", in J. James (ed.), *Women in American Religion* (Philadelphia: University of Pennsylvania Press, 1980) pp. 89–110
43. Serinity Young, *Encyclopedia of Women & World Religion*, Farmington Hills, (MI/US), Macmilean Library Reference, 1 Nov., 1998.
44. Renate Bredenthal and Claudi Coonz (eds.), op. cit., 1977.
45. Joan Kelly Gadol, "Did Women Have a Renaissance?" in R. Bredenthal and C. Coonz (eds.), op. cit., 1977.
46. Ibid.
47. Linda K. Kerber, "Daughters of Columbia: Educating Women for the Republic," in *The Hofstadter Aegis: A Memorial*, New York: Alfred A. Knopf, 1974.

    Joan Hoff Wilson, "The Illusion of Change: Women and the American Revolution", in Alfred F. Young (ed.), *The American Revolution: Exploration in the History of American Radicalism*, Dekalb: Northern Illinois University Press, 1976.

48. Gerda Lerner, op. cit, 1979, p. 175.
49. Ibid., p. 176.
50. Ibid.
51. See Barbara Evans Clements, "Images of Women: Views from the Discipline of History", in Michael Paludi and Gertrude Steuernagel (eds.), *Foundations for a Feminist Restructuring of the Academic Disciplines*, New York and London: Routledge, 1990.
52. Gerda Lerner, op. cit., 1979, pp. 145–46.
53. The terms 'Compensatory History' and 'Contribution History' used, in Marie J. Buhle, Ann. C. Gordan and Nancy Schrom, "Women in American Society: An Historical Contribution", *Radical America*, Vol. 5, No. 4, July-August, 1971, pp. 3–66.
54. Gisela Bock, "Women's History and Gender History: Aspects of an International Debate", in Robert Shoemaker and Mary Vincent (eds.), *Gender and History in Western Europe*, London: Arnold, 1998, p. 26.
55. Gerda Lerner, op. cit., 1979, p. 146.
56. Ibid., p. 147.
57. Gerda Lerner, op. cit., 1981, p. 19.
58. See Aparna Basu, "Methodology in Women's History: An Intergenerational Study of a Family", in A. Suryakumari (ed.), *Women's Studies: An Emerging Discipline*, New Delhi: Gyan Publishing House, 1993, p. 13.
59. Dierdre Beddoe, *Discovering Women's History*, London and New York: Longman, 1998.
60. See Catherine Hall, "Gender Divisions and Class Formations in the Birmingham Middle Class, 1780–1850", in R. Samuel (ed.), *People's History and Socialist Theory*, London: Routledge and Kegan Paul, 1981.
61. Joan W. Scott, "Gender a Useful Category of Analysis", in Robert Shoemaker and Mary Vincent (eds.), op. cit., 1998, p. 54.
62. Gisela Bock, "Women's History and Gender History", in Robert Shoemaker and Mary Vincent (eds.), op. cit., 1998.
63. Michelle Zimbalist Rosaldo, "The Use and Abuse of Anthropology: Reflections on Feminism and Cross-Cultural Understanding", *Signs*, 5 (Spring 1980), p. 400.
64. Gisela Bock, op. cit., p. 3.
65. See Gerda Lerner, op. cit., 1979, p. 173.
66. See A. Suryakumari (ed.), op. cit., 1993, pp. 68–88.
67. Maria Mies, "Towards a Methodology for Feminist Research", in Gloria Bowles and Renate Kleen (eds.), *Theories of Women's Studies*, London: Kegan Paul, 1983, pp. 117–39.

4

Resisting Logocentrism

Feminist Challenges in Sociology

Philosophy often tends to ignore what is actually there. So, its pervasive indifference to women is, in a measure, understandable. But if the same defect is found to mar the field of sociology, it is bound to look surprising, for this branch of knowledge is professedly the scientific study of the nature, structure and workings of human society, of which women are obviously as much a part as men. Yet, as feminist theorists have convincingly shown, sociology too has been sex-blind as it neglects the role of women in society. In detail, their protests run as follows:

> As it presently is, sociology describes and analyses only man's work and behaviour, thus giving skewed insights into human nature as a whole. It is deficient in concepts that could cover women's varied experiences, and so far it has regarded women as just an unchanging monolithic category utterly impervious to changes in time and space. The methodological and theoretical perspectives offered in ethno-methodology, structural-functional analysis (with its focus on system analysis), conflict analysis and other sociological approaches – all neglect women's perspectives just because women are not regarded significant enough for serious study.

As Millman and Kanter put it:

> With its focus on public, official, visible and dramatic role players, it [sociology] has produced a distorted view of social reality, thus ignoring the unofficial, supportive and invisible spheres of social life and organization which may be equally important.[1]

Feminists further protest against the dominant sociological tradition for placing a high value on reason and rationality, which are taken to be intrinsic or as inextricably tied to the male. Feminine capacity for emotional bonding and unerring, intuitive reactions are never taken into account. Even a quick look at the founding fathers of sociology should bear out what we say.

Some Eminent Sociologists on Women: Marx to Simmel

The value of the work done by the great thinkers in the field of sociology is, on the whole, unquestionable. They seriously addressed such vital matters as the nature and development of society; the occasional transformations it has undergone, may be as a consequence of the lead given by social reformers; major shifts in family life, specially in respect of relations between men and women; and construction of tenable concepts of masculinity and femininity. Yet, surprisingly, most of them have paid insufficient attention to issues of gender and sexuality, specially as they relate to women.

Karl Marx

To see this clearly, we may begin by referring to Karl Marx, who has greatly influenced feminist thinking through his theory of class struggle and concern for the proletariat. As is typical of his approach, Marx discusses questions of family and sexual relationships not abstractly, but in a historical and material context. His considered view is that such institutions and relations are neither fixed for ever nor consciously planned, but simply the products of a particular historical situation, and that, therefore, they can suffer changes only as incidentally to changes in conditions of production which are largely controlled by men of power. Thus, he views female subordination as a necessary feature of the overarching bourgeoisie scheme of things.

Now, the feminists here allege that in seeking to reduce everything to economic causes, Marxism has failed to grasp the all-encompassing nature of political power and its various manifestations in personal as well as in public life. Surprisingly, even the concept of 'productive labour', as interpreted by Marx, has ignored the domestic work performed by women. This becomes evident from his discussions on the reproduction of labour power in the first volume of *Capital*. He argues that labour must be 'reproduced' in two ways. First, the worker must be kept fit enough to work each day; and, second, the working class itself too must keep reproducing itself from the present generation to the next. All this seems sensible, but the oddity in both these emphases is that Marx ignores the indispensable role of women's labour in the private sphere.[2] How can a labourer be kept fit for the next day's work unless he is looked after properly at home, in terms of both nourishment and cordiality, and how can even the next generation be induced to take to productive labour unless the present generation sees it clearly that recourse to the work in question not only demands but in no way detracts from domestic peace?

Frederik Engels

Yet it was the thinking of Marx that formed the basis of Engels' well-known work, *The Origins of the Family, Private Property and the State*. Here, however, Engels had more to say about women than Marx. First, he totally rejected the claim that the modern family is 'natural'. Instead, he argued that in the earliest societies sexual relationships were totally promiscuous and unregulated; that they gradually took the form of 'pairing family' which characterized the subsequent forms of primitive society; that in these 'pairing families', the sexual division of labour did not involve any kind of subordination; and that, here, women reigned supreme in the home and even descent was determined in accordance with the female line, which came to be called (by Engels) the *mother right*. This egalitarian situation, we are told, changed with the emergence of a new way of acquiring wealth, that is, through the essentially male activity of the domesticating animals and tending. In so far as these activities are essentially outdoor and so inconvenient for women, men began to pass over his 'property' to their own male children, which resulted in a change in the traditional order of inheritance, and a preference for monogamy. As a consequence of these developments, women were gradually reduced to being mere possession of their husbands and simply machine to produce children. In Engel's words, "the overthrow of the mother right was the world historical defeat of the female sex". For him, the abolition of private property is the only way through which women could be emancipated, as men would then not be left with any effective means for exploiting them.

The feminists, however, allege that Engels does not present a complete picture of women's subjugation. In all his analyses he fails to acknowledge that the proletarian family too could be a scene of oppression and sexual exploitation, instead of just being a unit of equitable interpersonal relations. He had very little to say about domestic violence which received widespread publicity in the 19th century and was one of the central concerns of many feminists in

Britain and America. The truth indeed is that in the works of both Marx and Engels the overall lot of women remains ignored, essentially because neither of them gave as much value to the life-giving activity of procreation as to the material/economic activity of production, the obvious utility of which can be substantially outdone by unjust distribution or misappropriation of what is produced.

Max Weber

A similar neglect of women can be discovered in the work of Max Weber. For him, patriarchal authority is the oldest form of socially legitimate authority. Under this scheme of family life, it is the male head of the households who holds the reins of power, and has supreme authority over women and children. Weber never questions the propriety of the current division of work and authority between men and women as he always attaches greater value to the former than to the latter. His basic argument simply is that, according to current arrangement, men alone are sociologically significant because it is they who provide the link between mother and child on the one hand, and between family and society at large, on the other, besides lending a measure of respectability to the family.

Thus, Weber's works are dominated by the idea that women and children inhabit a private sphere, which is separate from the male dominated public sphere, but is yet dominated by a male at home. This, however, is not essentially what the feminists complain against. Their protests are rather the following: first, Weber's reflections on class completely overlook the gender dimension; and, second, he does not pay due attention to how men and women are differentially distributed within the occupational hierarchy, and how this hierarchy of class excludes those aspects of economic and social organization in which women have been traditionally active.

Durkheim

Another scholar, Emile Durkheim, not only views society as a neatly integrated functioning whole in which everyone has his (or her) due place but specifies home as the right place for women. His other major views may be listed thus: division of labour becomes more complex and diverse as society progresses; the roles of men and women become increasingly specialized, resulting in marked differences between them; these differences strengthen the conjugal bond, making men and women mutually dependent, the female contributing the affective functions and the male, intellectual ones to the overall health of the family.[3] At the same time, Durkheim comes very close to recognizing the fact of oppression of women where he says that married women have been more inclined to commit suicide than either married men or single women. Here, we may add, whereas Durkheim surely sees 'gender' as making for unhappy situations, he merely regards the state of affairs as a consequence of the inevitable and (supposedly) 'civilized' division of labour based on the fictitious assumption that, merely because of her sex, woman is inferior to man, instead of prescribing any remedy for the inequity.

Georg Simmel

As against all this, Georg Simmel's ideas came as a ray of light during this period. Although he took it for granted that man's orientation towards the public world and woman's towards the private domestic sphere reflected natural masculine and feminine proclivities, he was also clearly aware of the imbalance of power prevailing between women and men. He was acutely, almost painfully sensitive to the ways in which masculinity was treated as the human norm and femininity as just a deviation from it. Here is an extract from his own writings:

> The fact that the male sex is not only considered relatively superior to the female, but … is taken as the universal human norm … is, in many different ways, based on the power position of the male. If we express the historical relation between the sexes crudely in terms of master and slave, it is part of the master's privileges not to have to think continuously of the fact that he is the master, while the position of the slave carries with it the constant reminder of his [sic] being a slave. It cannot be overlooked that the woman forgets far less often the fact of being a woman than the man of being a man …. This fact is evident in the extremely frequent phenomenon that certain judgments, institutions, aims, or interests which we men, naively so to speak, consider purely objective, are felt by women to be thoroughly and characteristically masculine.[4]

This perceptive statement presages much modern feminist thinking about the ways in which men have been able to pass off their knowledge as objective when it is, in fact, merely and unfairly constructed from a masculine perspective.

Feminist Initiatives

The feminist tone which was feeble till this period became quite vocal in the 1970s when many scholars came forward and challenged the androcentric approach permeating sociological thinking. They referred to four major lacunae: (a) the omission and under-representation of women as subjects, (b) the focus on 'male' topics and relevancies alone, (c) a distorted presentation of women's experiences in the paradigms, models and methods of sociology, and (d) treating male experience as the norm.

As a challenge to this male bias in sociology, a huge quantity of feminist literature emerged. This upsurge can be divided into three periods:

1. Parsonian Period: Hegemony of Parsons' Theory
2. Post-Parsonian Period: Critique of Parsons and beginning of a feminist era in sociology.
3. Post-Post-Parsonian Period: A perceptible strengthening of feminist consciousness.

Now, in the first period (in the 20th century), the functionalist analysis of Talcott Parsons remained dominant. Parsons put forth the view that there is a complementary division of labour between husbands and wives and that it is this which not only stabilizes the family but also integrates it with the society at large. Men in their instrumental (goal-oriented) roles and women in the their affective (emotional) roles conjoin to minimize the potential strain between the instrumental ethos of industrial society and the emotional character of family life.

In subsequent years, however, such views began to be challenged critically. In her work, *Sex and Temperament in Three Primitive Societies*. Margaret Mead questioned the naturalistic assumptions about sex differences. She made a study of three New Guinea societies and discovered that gender is always a constructed category, not a natural one. The first of these societies, the Arapesh, was characterized by her as androgynous in temperament, with both men and women exhibiting the nurtural, caring qualities which are regarded as essentially feminine in Western culture. The second tribe, namely, the Mundugamor, was equally androgynous, but here (by Western standards), both men and women were 'masculine' as they were both very aggressive. The third tribe that Mead studied was that of Tchambuli. The study of this tribe reversed the whole idea about 'masculinity' and femininity, because here women were the practical doers and men remained largely preoccupied with idle gossip and self-adornment. Mead's work provided useful insights and data for a later generation of sociologists and so it was widely referred to with an eye to demonstrate the cultural malleability of gender and thus to illustrate its disconnection with biological sex.

In the following years, various other theories in sociology came to be challenged. The first four ventures of sociological work by feminists, which had a great impact on mainstream sociological work by feminists, were authored by Betty Friedan, Jessie Bernard, Joan Acker, Ann Oakley and others. Bettty Friedan[5] presented a critique of functionalism – of the work of Parsons in particular; and she labelled the era of the 1950s as one of "functional freeze in social science". Jessie Bernard[6] put forward powerful criticism of sexism in sociological theory and methods through her work on the autobiographical history of the ASA (American Sociological Association). Joan Acker[7] brought out the sex bias in stratification theories, class theories and specially the research methods of sociology and Ann Oakley[8] highlighted the sexism pervading sociology in general, and specially the work done on deviance, stratification, power, family and industry.

Even before 1980s it was realized that "the conflicts between home and work were not purely a personal concern, but had enormous social structural ramifications."[9] This could be clearly seen in what Myrdal and Klein[10] wrote on women's two roles; M. Hewitt[11] on working class wives and mothers in Victorian industry; Jephcott,[12] a little earlier, on growing-up girls; and Margery Spring Rice[13] on working class wives. In the field of community studies Frakenberg[14] Littlejohn[15] and Stacey[16] discussed the status of women at length. However, the greater part of these studies was devoted to the family, and this from the viewpoint of the implications that women's role in the family had on the status of women in society at large. In all these studies, discussion of women's work outside the home was but infrequent. What was focused on was largely the role of women in their families, probably because it was only here that the visibility of women was extraordinarily high; and that of men, extraordinarily low.[17] In scholarly sociological studies, therefore, woman still remained at the periphery.

On such matters as those that relate to childbirth, very significant work in the field of sociology of health was done by Ann Oakley[18] and Hilary Graham.[19] Some other authors' work was not so restricted in its concern. Lesley Doyal and Imogen Pennell[20] provided a careful analysis of the general condition of women in their *Political Economy of Health*; Carol Smart[21] produced works on deviance; Sheila Allen[22] on work and race; and Margaret Stacey and Marion Price[23] on power.

Feminist consciousness was further intensified when a number of feminist movements emerged in different parts of the world. This naturally resulted in production of many more feminist works.[24]

Various journals like *Signs, Sex Roles, Feminist Studies, Gender and Society* and *Women's Studies International Forum* appeared on the scene. Besides journals, countless scholarly works saw the light of day, so enlarging the horizons of sociology that the role of women in society[25] was fairly comprehensively covered. By way of summing up the development of feminist thought from the 1960s onwards, Alexander and Turner have spoken thus:

> Sociological theory is entering a new and important phase. In the (first) postwar period, European theory ... was diminished [in importance] and Parsons' structural-functional approach held the day. In the 1960s, there developed ... [some] challenges to Parsons' hegemony that became the major traditions in the *second*, post-Parsonian period ... [These challenges may be listed thus:] constructionist and logico-deductive trends, new waves of micro-theorizing; and the re-emergence of marco-structuralist approaches. The polarization that defined these first two periods has come to an end. We are in the beginning of a *third* phase that has [presently] a much less clearly defined character .... What will emerge from this [third] period of theoretical ferment remains to be seen.[26]

Feminist Challenges to Sociological Theories

It would now be of help to deal with all those sociological theories, one by one, which came under the direct attack of feminist thinkers. To begin with, we take the theory of socialization.

Socialization

Feminists have challenged the basic assumption of the early socialization model which believes that personality is formed, once for all, pretty early in life and is thereafter relatively unmalleable. They argue that:

(a) such a model is static rather than an evolutionary one, and so makes no provision for an individual's self-improvement which runs counter to the evidence of fact;

(b) it has simply banged the door on one direction of sociologists' work, that is, the study of how personality changes, under new structural conditions; and

(c) it has wrongly claimed that a person's positive or negative self-image and self-confidence are always determined by what happens in the first decade, or in the first six years and more importantly by the first eighteen months of his life;

(d) if has seriously damaged the status of women and minorities, because if they admit the assumption in question as true, they cannot hope for any improvement in their life if it has been miserable so far; and

(e) finally, if accepted as true, it strikes at the very root of the possibility of transforming people through education. How is than any hope left for the weaker sections of the society?

The above critiques find their very clear expression in the writings of Cynthia Fuchs Epstein. In her well-known work, *Women in Law*[27] she has tried to prove that "women changed radically when they began a profession and even more radically if they were successful". Many who were insecure became confident; the unmotivated became ambitious; and the timorous became steady and self-possessed. Many other social scientists also came to similar conclusions. Melvin Kohn, Carmi Schooler, Jeylan Mortimer[28] and others have shown how the mere gaining of some occupation produces some very happy effects, such as attainment of enormous amount of autonomy and self-confidence, specially if the occupation in question entails the doing of such work as is complex and interesting. Oppositely, if the occupation is boring and insecure, they become unhappy and lose in self-esteem.

Some other thinkers like Merton and Goffman have also shown that women are affected quite adversely if people do not think well of them. Thus, when they are regarded as deviants, they actually begin to behave as deviants; and what causes women to behave so is not any 'natural' tendencies or early conditioning by circumstances or parental influence. In this regard, Rozabeth Kanter's study, *Men and Women of the Corporation* is a variable milestone. She forcefully argues that women behave in a petty or narrow manner only when they are locked in enervating jobs, and that men would have behaved in the same manner were they put in similar positions. She concludes that differences in behaviour in corporations depends on the controlling power or its lack that goes with individual's specific position. In her words,

> Visibility tends to create performance pressures on the token [that is, something that indicates authority]. Contrast (of one performance with others] leads to heightening of dominant cultural boundaries, including isolation of the token. And assimilation results in the token's role encapsulation (or condensed expression of its essential significance).[29]

Robert. K. Merton[30] located this dual process in a sociological phenomenon linked to the maintenance of group boundaries whereby in-group virtues became out-group vices. For example, display of anger, and pulling strings for success by women were all seen as adoption of male values, and recourse to deviant behaviour.

In a similar theoretical framework, Cynthia Fuchs Epstein in her book, *Woman's Place*[31] shows that since women in professions did not share men's sex status, they were regarded as 'deviants' and so they actually reacted as 'deviants'. She further explains that such deviance did not result from natural tendencies, personality variables or early socialization but from consciousness the backstage positions they were forced to take, as against the better positions occupied by men.

Political Sociology

A similar neglect of women can be discovered in the study of political sociology. Descriptions of political processes ignored the role of women. It was always assumed that, by their very nature, women were unsuited to politics. Feminist theorists have challenged this view of political socialization by arguing that:

(a) It has attributed stereotyped motivations to women's behaviour, thus ignoring the large number of women who actively take part in politics and not without success.
(b) It has tended to regard electoral politics as the sole arena of political behaviour, excluding the political activity performed by voluntary organizations, such as the League of Women Voters, Consumer Groups, Community Action Groups, and other organizations comprising large number of women as members.
(c) It has wrongly assumed that women's political behaviour is almost entirely determined by the influence of men, children, parents, and has totally ignored those fields of activity where women may act independently or may even influence their husbands' political choices.

Feminists contend that instead of admitting the possibility and significance of such independent feminine activity women's work, where it was at all recorded, was always regarded as a kind of 'deviance'. Marcia Millman has shown it clearly that this so-called 'deviance' has been totally ignored in works on sociology.[32] Cynthia Fuchs Epstein points out that such indifference has resulted in a total failure to account for the influence of such 'deviant' behaviour of women on the prevalent social norms,[33] and that at all levels, in the public sphere, woman has been relegated to a marginal position. Richard Cloward and Frances Fox Piven[34] are therefore justified in arguing that instead of merely ignoring the fact that women did not engage in collective forms of resistance, the category of the deviant should be expanded to include the self-directed and private kinds of 'deviance' women have engaged in. What is more, sociologists should also have made it clear how this tendency to dub women's independent activity as merely deviant arose out of the self-interest of the powerful mental health industry; and were this need duly met, the discipline of sociology could well claim to have done justice to the long oppressed half of the human population.

Stratification

Instead of moving in the desirable direction just referred to above, sociologists have shown a male bias even in stratification of society, that is, in fixing the value level of different sections of society. Their attitude, here, rests on the following (not quite fair) assumptions about the social position of women:

1. The social position of the family, which is obviously the basis of the stratification system, is determined by the status of the male head of the household.
2. In so far as most females live in families, (women's) status too is determined by that of the males to whom they are attached.
3. Women are able to determine their own social status only when they are not attached to a man.
4. Women are unequal to men in many ways, and so have to be differentially evaluated on the basis of sex.

Now, the very first assumption, that the family is the unit in stratification, is basic to the other three; and all of them rest on the idea that the fate of the female in the class system is determined by the fate of the male. Therefore, they neatly dispense with the need for considering the position of women in studies of social stratification for considering gender as a dimension of stratification.

Feminist scholars have challenged the stratification model (as outlined above) on the following grounds:

(a) it neglects the contributions women have made in understanding class structure, and the place of the family in this structure;
(b) it fails to recognize the important interplay that freely occurs between the institution of family and the occupational sphere outside the family;
(c) it also makes it impossible for us to see that women's activity at home too can be truly economic productivity, because it assumes that activity away from home alone could be economic activity, properly so called; and
(d) it assumes that independently of their family roles and ties to men, females have no relevant role in stratification processes.

To illustrate, in her milestone essay, 'Women and Social Stratification,' Joan Acker [35] contends that all the assumptions made about women's position in stratification are faulty. Carrying the criticism further, Sylvia Walby argues that critics of androcentric approaches to stratification have often not gone far enough. In just putting women into occupational hierarchy, they simply ignore the specific social location of wives[36] in the family circle.

Binarism in Sociological Theories

In the postmodern era, that is, after 1960s, it was discovered that most of the lacunae in the prevailing sociological theories arise because of their innate binarism. There is a tendency to view everything within the two extremes juxtaposed against each other, whereas the fact really is that two seemingly independent concepts and two different modes of thought may yet be held as one by some hidden, underrunning link.

Instrumental vs Expressive

In the 1960s and 1970s Talcott Parsons faced severe criticism from the feminists for his functionalist theory, and especially for his work on family. Through this theory, he maintained that, within the family it was functional (or practically helpful) for wives and husbands to keep to this judicious division of functions, for thereby the possibility of disharmony in the family will be naturally minimized, because wifely love and husband's economic support would need, instead of colliding with each other. On the other hand, if a husband and his wife both become wage-earners, the higher earning of any one of them could easily lead to the attitude of dominance of one over the other and so lead to disharmony in the family.[37] Indeed, the evidence of family life, as it is seen in its changing form today, supports the conclusion that where the wife/mother takes the expressive role, she helps in cementing relationships, provides emotional support, nurture and care etc. and so sustains the household; and that where a deviation from these roles occurs, family system comes to suffer a temporary state of disequilibrium.

However, it is precisely this dichotomy or of exaggerated difference posited between the expressive and the instrumental, which was criticized by feminists. Focusing on the limitations of Parsons' functionalist theory, Betty Friedan[38] labelled the era of 1950s as one of 'functional freeze' in social science. In other words, thinkers in this era were accused of limiting quite arbitrarily the earning capacity of a wife and a husband's potential for showering love on the family. The feminists' challenge, here, is indeed quite warranted. Where a husband is somehow incapacitated physically, will not the wife be justified in trying to become a wage-earner herself? And does a husband's protective attitude necessarily exclude an attitude of loving tenderness for the family? Linda. L. Lindsey[39] put forward a critique of Parsons' work on the family and labelled it as 'inherently conservative' as it does not account for a variety of existing family systems that can be said to be functional. Is not a single parent often seen to provide both love and material. sustenance to his/her dependents? Such cases are surely instances of deviations from the functional perspective as traditionally conceived.[40]

Disagreeing with Lindsey, Miriam Johnson[41] reexamined Parsons' work on the family and argued that Parsons was well aware of the 'structured strains in both male and female socialization'. She revisited Parsons' study to show how one can revise his evolutionary change theory and analysis of family roles in a way that could help understanding the recent changes in women's roles.

Moving away from both Mirian Johnson and Talcott Parsons, Dorothy Smith envisages a "distinctive standpoint for women not necessarily as a general attribute of women as *a class of persons*, but *as a mode of experience* that is distinctive to women and in important ways an experience that has marked ... off [women] from men and still continues to do so."[42] She argues thus that Parsons' adaptation of psychoanalysis "as a theory of internalization of practically everything" resulted in an individual's treatment merely as an expression of a socio-cultural system. She criticizes Parsons for his view that what is social is at once internal to the particularities of people's lives – a view which just leaves no room for regarding an individual as embodied, and so as resisting, and not merely yielding to influences from the outside.

Rationality vs Emotionality

The second binarism of crucial significance in sociological theory (quite other than that of expressive-functional) is that of reason/emotion. Modern western culture identifies rationality with the masculine and emotionality with the feminine, and the rational has always been regarded as superior to the emotional. Further, in respect of rationality itself, a distinction has been drawn by Max Weber,[43] one of the founding father of sociology. He distinguishes (merely) formal and instrumental rationality from substantive or value rationality, and the difference is put as follows. Whereas the former is determined by 'calculated ends', the latter is determined by emotions. In everyday speech, it is the instrumental rationality that is at work, for here we use reason simply for the sake of conveying our thoughts, intention, or feelings to others. Value rationality, on the other hand, makes for loving relations with others, just because such relations are pleasing in themselves. Both have their own value, but the tendency to assign greater value to the rational than to the emotional generally makes for the view that the male is superior to female.

Similarly, Habermas' theory rests on the view that rationality is essentially a male attribute. This is a clear emphasis in his work, *The Theory of Communicative Action*, which provides a detailed account of his view of human reason taken as a whole. Here, he also favours the view that all truths need the support of rational argument. Young[44] and Meisenhelder[45] acclaim Habermas for adding considerably to the previous analyses of rationality because he traces the operation of reason not only in mere argumentation, but in art, morality, and evolution of the sense of personal identity. However, at the same time, they criticize him for failing to trace the role of reason in emotional life. The truth in fact is that, for Habermas, emotionality is utterly non-rational and therefore not importantly human. What is, however, a little more striking in the work of Habermas is that, as Merchant[46] points out, the following three qualities are identified (by Habermas) as universal characteristics of reason:

(i) To visualize reality as a structure composed of essential dualities or divisions as between intellect and emotion, head and heart, mind and body. In all these dualities, whereas the former is supposed to be the source of knowledge and truth, the latter is taken as a quite unpredictable region characterized by sentimentality, untruth and the absence of reason.

(ii) To press for what is objectively verifiable and to look at the emotional as the merely subjective. This emphasis naturally heightens the subject-object duality and the difference between nature which surrounds us as an uncomprehended something and science which aims at understanding nature and so is higher than a mere unthinking communion with nature.

(iii) To regard the patriarchal mind as essentially the source and locus of objective knowledge which is why the male mind is able to control production. Be that as it may, Habermas favours the view that reason is devoid of emotionality. Contemporary feminists like Harding are also of the view that Habermas's model of reason is patriarchal because it ranks the scholarly thinking done by man as higher than women's thinking even if it is truly of the same quality.

As a corrective to this judgmental injustice, Meisenhelder suggests that if practical and instrumental rationality has to be checked for the sake of freeing society from a political economy of domination, a balanced and truthful theory of emotional reason is also necessary, that is, if we are to get rid of social repression.[47] Many other feminist theorists; notably Dorothy Dinnerstein[48] and Nancy Chodorow[49] have also tried to redeem sociological theory from the patriarchal bias referred to a love. This corrective thinking has been dealt with at length in the chapter on psychology and feminism.

Public vs Private, Work vs Family

Besides the distinction we have just dealt with, another important distinction which has prevented an objective analysis of sex roles in sociological theories is the distinction drawn rather exaggeratingly, between the public and the private. These two 'worlds' are conceived as separate and often conflicting realities, with different inner structures, outlooks and world views. Thinking where this distinction rules confines the 'female' wholly to the private sphere, and the male, just as rigidly, to the 'public'. Such a sharp dichotomy naturally fails to accord the title of economic productivity to women's work in the home and at workplace, simply because only those who inhabit the public sphere – that is, men – are regarded capable of doing productive work. Naturally, quite a few feminist scholars have challenged this public-private dichotomy. Some of them criticize Marx for taking into cognizance the work done in public alone and for ignoring the unpaid work at home. They add that it is this attitude of Marx which makes the history of labour merely an account of men's work at public places. The 'economics' of Marx is indeed confined to the masculine, public realm of industry and labour, and utterly ignores not only nature, the frequent changes in which can influence productivity greatly, but even the visibly life-giving feminine labour of reproduction at home.

Now, the postmodern feminists see the public-private distinction as a false dichotomy, and claim that these two spheres freely get fused into one overlapping set of experiences that constitute the life-world in late capitalist societies.[50] Indeed, the fact today is that whereas numberless women are making a mark in public economic activity, such as the garment industry, husbands are no longer wholly averse to share indoor responsibilities to ease the burden a little on their working wives.

Closely related to the public-private split is the work-family dichotomy. It assumes two things: (a) that outdoor productive work is superior to looking after family affairs, and (b) that what is done in the family, however time-consuming it be, cannot be regarded as work, truly so called. Now, protesting against this simplistic distinction between work and mere activity, Gladys L. Symonds outlines six types of labour regarded as what is done to sustain a family: (1) economic support, (2) domestic labour, (3) emotional work, such as providing relief and encouragement, say, by giving a pat on the back or gifts, kissing, and verbal exhortation, (4) reproduction, (5) general care of dependants, and (6) personal service, such as nursing the sick and running errands. What is noteworthy, however, is that these different types of work may well be done in the same field of activity. Thus, whereas in the protypical patriarchal family[51] or the 'breadwinner family'[52] the husband is the economic wage-earner and wife is responsible for the care of home and children, in the dual-earner family (say i.e., typical North American family), both husband and wife participate in the labour market and work for a wage. What is more, here women do the housework as well as provide economic support to the family. To conclude, none of the dichotomies we have discussed above is quite true to the actual state of work done by the two sexes.

Feminist Perspectives in Sociological Theories

Feminist theorists are indeed able to criticize, quite fairly, the sociological theories we have so far dealt with, say, as follows:

(a) The Marxists attach value only to wage-earning labour. How are they justified in ignoring the non-wage-earning labour performed by women? The feminists theorists also allege that oppression for women results equally from patriarchy and from class structure, not simply as a by product of class relationships.

(b) Nor are the Marxist world systems and dependency theories quite satisfactory. They are not equally applicable to all nations. They ignore, for instance, the aberration that the capitalist slant of core nations has penetrated the peripheral ones, and thus denigrated the general condition of women as reflected in such disturbing conditions as high fertility rates, poverty, and income inequality in the peripheral nations. Ward criticizes the world system theory for its assumption that women's participation in the modern world economy occurs only in members of those households in which the male 'head' dominates. Such an assumption simply ignores the direct participation of women in global economy and also their contributions in the informal labour market as well as in the household.[53]

Interesting developments are indeed taking place in the work area and they are being duly noted by researchers. Thus, in an attempt to chart out a feminist theory of development, Blumberg has attempted to bridge the macro-micro gaps prevalent in development theory. He further explains how both the competing paradigms of development – namely, a neo-classical modernization approach and a more radical alternative (embracing Marxist dependent-world system variants) – rarely pay due attention to women, in spite of regarding the household as a basic unit of analysis.[54]

On the other hand, feminist theorists demonstrate the centrality of gender as a concept, along with recognizing the concept of class, in understanding exploitation/oppression in capitalist systems and also in understanding how these capitalist systems are maintained and strengthened.

Not only this, feminist theorists have also contributed to and challenged the macro-structural theory which explains variations in the level of gender stratification across time/space. They provide important insights concerning the links that can be drawn between gender stratification and other macro-level structures and processes that should be incorporated into general structural theories. They also demonstrate that the different aspects of socio-cultural structure in all types of societies are covered in the gender system.[55]

> Theories concerning technology, work, ideology, family structure, demography, political economy, not to mention social inequality, that ignore the ubiquitous phenomenon of gender are radically incomplete, as are theories that attempt to explain social change and/or stability without gender.[56]

Similarly, several feminist scholars have targeted the rational choice and exchange theories,[57] and the criticisms here mainly are that they are all mainly rooted in an essentialist logic; that they assume a selfish, separative and non-emotional actor who is masculine, thereby ignoring the connective, altruistic and emotional motivations, characterized as feminine.[58] Friedman and Diem, however, argue that the rational choice theory can be of use in analysing gender issues. So they advocate such an enlargement of this theory as may include altruism (or its absence) as a variable and also give due attention to the role of emotion and interpersonal preferences.

Feminists also use the exchange theory to understand gender inequality. They claim that wives balance exchanges with their husbands by providing compliance and deference in return for financial support and access to other externally generated resources.[59]

In a similar way, feminist versions of status expectations and network theories explain how interactive relationships are shaped along structured gender lines and how they result in gender differentiation and inequality.[60] Likewise, feminist interpretation of symbolic interaction focuses on gender as an ongoing accomplishment that emerges during interaction: By demonstrating that both *cross* and *same* sex interactions normally entail gender,[61] they suggest that gender is an outcome of all interaction, one that should be regarded as a central component of general interaction theories.

As a subset of symbolic interaction, ethnomethodology demonstrates how we create and share our understanding of social life. For example, the categories of gender, race and class are first socially constructed and then gradually take the forms of objective reality. Feminist versions of ethnomethodology focus on micro-level processes by which gender differences and inequalities are constantly re-created in everyday life.[62]

Feminists also attack the neo-Freudian and role theories for being male-centric. By 1970s, a new sociology of sex roles was developed by feminist sociologists. In this context, Chodorow's[63] neo-Freudian account of gender differentiation and inequality is very significant.

The recent strand in feminist theorizing is "the intersection of race, class and gender". The central contention of this emerging focus is that the "three forms of oppression are not separate and additive, but interactive and multiplicative in their effects."[64]

Having discussed the theories at fair length, we shall now focus on a pioneering critique of the androcentric assumptions underpinning mainstream sociology, made by the standpoint theorists who try to explore how sociology might be reconfigured from women's perspective.

Towards a Feminist Standpoint Theory

As an alternative to the mainstream, 'masculinist', 'objectivist' and 'positivist' sociological theory some contemporary sociologists have developed a standpoint theory. The publication of Nancy Hartsock's *Money, Sex, and Power*[65] has changed the very landscape of feminist theory. It defines the nature of truth claims advanced by the new feminists and provides a methodological base to give validity to those claims. This has been defined by Hartsock as the feminist standpoint. In the succeeding decades this feminist standpoint theory became a staple of feminist theory.

Of all those who swear by this theory, the two most widely cited feminist sociologists are Dorothy Smith and Patricia Hill Collins. While Smith[66] has developed a generally relevant "women's standpoint", Collins[67] articulates a specifically Afrocentric feminist standpoint. Both argue that the feminist standpoint is discursively constituted but the material lives on which it is based are not so. They claim that until recently the knower in sociology had a common standpoint – that of white, middle class male. Recognizing the diversity of experiences among women, both Smith and Collins maintain that each gender has a standpoint that results in profound differences between the ways men and women think, in addition to what they think about.[68] Smith refers to "male created discourse" and talks about male thinking as "objectifying" experience, thereby creating "lines of fault" between women's subjective experience and the way women sociologists write about them. She posits an absolute dichotomy between abstract concepts on the one hand and lived reality on the other. So, she says that women's everyday world is alienated and objectified by the very categories of analysis, that is as sociologists, scholars are taught and expected to bring to their work categories that reflect and support the "social relations of ruling" that oppress them. In this context, Smith arrives at two conclusions: first, that the lived reality of women's lives is absent from sociology, perhaps because it is just invisible to the sociologists; and, second, that the woman sociologist experiences a bifurcated consciousness, that is, the abstract, conceptual world she encounters in the capacity of a sociologist as opposed to her lived reality as a woman. So, Smith claims that, as a sociologist, the grasp and exploration of her own experiences as a method of discovering society restores to her a centre which is wholly hers.[69]

Here, it must be noted that taking a feminist standpoint may sometimes serve to privilege particular women's perspectives at the expense of others, as happened with the Black feminist thought. Patricia Hill Collins has taken special interest in theorizing a unique standpoint of black women without denying the differences among them. She speaks of a distinctive "androcentric women's culture of resistance which represents the simultaneity of race, class and gender oppression" in a "matrix of domination". Collins describes "positivism" of sociology as "a Eurocentric masculinist epistemology" that is highly problematic for understanding African-American women's lives. She argues:

> [Scientists] aim to distance themselves from the values, vested interests and emotions ... (and thus) decontextualise themselves (in order to become) detached observers and manipulators of nature.

Collins criticizes this epistemology not only because it treats the subjects of research as objects (as does Smith) but also because of the absence of emotion, ethics, and values in establishing knowledge claims.

To both Smith and Collins, the taken-for granted concepts, language and style of writing and making truth-claims in sociology are male-created, alien to women, and function simply to support patriarchy, specifically "relations of ruling" as described by Smith or "matrix of domination" as argued by Collins more generally. Pointing to the significance of standpoint theory for women worldwide, Judith Grant says:

> Though women speak from multiple standpoints, producing multiple knowledge, ... the similarities among them can [yet] be cultivated to help them speak across suppressed differences.[70]

All the above critiques project that women's inferior position is due to the ways in which gender roles are constructed within society. The masculine is always seen as superior to the feminine. The next chapter explores the various ways in which such a mindset is created and reinforced in society.

Notes

1. See Marcia Millman and Rosabeth Kanter (eds.), *Another Voice*, New York: Doubleday, 1975.
2. Karl Marx, *Capital*, Vol. I, Harmondsworth: Penguin, 1976, pp. 717–18.
3. Emile Durkheim, *The Division of Labour in Society*, New York: Free Press, 1964.
4. Simmell quoted in V. Klein's *The Feminine Character*, London: Routledge, 1946, pp. 82–83.
5. Betty Friedan, *The Feminine Mystique*, New York: Dell, 1963, pp. 117ff.
6. Jessie Bernard, "My Four Revolutions: An Autobiographical History of the ASA", *American Journal of Society*, 78, 1973, pp. 773–801.
7. Joan Acker, "Women and Social Stratification: A Case of Intellectual Sexism", in John Huber (ed.), *Changing Women in Changing Society*, Chicago: University of Chicago Press, 1973, pp. 174–83.
8. Ann Oakley, *The Sociology of Housework*, London: Martin Robertson, 1974.
9. Helen Roberts, "Some of the Boys Won't Play Any More: The Impact of Feminism on Sociology", in Dale Spender (ed.), *Men's Studies Modified*, London: Pergamon Press, 1981.
10. A. Myrdal and V. Klein, *Women's Two Roles*, London: Routledge and Kegan Paul, 1956.

11. M. Hewitt, *Wives and Mothers in Victorian Industry,* London: Rockliff, 1958.
12. Pearl Jephcott, *Girls Growing Up*, London: Faber and Faber, 1949.
13. Margery Rice Spring, *Working Class Wives,* London: Penguin, 1939.
14. R. Frakenberg, *Village on the Border,* London: Cohen and West, 1957; *Communities in Britain*, London: Penguin, 1966.
15. J. Littlejohn, *Westrigg: The Sociology of a Chevist Parish,* London: Routledge and Kegan Paul, 1963.
16. M. Stacey, *Tradition and Change: A Study of Banbury,* Oxford: Oxford University Press, 1960.
17. Ann Oakley, *The Sociology of Housework,* London: Martin Robertson, 1980.
18. Ann Oakley, *Becoming a Mother,* London: Martin Robertson, 1979.
19. Hilary Graham, "Women's Attitudes to Conception and Pregnancy", in R. Chester and J. Peels (eds.), *Equalities and Inequalities in Family Life.* London: Academic Press, 1977.
20. Lesley Doyal and Imogen Pennell, *The Political Economy of Health,* London: Pluto, 1979.
21. Carol Smart, *Women, Crime and Criminology,* London: Routledge and Kegan Paul, 1976;

    C. Smart and B. Smart (eds.), *Women, Sexuality and Social Control,* London: Routledge and Kegan Paul, 1978.
22. Sheila Allen, "Perhaps a Seventh Person", in *Women's Studies International Quarterly,* Vol. III, No. 4, 1980.
23. Margaret Stacey and Marion Price, The Law is Not Enough: The 'Continued Oppression of Women.' Paper presented at the British Sociological Association Conference, University of Warwick.
24. Gloria Bowles and Renate Kleen (eds.), *Theories of Women's Studies,* London: Routledge and Kegan Paul, 1983.

    Julia Bramen and Gail Wilson, *Give and Take in Families,* London: Allen and Unwin, 1987.

    Patricia Hill Collins, *Black Feminist Thought,* London: Allen and Unwin, 1990.

    Liz Stanley, *Feminist Praxis: Method, Theory and Epistemology in Feminist Sociology,* London: Routledge and Kegan Paul, 1990.
25. Post-second wave feminism saw a profusion of feminist scholarship in the field of sociology. Some of the relevant works here are:
    - Jessie Bernard, *The Female World,* New York: Free Press, 1981.
    - Janet. S. Chafetz, *Feminist Sociology: An Overview of Contemporary Theories,* Ithaca, IL: F.E. Peacock, 1988.
    - Ruth A. Wallace, *Feminism in Sociological Theory,* London: Sage Publications, 1989.
    - Dorothy Smith, "A Sociology for Women", in J.A. Sherman and E.T. Beck (eds.), *The Prism of Sex: Essays in the Sociology of Knowledge,* Madison: University of Wisconsin, 1979.

- Arlie Hochschild, *The Managed Heart,* Berkeley: University of Calfornia Press, 1983.

26. J.C. Alexander and J. Turner (eds.), "Key Issues in Sociological Theory", (editorial statement) in J.C. Alexander (ed.), *Neofunctionalism,* Beverly Hills, CA: Sage, 1985, p. 2, bracketed words added.
27. See Cynthia Fuchs Epstein, *Women in Law,* New York: Basic Books, 1981; "Women and Power: The Role of Women in Politics in the United States", in C.F. Epstein and R.L. Coser (eds.), *Access to Power: Cross-National Studies on Women and Elites,* London: George Allen and Unwin, 1981, pp. 124–46; "Institutional Barriers: What Keeps Women Out of Executive Suite?" in F. Gordon and M. Strober (eds.), *Bringing Women into Management,* New York: McGraw Hill, 1975, pp. 7–20.
28. See Melvin Kohn and Cami Schooler, "Occupational Experience and Psychological Functioning: An Assessment of Reciprocal Effects", *American Sociological Review,* (February 1973), pp. 97–118. Also J.T. Martimer and J. Lawrence, "Work Experience and Occupational Value Socialization: A Longitudinal Study", *American Journal of Sociology,* Vol. 84, No. 6, May 1979, pp. 1361–85.
29. See Rosabeth Kanter, *Men and Women of the Corporation,* New York: Basic Books, 1977, p. 212.
30. Robert. K. Merton, "Self-Fulfilling Prophecy", in *Social Theory and Social Structure,* Glencoe, Illinois: The Free Press, 1957.
31. See, Cynthia Fuchs Epstein, *Woman's Place,* Berkeley, Los Angeles, London, University of California Press, 1970.
32. Marcia Millman, "She did it all for Love", in Marcia Millman and Rosabeth Kanter (eds.), op. cit., 1975.
33. Cynthia Fuchs Epstein, op. cit.
34. "Hidden Protest: The Channeling of Female Innovation and Resistance", *Signs,* Vol. 4, (Summer 1979), pp. 651–69.
35. Joan Acker, "Women and Social Stratification", *American Journal of Sociology,* 78(4), 1973, pp. 936–45.
36. Sylvia Walby, "Gender, Class and Stratification", in R. Crompton and M. Mann (eds.), *Gender and Stratification,* Cambridge: Polity Press, 1986.
37. See Talcott Parsons, "Age and Sex in the Social Structure of the U.S.", in *Essays in Sociological Theory,* Glencoe, Illinois: The Free Press, 1954.
38. Betly Friedan, op. cit.
39. Linda. L. Lindsey, *Gender Roles: A Sociological Perspective,* New Jersey: Prentice Hall, 1997, p. 6.
40. Ibid., p. 6.
41. Miriam Johnson, J. Stockard, J. Acker and C. Naffziger, "Expressiveness Reevaluated", *School Review,* 83, pp. 617–43. Also see, Miriam M. Johnson, "Feminism and Theories of Talcott Parsons", in Ruth A. Wallace (ed.), op. cit.

42. Dorothy Smith, *The Everyday World as Problematic: A Feminist Sociology*, Boston: North Eastern University Press and Milton Keynes: Open University Press, 1987.
43. Max Weber, *The Theory of Social and Economic Organization*, New York: The Free Press, 1947.
44. I. Young, "Impartiality and the Civic Life", in S. Benhabib and D. Comell (eds.), *Feminism as Critique*, Minneapolis: University of Minnesota Press, 1987.
45. Thomas Meisenhelder, "Habermas and Feminism", in Ruth A. Wallace (ed.), op. cit.
46. C. Merchant, *The Death of Nature*, London: Harper and Row, 1980.
47. Thomas Meisenhelder, op. cit.
48. Dorothy Dinnerstein, *The Mermaid and the Minotaur*, New York: Harper and Row, 1976.
49. Nancy Chodorow, *The Reproduction of Mothering*, Berkeley: University of California Press, 1978.
50. Gladys L. Symonds, "Post Modern Feminism Challenges Organizational Theory", in Vasilikie Demos and Marcia Pexler Segal (eds.), *An International Feminist Challenge to Theory*, London: Elsevier Science, 2001.
51. The family needs to be qualified, for rapid and complex changes have produced many different forms, including reconstituted families, solo-parent families as well as same-gender-parent families.
52. M. Eichler, *Families in Canada Today*, Toronto: Sage, 1988.
53. See K. Ward, *Women in the World System: Its Impact on Status and Fertility*, New York: Praeger, 1984;
    Women Workers and Global Restructuring, Ithaca, New York: ILR, 1990;
    "Reconceptualising World System Theory to include Women", in P. England (ed.), *Theory on Gender/Feminism on Theory*, New York: Aldine De Grutyer, 1993.
54. R.L. Blumberg, "Towards a Feminist Theory of Development", in Ruth A. Wallace (ed.), op. cit., pp. 161–99.
55. J.S. Chafetz, "Feminist Theory and Sociology", *Annual Review of Sociology*, Vol. 23, 1997, pp. 97–120.
56. J.S. Chafetz, "Feminist Theory and Sociology: Underutilized Contributions for Feminist Theory", *Annual Review of Sociology*, Vol. 23, 1997, pp. 97–120.
57. See P. England, "A feminist Critique of Rational Choice Theories: Implication for Sociology", *American Sociologist*, Vol. 20, 1989, pp. 14–20.
58. This and other related criticisms of rational choice theory are discussed and rebutted by Friedman and Diem. "Feminism and Pro (Rational) Choice Movement; Rational Choice Theory, Feminist Critiques and Gender Inequality", in P. England (ed.), op. cit., 1993.

59. See S. Parker and H. Parker, "The Myth of Male Superiority: Rise and Demise", *American Anthropology,* Vol. 81, pp. 289–309.

    R. Curtis, "Household and Family in Theory on Inequality", *American Sociological Review,* Vol. 51, pp. 168–83.
60. See Lynn Smith Lovin and L. Miller McPherson, "You are Who You Know: A Network Approach to Gender", in P. England (ed.), op. cit., 1993; and

    B.F. Meeker and P.A. Weitzel-O'Neill, "Sex Roles and Interpersonal Behaviour in Task Oriented Groups", *American Sociological Review,* Vol. 42, pp. 92–105.
61. C. West and D.H. Zimmerman, "Doing Gender", *Gender Society,* Vol. 9, 1995, pp. 8–37.
62. See M. De Vault, *Feeding the Family: The Social Construction of Caring as Gendered Work,* Chicago: University of Chicago Press, 1991. Also see M. De Vault and K. Ferguson, *Self, Society and Womankind,* Westport, CT: Greenwood, 1980; and P. Fishman, "Interaction: The Work Women Do", in R. Khan-Hut et al. (eds.), *Women and Work: Problems and Perspectives,* New York: Oxford University Press, 1982.
63. For further details, see Chapter on Psychology.
64. For this perspective,

    see E. Almquist, "The Experiences of Minority Women in the United State: Intersections of Race, Gender and Class", in J. Freeman (ed.), *Women: A Feminist Perspective,* Mountain View, CA: Mayfield, 1989, pp. 415–45; and E. Almquist, M.L. Anderson and P.H. Collins (eds.), *Race, Class and Gender: An Anthology,* Belmont, CA: Wordsworth, 1995.
65. See, Nancy Hartsock, *Money, Sex and Power,* New York, Longman, 1983.
66. Dorothy Smith, *The Everyday World as Problematic: A Feminist Sociology,* Boston: North Eastern University Press, 1987.
67. Patricia Hill Collins, *Black Feminist Thought: Knowledge, Consciousness and the Politics of Empowerment,* Boston: Unwin Hyman, 1990.
68. J.S. Chafetz, "Feminist Theory and Sociology", *Annual Review of Sociology,* Vol. 23, 1997, pp. 97–120.
69. Dorothy Smith, "Women's Perspective as a Radical Critique of Sociology", in Stevi Jackson and Sue Scott (eds.), *Gender: A Sociological Reader,* London and New York: Routledge, 2002.
70. Judith Grant, *Fundamental Feminism: Contesting the Core Concepts of Feminist Theory,* New York: Routledge, 1993.

5

Rupturing the 'Masculine'

Restoring the 'Feminine' in Psychology

Feminists have challenged the discipline of psychology through and through. Both its fundamental assumptions and methodologies have been contested and labelled as androcentric. They argue that psychology and its practitioners have downgraded the woman in both theory and practice. In theory, she is portrayed as 'irrational' and 'overemotional', whereas in practice, she is devalued for being disunited, illogical and ignorant. Historically, it has been discovered that even the primary concept of the human subject that psychology used till 1960s was deeply gender-based. To illustrate, all published books over a decade ago have defined psychology in male-centric terms, that is, "as the scientific study of man" and all individuals have been referred to as 'he' only, as if women just do not exist. Moreover, it is men who are always treated as the normative population and all females are judged by comparing them with this arbitrary conception of the normative. This is why, M. Crawford and J. Maracek allege that the mainstream psychology has "not only omitted the consideration of women and women's activities, it has also validated the view that [only] those activities in which men engage are activities central to human life."[1]

Contesting Androcentrism: Feminist Contributions

Gender interrogations within the discipline of psychology began from the late 1960s. Earlier, stereotyped sex differences were either simply assumed or, when measured, they were assigned axiomatically to biology.[2] This assumption of stereotyped sex differences among men and women was challenged by the landmark work of Maccoby and Jacklin published in 1974. It revealed that there were more similarities than differences between the sexes, and that these differences could be attributed to environmental processes rather than to biology.[3] Some years later, Kay Deaux, continuing the trend of psychological research in the previous decade, concluded that the sex differences between men and women were "surprisingly small in most cases".[4]

From outside the field of psychology, the first attack on the discipline came from assault of major feminist writers, such as Simone de Beauvoir (1953)[5], Millett (1971)[6], Greer (1971)[7] and Firestone (1971).[8] Others focused on psychoanalysis in particular. However, it was the publication of Weisestein's article (1971)[9] that proved to be a landmark in exposing deep-seated biases in psychology. She contended that "psychology has nothing to say about what women are really like, what they need and what they want, essentially because psychology does not know."[10]

This was followed by a number of publications in the field. In 1970s, various journals like *Sex Roles: A Journal of Research, Psychology of Women Quarterly, Feminism and Psychology: An International Journal, Journal of Women and Aging, Journal of Gay and Lesbian Psychotherapy;* and *Women and Therapy* appeared on the scene and pushed forward the task of exposing the male bias in psychology. To speak generally, the feminists condemned all psychological theories as 'discourses of masculinity'. However, they did not stop at such generalities; and, as we now set out to show, challenges were posed to every aspect of psychology, from theory to specific research methodology and therapeutic practices.

Male Bias in Freudian Psychoanalysis

Freudian psychoanalytic theory has been criticized by feminists as misogynist, ahistorical, and acultural, as it is fraught with male bias, and so is quite untrue to the evidence of history and culture. Donovan voices the view that what Betty Friedan called the 'feminine mystique' could just as easily be called the 'Freudian mystique'.[11] Feminists claim that Freud explains men's and women's relative social and psychical positions in terms of their anatomy and takes masculine characteristics as a psychoanalytic norm; that he regards the feminine simply as a lesser, 'castrated' version of that norm; and that he sees male development as the prototype, the penis being central to an understanding of the Oedipus complex and all subsequent development. Moreover, as Freud visualizes it, the resolution of the Oedipus complex is essential for the development of the moral component of the personality (the superego) and is central also to the repression of all the earlier phases of development which, by virtue of their denial to consciousness, recur to haunt us in our subsequent growth throughout life. Thus, for both males and females, development is to be understood in relation to penis – for males because of its presence, and for females in virtue of its absence. It is to this sheer physical lack that Freud ascribes the female's sense of inferiority, her passivity, her underdeveloped ego and subsequent dependence on the male. Feminists therefore challenge Freud's psychoanalytic theory as just "another weapon in the armoury of patriarchy". Nevertheless, instead of abandoning psychoanalytic theory completely and developing radically alternative models of psychical development, feminists attempted to "reform, re-read or reinterpret psychoanalytic doctrine" to explain the ways in which males and female acquire their socially ordained sexual roles and their correlative psychical attitudes and structures.

To understand the critique of Freud, one has to reflect on the two major classes of psychoanalytic feminists: Freudian feminists and Lacananian feminists. Freudian feminists[12] are those who, unlike Freud, emphasize the significance of 'the father' in shaping psychic (unconscious) life, and also the prior (pre-linguistic) importance of the mother. They emphasize the impact of women's primary care-giving responsibilities on personality and social relations, focusing on the fact that in all societies women's primary task is nurturing and parenting. Drawing on the work of Sigmund Freud in their discussions of how it is that women become feminine and motherly, they also offer a reinterpretation of his account of how the (sexed) self is formed.

In the writings of Freudian feminists[13], the psychological and cultural influence of women on the constitution of subjectivities and social relations is largely viewed as active and positive, despite their oppressed status. Instead of conceiving women as unconsciously shaped by envy for what appears to belong exclusively to men, and in relation to a male standard against which they must appear deficient, women are here regarded as contributing positively an alternative psychological order.[14] Accordingly, women are viewed as having much to offer to a programme for political change.

The Lacanian feminists are those who, unlike Freud, describe the development of the (sexed) self in linguistic or symbolic cultural terms rather than in more concrete, literal or even biological terms. This mode of thought is particularly evident in the works of French feminists like Irigrary, Cixous and Kristeva, who concentrate on reworking of Freudian psychoanalysis and also build on the approach of French psychoanalyst Jacques Lacan.

Feminists have been presenting a critique of mainstream psychoanalysis right since 1920s. Many new perspectives have been added. A total picture of these critiques can only emerge when they are presented in a chronological order, and this is precisely what we now set out to do.

Early Psychoanalytic Feminism

The earliest contribution was made during the 1920s and 1930s by Karen Horney, Melanie Klein and Ernest Jones. They all argued against the Freudian account of masculinity and femininity mainly on three grounds: (a) it exaggerated female inferiority; (b) it wrongly conceives the distinction between the sexes as naturally given, rather than as a psycho-social construction, and (c) it envisages people as born masculine or feminine predeterminately, and as impervious to the impact of subsequent interaction with society.

Karen Horney

To turn now to individual challengers to Freud's views, Karen Horney contended that "woman's capacity to reproduce constituted an undeniable physiological superiority". She attributed the cultural devaluation of women to two factors: first, the male envy of female reproduction capacity and second, women's own envying men for what they do not possess, that is, a penis. Penis envy, however, is not a product of Horney's mind. It is one of Freud's psycho analytic concepts, and it postulates envy of the penis as the cause for some of the characteristics of femininity. Horney, we may note, does not oppose this particular notion of Freud, but she does bemoan that "the girl begins to measure herself by pretensions and values that are foreign to her specific biological nature and confronted with which she cannot but feel herself inadequate".[15]

Melanie Klein

Melanie Klein[16] too had a considerable impact, particularly on British psychoanalysis of her times. She revised and extended several Freudian categories in the light of her child analysis findings during 1940s and 1950s, most notably by means of the idea of a pre-oedipal realm. According to Klein, child is oedipal much earlier than Freud visualized. She emphasized the role of pre-oedipal stage in the development of personality, as also of the child's relationship with the mother in the first year or so of its life. She argued that the infant feels envy not for paternal penis but for maternal plenitude, that is, for how full the mother's figure is and for how much she provides. Placing great importance on maternal functions and on the breast, she identified the existence of a peculiar trait in men too, that is, 'breast envy'. Klein sees femininity as an innate drive and posits a primordial infantile feminine sexuality, based on the girl's biological sex, which could then get modified according to the girl's relationship with others.

Until the early 1970s most feminists (for example, Simone de Beauvoir, Eva Figes, Betty Friedan, Shulamith Firestone, Germaine Greer and Kate Millett) treated Freud with hostility for his theory of psychoanalysis. For example Figes writes:

> Of all the factors that have served to perpetuate a male-oriented society, that have hindered the free development of women as human beings in the western world today, the emergence of Freudian psychoanalysis has been the most serious.[17]

Simone de Beauvoir[18] surely valued some insights of psychoanalysis but she strongly disagreed with the psychoanalytical method. She argued that the theory of psychoanalysis needed to be placed in a philosophical and historical context. The intrinsic weakness of the psychoanalytical theory, according to her, was its too much emphasis on the male. She criticized Freud for setting up a masculine model of individual development and for identifying human with male and so regarding female as merely the 'other'.

Friedan[19] too argued that Freud's psychoanalysis was largely responsible for the way in which the derogatory mystique of femininity had flourished in America since the 1940s.

Contemporary Psychoanalytic Feminism

Kate Millett and Phyllis Chesler

Contemporary psychoanalytic feminism begins from 1970s with Kate Millett's well-reasoned protests against Freud's views, and Phyllis Chesler's well-known work *Women and Madne*ss (1972). Millett[20] made an explicit attack on Freud's biological determinism. She accused Freud of a 'gross male-supremacist bias' and made a specific sarcastic comment: "It is interesting that Freud should imagine the young female's fears centre about castration rather than rape – a phenomenon which girls are in fact, and with reason, in dread of, since it happens to them and castration does not."

In *Sexual Politics* (1971) and subsequent writings Millett widened the concept of politics to refer to power structuring in general and showed how patriarchal power creates a sexist society. Millett has made a very significant analysis of the modes in which patriarchy operates, that is, as biology, sexual violence, class distinctions and inequity in respect of opportunities for education and she has thereby transformed contemporary thinking about women's roles significantly.

As for Phyllis Chesler in her work, *Women and Madness* (1972)[21] put forward the intriguing idea that in contemporary society female identity is routinely described in motifs of sickness and insanity. She argued that psychoanalysis regards sickness as a normative characteristic of femininity, and that women's mental illness is very probably a result of sex role stereotyping. Chesler explained that when women do not act in conscious or unconscious conformity with gender norms, their activities are regarded by society as examples of sickness and psychological deviance. If only incidentally, this particular view of Chesler dovetailed with a major emphasis of 'second wave feminism', besides challenging the social norms of the 'feminine' prevalent in the 1950s and 1960s. It also stimulated fresh thinking on alternative meanings of feminism such as the overall upraising of women's consciousness in respect of their present lot and the possibilities of its amelioration.

Current Psychoanalytic Feminism

However, the rejection of Freudian theories by Millett and early second wave feminists was itself challenged, a little later by Juliet Mitchell, who focused on the difference between psychodynamic and social structures, and not on mere psychoanalyis. Further, in response to women's movement, Dorothy Dinnerstein,[22] Jean Baker Miller,[23] Adrienne Rich[24] and Nancy Chodorow[25] created new psychoanalytic theories with reference to heterosexual relations, and it is their writings in the period 1970–78, together with Mitchell's work, which provide the basis for current psychoanalytic feminism.

Juliet Mitchell

Juliet Mitchell's text has served as a call for feminists, first, to reconsider Freud's work in order to explain the basic ways in which the 'unconscious' contributes to gender identity and hence to women's social oppression; and, secondly, to develop a concrete materialist feminist theory of gender and sexuality. She argues that "psychoanalysis is no recommendation for, but analyses the phenomenon of a patriarchal society."[26] At the same time, Mitchell is one of the first feminists to make a constructive use of Freud's theories. She not only concedes that psychoanalytic theory was, on the whole, valuable as an analysis of the individual within a patriarchal society, but also contends that far from being an unavoidable stage in personality development, the castration complex is only a theoretical tool constructed in response to the demands of a culture which sought to enforce rigid sexual differentiation. She thus argues that Freud's ideas (and Lacan's reconstruction of Freudian concepts)[27] did explain the attitudinal consequences (for women) of penis envy and oedipus complex in a phallic culture – attitudes like 'masochism' and 'fear of success'.

Dorothy Dinnerstein

Dorothy Dinnerstein was one of the first American feminists to devise a theory of social psychology to describe the effects of women's mothering and child rearing practices. She claimed that these practices are the central force in, and determinants of, gender identity throughout history. In her account of the pre-oedipal stage of gender development, Dinnerstein argued that the current family arrangements, where women do only the mothering, turn women into 'mermaids' and men into 'minotaurs'.[28] The only difference between men and women, according to her, is biological. Hence, women have a responsibility to establish the reasons for their compliance with a division of labour where they 'rock the cradle', and rule over childhood, while men 'rule the world', and exert public dominance.[29] Dinnerstein, while regarding Freud's legacy as potentially revolutionary, distances herself from the inevitability he sees in the construction of gender difference. Instead, she holds that the experiences of dependence and fear are locked deep into the unconscious mind and resurface in men's ambivalent fear of female authority and love of female flesh, and that of it is these fears that are at the root of creating social controls over women's public activities. Dinnerstein argues that a solution to this universal dilemma lies in the abolition of sexual division of productive labour.

Jean Baker Miller

Jean Baker Miller examined the psychological effects of social oppression on women and devised a 'new psychology' of women based on the concepts of 'affiliation' and 'care taking'. She argued that women develop these qualities in order to compensate for their lack of social power. In her book, *Toward a New Psychology of Women* (1986),[30] Miller suggests, like Nancy Chodorow, that women's capacity for emotional understanding derives from the early symbiotic bond with the mother and that it is precisely this bond which is unduly devalued by the dominant masculine culture. Miller develops the political implications of her new women-centred theory. For example she claims that women learn political skills in playing a subordinate role such as the skill of maintaining interpersonal a relationship even at the cost of personal hardship. She also argues that skills of 'peer support', which women are forced to acquire – and which men somehow deny to themselves – can produce new social communities partly as a defence against the insensitivity of androcentric culture.

Nancy Chodorow

Nancy Chodorow provided an influential reinterpretation of Freudian theory. Focusing primarily on sociological facts, Chodorow argued that the desire to be mother and the way a woman actually does the mothering cannot be adequately explained by biological arguments or socialization theories of role learning. For this purpose, she contends, an understanding of the unconscious process of parenting is necessary. In supporting her argument, she says that psychoanalysis may well be taken to provide an explanation of how mothering is reproduced from generation to generation, but it does not explain how women, from one generation to the next, take on the role of nurturing and caretaking happily and quite without any husband's coercion or social pressure.[31] In this context, she rejected the physiological, biological and even sociological theories as unconvincing and found the *object relations theory*[32] to be the best means to understand "the reproduction of mothering as a central and constituting element in the social organization and reproduction of gender."[33] What this theory says may be put quite simply as follows: We all see that it is always a female who, as the mother, brings up the little ones. This serves as an object lesson to girls. Of course, male children too are brought up by their mother's, but this very perception that the basic nurturing is done only by a female encourages girls to follow suit. They see that "women mother daughters [and not only sons; so] when they become women, [they too begin to] mother."[34]

Chodorow further says that the development of child's subsequent social identity is based on two unclearly separated relations – to its own corporeality and bodily sensations, and to the world of objects. The first relation derives from "an inner physical experience of body integrity and a more internal 'core of sense'"[35] while the second is the result of a "sense of personal psychological division from the rest of the world".[36] To put it all simply, the sense that one is a distinct individual depends, first, on the natural tendency to regard oneself as a distinct bodily existence; and secondly, on the experience that one's thoughts, attitudes and preferences differ from those of others.

French Psychoanalysts

More recently, psychoanalysis has been usurped by feminist literary critics to visualize how the 'feminine' is represented and organized in language. This trend was started by Jacques Lacan, who described the development of the (sexed) self in linguistic or symbolic cultural terms, rather than in more concrete, literal and biological terms the way Freud has done.[37] Lacan's re-reading of Freud has had enormous influence on French intellectuals. Julia Kristeva, Luce Irigracy and Helene Cixou, in particular,[38] are among the prominent French feminists who challenge 'phallogocentrism'[39] and share a common interest in a feminine language.

Lacan's contribution to the feminist theory lies essentially in his radical suggestion that Freud's hypothesis must be interpreted symbolically. In Lacan's own work 'penis envy' is no longer seen as involving envy of the literal biological organ, as it is in Freud's thinking; but has a thoroughly symbolic-cultural meaning, rather more along the lines of a psychological positioning as 'lacking' in relation to the authority power associated with the masculine. In this context, Lacan refers to 'the phallus' rather than to the penis, and he says that phallus is not so much a thing (though it may be represented by the penis or father) as the symbol of that which is not-the-mother. While the child initially does not distinguish his self as distinct and exists in a symbolic relationship with the mother, the phallus provides the means by which the child learns that all is not one and the same, and that distinctions can be made. In other words, the phallus enables the child to discover sexual difference. The phallus, therefore, breaks up the seamless interconnecting world of mother-child and alerts the child to the meaning of difference *per se*. Further, because (for Lacan) language, culture and meaning itself make an organized symbolic system of differences, he looks at the phallus as the basic determinant of meaning or significance. Further, since it provides the key by which the child encounters the difference, it is the phallus which is said to make for the child's entry into culture and society by the development of self (an 'I' recognized as being distinct and different from others). All children thus become 'subjects' and develop a self through the operation of a masculine regulatory principle. According to Lacan, 'civilization' itself is the 'Law of the Father'. For him, language, which is obviously a system of differently meaningful words, is the necessary first step by which the child enters the realm of. It is also viewed as a sign system which organizes or shapes culture by directing what can be known and recognized and what cannot be apprehended. As such language is conceived as the foundation of or as encapsulating culture. Culture is essentially a system of values, attitudes and pursuits, but how can all this be apprehended and articulated except in terms of language? Further, according to Lacan, there can be no (sexed) self – on masculine or feminine person – prior to the formation of the subject in language.[40] The argument here simply is that one cannot think of oneself as masculine or feminine unless one regards oneself as 'I' as opposed to the other, and the notion of self-identity develops essentially, if partly, through the repeated use of words like *I*, *me* and *mine*. Further, in so far as society is nothing without a number of individuals, and because, as we have just argued, the sense of being a distinct individual itself develops through a self-referent use of language, society itself may be regarded as a product of language, but indirectly. The superior status of the male in society can also be ascribed, in part, to a detail of linguistic usage say, the very free tendency to use the words humanity and man interchangeably.

The Ecriture Feminine School

If in Nancy Chodorow's *The Reproduction of Mothering* (1978), psychoanalysis is made to serve feminism by turning pre-oedipality into an explanation of the social relations of gender, in French feminist theory, psychoanalysis is done to serve the same end by making pre-oedipality on the basis of a unique feminine imagery or language. In both versions, the displacement of the father is further elaborated, and psychoanalysis is made to focus on the figure of the mother, seemingly displacing the father as the central figure of that discourse.

Influenced by the significance accorded to language in Lacan's work, French feminists (including writers like Luce Irigraray, Helene Cixous and Julia Kristeva) have concentrated upon a reworking of

Freudian psychoanalysis. These Lacanian feminists are described as engaged in the project of 'ecriture feminine' and as attempting embodied feminine writing, or writing from the viewpoint of the female body in a manner that challenges the way in which woman is construed, more or less abstractly, in language and culture. Whereas Lacan, in common with Freud, depicts femininity as a castrated state, that is, as lacking or deficient in comparison with the masculine, these French feminists start from, but provide a powerful critique of this negative assessment.[41] They question the assumption that femininity can only be seen from the point of view of phallic culture (culture as masculine dominance) and argue for other possibilities.[42] They propose the development of an alternative language, a way of thinking, which might make use of the 'outsider status' of the feminine implying that, because of its cramped vision, the phallic order of language[43] does not admit a 'feminine outsider' though it is unmistakably there.

For the 'ecriture feminine' writers, the general notion of 'woman' looks on her as inferior just because she does not fit the masculine norm of character and identity. It does not admit that there may well be beings who are just as human as men but with qualities and attitudes that are quite different from those of men, and not only in respect of sex. On the other hand, the living reality of "woman demonstrates the operation of hierarchical differentiation within phallic culture rather than bearing a set content. Thus, in 'ecriture' writing, femininity is celebrated as offering the potential for interrogation of the singular yardstick of the symbolic order (the Rule of the Father). In other words, femininity offers a possible procedure for subverting the marginalizing mechanism of power, thereby breaking it up.[44]

In this way, French feminist theorists have reasserted the concepts of difference and revalorized, so to say, both femininity and maternity within the ambit of psychoanalysis.

Having discussed the various contributions and challenges to the Freudian psychoanalytic approach, we may now turn to the stereotypes that the male-centred approach has brought about. In this context, we shall discuss the theories of human development as propagated by Freud, Kohlberg and Erikson, and then present the feminist critique of these theories. Later, we shall focus on the contemporary theories of human development which aim at a gender-free psychology by dismantling the stereotypes in question.

Resting Stereotypes of Male Bias in Theories of Human Development

Ever since the work of Freud psychology has adopted quite a few stereotypes in characterizing women's 'feminine' roles in terms of overworked words like *emotional, passive, subjective* and *dependent,* and men's roles as 'masculine', i.e., *practical, active, independent, strong* etc., always privileging the latter over the former. These stereotyped conceptions about what is appropriately masculine or feminine can cover at least five areas of behaviour:[45] personality traits (e.g., aggressive or *gentle*), family roles (e.g., breadwinner or *homemaker*), leisure activities (e.g., football or *knitting*), work roles (miner or *manicurist*) and personal styles and appearance (swaggering or *hip swinging*) etc. These stereotypes emphasize the distinctiveness of the sexes and serve to maintain the different status accorded to men and women.

Through its theory and practice psychology has itself contributed in a number of ways to the reinforcement of these sex role stereotypes. This has been detrimental to women in the following ways:

(a) Masculine traits have come to receive more positive evaluation than the feminine ones,[46] outweighing the desirability of being complaint, emotional and submissive. Evidences point out that, if only unknowingly women themselves tend to accept this societal bias towards typed feminine traits. Thus, those of them who rate themselves higher on masculine than on feminine traits have higher self-esteem than women who continue to describe themselves in feminine typed terms.[47]

(b) The conformity to sex role expectations tends to bring about permanent changes in a person's self-concept and behaviour, thus producing a 'self-fulfilling prophecy'[48] – or providing added warrant – to the stereotype.

(c) Stereotyped expectations about women's competence, emotionality, or physical characteristics frequently result in biased evaluations and artificial barriers to women's achievement.[49]

Thus, societal stereotypes need to be considered in earnest in order to evaluate the influence of these expectations on women's psychological development. Between men and women, the chromosomal, gonadal and hormonal sex differences are universal. While a normal woman has two x chromosomes, a normal man, an x chromosome and y chromosome. The internal and external reproductive sex organs, of course, differ in normal men and women. The sex hormones secreted and the timing of secretion also differ, with the woman exhibiting a cyclical pattern. These differences have provided the basis for a number of traditional theories concerning psychological sex differences, like the theories of Frued, Erikson, Kohlberg etc., who all support societal prescriptions for male dominance and privilege, by regarding women not only as biologically different from, but also inferior to men. They hold that women themselves tend to internalize the biological superiority of men, thus diminishing their self-image, their sense of self-worth and their own expectations of what they can become.[50] Thus, the traditional theories confine women to traditional roles of work and behaviour and view any alternative lifestyle as a mark of 'deviance' however sensible it may be in itself.

Traditional Theories: "Anatomy is Destiny"

Theory of Freud[51]

Frued's theory of development differentiation is based on the biological differences between girls and boys, primarily on the presence of penis in the boys and the capability of women to bear children. He calls the penis the organ of "power and creativeness"[52] whereas the female's lack of it, an "anatomical tragedy".[53] Further, he says that, around the age of three, all boys begin to lust after their mother, (a symptom which he calls the oedipus complex) and view their father as a competitor for her affection. Sensing his father's retaliation in the form of emasculation (the castration complex), the boy renounces his mother as an object of complete love. In self-defence and to placate his father, the boy then identifies himself with the father, taking on his qualities and standards of masculinity or what it means to be a man. In this manner, the boy becomes socialized into the prevailing culture and develops a conscience and a set of moral standards (the superego). However, Freud does not clearly explain the mechanisms responsible for sex role development in girls, but remains committed to a genital view of identification. The little girl, observing that she does not possess a penis, realizes her deficiency and blames her mother for it, and in this process she develops 'penis envy' and a basic sense of inferiority, resolving her genital loss by transferring her affections to her father. In course of time, she recognizes that, in a way, she can own a penis by accepting it passively from a male, and she transfers this envy into a desire to have a child, preferably male.

Her identification with her mother and with the feminine role in general develops not only out of her competition with the father but also out of the fear of losing mother's love completely. This process has a number of effects on female psychology; one of them, according to Freud, being the fact that women do not develop strong superegos.

> In the absence of fear of castration, the chief motive is lacking which leads boys to surmount the Oedipus complex. Girls remain in it for an indeterminate length of time, they demolish it late and, even so, incompletely. In these circumstances the formation of the superego most suffers it cannot attain the strength and independence which give it its cultural significance ...[54]

In Freud's thought the development of the superego and the development of civilization are closely bound together. He further states that "since penis envy is never entirely sublimated in normal women, envy and jealousy play a greater part in the mental life of women than in that of men".[55]

Feminist theorists see this theory as essentially one of male development because of Freud's male-centric perception describing women as inferior to men, having a lesser sense of justice, and remaining more influenced by their emotions than by logical reasoning. Further, the feminists contend that Freud's theory of sex role development has very little scientific or empirical support.[56] However, at the level of practical application to human problems, the theory continues to influence the practices and assumptions of many professional mental health specialists in their dealings with women under treatment.[57] One distinct result of viewing women from a Freudian perspective may also be the tendency to see even the 'normal' – or quite sensible – behaviour of women as a kind of 'deviance'.

Erikson's Theory

A number of psychologists and psychoanalysts agree with Freud that women and men are psychologically very different, but they do not all accept the notion of 'penis envy'. According to Erik Erikson, a well-known critic of the notion in question, women's psychology is determined not by the missing penis but by the existence of a "productive inner-bodily space".[58] He explains that woman's "somatic design harbours an 'inner space' destined to bear the offspring of chosen men and, with it, a biological, psychological, and ethical commitment to take care of human infancy".[59] His emphatic view is that women's impressive activity in non-male ways, such as bearing and taking care of babies, is not masochist, but is rather a natural consequence of their "ability to stand [and to understand] pain as a meaningful aspect of human experience in general and of the feminine role in particular".[60] Erikson's theory develops around his concept of the "eight stages of man" (see Table 1).[61] Elaborating this concept, he explains that human development proceeds throughout life in the way of stages in which polarities determine the formation of our personality. Each stage consists of polarities such as trust-mistrust, autonomy-shame and industry-inferiority. Two of

Table 1
Eight Stages of Psycho-social Development

Stages (Ages are Approximate)	*Psychosocial Crises*	*Radius of Significant Relations*	*Psychosocial Modalities*	*Favourable*
1. Birth-first year	Trust vs mistrust	Mother or mother substitute	To get To give in return	Drive and hope
2. Second year	Autonomy vs shame, doubt	Parents	To hold (on) To let (go)	Self-control and willpower
3. Third year-fifth year	Initiative vs guilt	Basic family	To make (going after) To "make like" (playing)	Direction and purpose
4. Sixth year-onset of puberty	Industry vs inferiority	Neighbourhood school	To make things (completing) To make things together	Method and competence
5. Adolescence	Identity and repudiation vs identity diffusion	Peer groups and outgroups; models of leadership	To be oneself (or not to be) To share being oneself	Devotion and fidelity
6. Early adulthood	Intimacy and solidarity vs isolation	Partners in friendship, sex, competition, cooperation	To lose and find oneself in another	Affiliation and love
7. Young and middle adulthood	Generativity vs self-absorption	Divided labour and shared household	To make become To take care of	Production and care
8. Later adulthood	Integrity vs despair	"Mankind" vs "My kind"	To be, through having been To face not being	Renunciation and wisdom

Source: Erikson (1963); modified from original.

these stages – identity vs diffusion and intimacy vs isolation – provided a difficulty for Erikson when he attempted to understand how women's development fitted his scheme of things. In normal development, according to him, the adolescent achieves a sense of personal identity rather than that of identity diffusion, by embracing a philosophy of life and commitment to a career. In the next stage of young adulthood, intimacy is achieved by relinquishing one's autonomy in the fusion of self with another and committing oneself to "affiliations and partnerships".[62] However, Erikson could not relate this view of life progression to women. Instead, he concluded that women defer developing a sense of identity until "they know whom they will marry and for whom they will make a home".[63] Thus, according to Erikson, woman's identity is not defined in terms of commitment to a career, but in those of her commitment to the roles of wife and mother, and to her search for a man to give both meaning and direction to her life.

Feminist theorists naturally oppose Erikson's theory because of its androcentrism and gendercentrism. They contest the very division of life goals as career for men and intimacy for women.

Kohlberg's Theory

Kohlberg's theory of sex and moral development[64] represents a third approach to traditional understanding of how men and women develop in a society. Of particular interest to the feminist theorists is his view as to how individuals develop a sense of moral understanding and the capacity for mature ethical judgment (see Table 2).

Kohlberg developed his theory using the responses of young men to a set of ethical dilemmas. On the basis of their responses to hypothetical situations, he concluded that some moral decisions were more advanced or mature than others. When men and women were compared across levels of moral maturity, it was discovered that women tended to score at 'lower' level than men. Men solved moral dilemmas in terms of appeals to individual rights and principles of abstract justice; on the other hand, women tended to focus on concern for, and responsibility to others, emphasizing relationships, reciprocity and interdependence.[65] He assumed that decisions based on the laws of society and abstract principles were more advanced morally than those based on concern for others. As a challenge to Kohlberg's theory, Carol Gilligan[66] wrote an impassioned essay pleading for a recognition of the value of women's morality that implies an ethics of caring and attachment, which is so

Table 2

Stages in the Development of Moral Values

	Levels and Stages	*Illustrative Behaviour*
Level I. Pre-moral		
1.	Punishment and obedience orientation	Obeying rules in order to avoid punishment
2.	Naive instrumental hedonsim	Conforming with a view to obtain rewards, to have favours returned
Level II. Morality of conventional role-conformity		
3.	"Good-boy" morality of maintaining good relations, approval of others	Conforming for avoiding disapproval, dislike from others
4.	Authority maintaining morality	Conformity aiming at avoiding censure by legitimate authorities and the resultant guilt
Level III. Morality of self-accepted moral principles		
5.	Morality of contract, of individual rights, and of democratically accepted law	Conformity which aims at maintaining the respect of the impartial spectator judging in terms of community welfare
6.	Morality of individual principles of conscience	Conformity which aims only at avoiding self-reproach

vital for the very survival of humanity, and which shows that women are not less moral than men, but only speak "in a different voice". Gilligan focuses on the attitudes of social concern and non-violence as providing the very bases of women's moral reasoning, and on others' neglect (in previous descriptions) of sex differences as they relate to morality. Recent analyses of many studies on stages of moral development have supported Gilligan's assertion that neither of the two orientations – that is, women's ethics of love and concern and men's emphasis on justice and independence – represents any important facet of men's development and can be deemed as superior to the other.[67] These studies also revealed that sex differences in moral judgement may vary at different educational levels.[68] Feminist theorists argue that had Kholberg developed his theory on the basis of the responses to both men and women, he might have arrived at very different conclusions.

Contemporary Theories

As against the traditional theories of Freud, Erikson and Kohlberg that portray women as inferior and also morally deviant, quite a few contemporary scholars propose some intriguing alternatives and argue that currently observed gender differences are not quite defensible because they reflect societal stereotyping. Not only these alternative gender-free theories view women and men as similar in psychological make-up and goals which promote growth and human potential, they also avoid language that labels one gender as more socially respectable than the other. Unlike traditional theories' emphasis on biological factors, the contemporary ones explain psychological differences between men and women as stemming from three major factors:[69]

1. Normal cognitive processing of incoming information to the developing child.
2. The visible organization of current social roles that provide models for children to imitate and follow.
3. Prevailing societal forces that differentially reward males and females for sex-stereotyped behaviours and ignore or punish ethnic or alternative lifestyles, and restrict opportunities for role innovation.

These theories enable the individual to move towards a desirable self-modification of stereotypic behaviour.[70] Some of them – specially the social learning theory, androgyny theory and gender schema theory – offer an optimistic view of the possibilities for such a psychology of human development as may fairly be said to regard both women and men as strong, caring, connected to one another, and equal.

Social Learning Theory: Society as Destiny

The social learning theory[71] challenged the earlier notion that gender differences are a natural result of innately determined individual development. Pant H. Mussen summarizes this theory in the following words:

> ... social learning theory holds that sex-appropriate responses are rewarded [reinforced] by parents and others, and hence are repeated [increased in frequency]. Sex-inappropriate behavior, on the other hand, is likely to be punished and hence to diminish in strength and frequency, i.e., to become extinguished.[72] Social learning approaches theorize that we pattern our behaviour, including our sex roles, according to the messages we receive from the social environment. These messages take the form of models for behaviour of others, and social responses to our own behaviour as we attempt to imitate these models. Social responses to our behaviour can be positive [rewarding] or negative [punishing], and they gradually shape our

> behaviour, thoughts and feelings. Since the images in the social environment are largely Caucasian, heterosexual and gender-typed, children soon learn what behaviours are normative and they fashion their own behaviour accordingly.

In this manner, the social learning theory provides both for sex role conformity to traditional images, as well as the possibilities of change through provision of new models for behaviour, opportunities for self-determination and skill development, and a revised system of social rewards.[73] Research in social learning theory has clearly demonstrated that when observed models change their sex-typed behaviours, children also revise their stereotyped expectations. For example, children exposed to textbooks in which all words and pictures about boys and girls being egalitarian were less stereotyped in their expectations about gender roles than were children exposed to traditional texts.[74] Similarly, research on the school-age daughters of working mothers shows that these girls have more flexible ideas about the roles of women and men, in so far as they believe that both sexes should share equal roles in family and business settings.[75] Thus, the image of women that emerges from the social learning theory is one of equal potential, with each individual female potentially free to choose her own identity and destiny.

Feminist theorists argue that if women are naturally passive and dependent and men naturally aggressive and independent, anthropology should provide evidence of this. Margaret Mead's study of three New Guinea tribes has ruled out such assumptions about the normal female and male psychology. In two of the tribes, the males and females are not expected to – and in fact do not – display different personality traits. All members of the Arapesh society are "trained to be cooperative, unaggressive, responsive to the needs and demands of others".[76] Males as well as females are (in personality) very like our notion of the normal nurturing woman. On the other hand, among the Mundugomor, "both men and women developed as ruthless, aggressive, sexed individuals, with the maternal cherishing aspects of personality at a minimum. Both men and women approximated to a personality type that we in our culture would find only in an undisciplined and very violent male".[77]

In the third tribe, the Chambulli, sex-linked personality differences are clearly visible. "The women [are] the dominant, impersonal, managing partner, the man the less responsible and emotionally dependent person".[78] From an essentially psychological perspective, Chambulli men are feminine, whereas women, masculine. Thus, Mead concludes: "Many, if not all, of the personality traits which we have called masculine or feminine are as lightly linked to sex as are the clothing, the manners, and the form of headdress that a society at a given period assigns to either sex".[79]

Androgyny Theory

The androgyny theory, which visualizes the presence of both male and female characteristics in the same individual, was developed by Sandra Bem.[80] She observed that the traditional theories of personality defined healthy development in terms of 'appropriate sex typing' which posits a clear separateness between the two kinds of characteristics. Thus, well adjusted boys were expected to be 'masculine', i.e., aggressive, independent and achievers; and girls were expected to be 'feminine', i.e., nurturing, passive and compliant. Further, it was assumed that as masculinity increased, femininity decreased and that one could not possess both sets of characteristics. Against this traditional conception, Bem suggested that a healthier outcome for development for all individuals would be to display the personality characteristics expected of both males and females. It is precisely this amalgamation of masculine and feminine attributes that the term 'androgyny' signifies.[81] Bem demonstrated that persons who described themselves as androgynous on the Bem Sex Role Inventory were more likely to be flexible and adaptive across a range of differing situations than persons who saw themselves in sex-typed terms.

Further, androgynous males were found to exhibit higher levels of nurturant and playful behaviour than merely masculine males[82] and androgynous men and women were more interpersonally responsive than sex-typed individuals.[83]

The androgyny theory assumes that access to both masculine and feminine capabilities is equally advantageous to both women and men. Unfortunately, in a society where male-typed behaviours of assertion, independence and competition are privileged over nurturance and cooperation, an individual emphasizing the feminine domain in his personality styles has little chance to gain in social prestige and power.[84]

Gender Schema Theory

More recently, Sandra Bem has proposed a gender schema theory[85] which emphasizes the cognitive process of sex-linked information from the environment and its relation to an individual. It says that all individuals possess a natural readiness to form categories about the external world, and that on the basis of what they observe in a sex-typed society, children will spontaneously sort out persons, attributes and behaviours (which catch their fancy) into masculine and feminine categories. These categories are then assimilated into the self-concept, forming a kind of gender identity which colours their perceptions and behaviours. Thus originates a predisposition to view the world in dichotomous gender terms, promoting a 'self-fulfilling prophecy' in which the world indeed appears to be organized in terms of male- or female-typed activities.

In this context, Bem proposes an alternative to a gender schematic society in which both women and men conform to societal stereotypes, by raising gender-schematic children. She prescribed a set of childbearing activities designed to provide gender-free parental models. She suggested that parents should interpret the societal models for the child by means of challenges to existing stereotypes, and by providing 'subversive' schemata in their place. For example, parents should divide childcare and household roles between themselves, so that children do not observe their parents conforming to stereotyped roles.

Bias in Psychological Research

As a science of human behaviour psychology requires that we test hypotheses and arrive at conclusions by means of carefully conducted research studies. The fact, however, is that scientific research can easily become biased by the chosen methods and procedures of the individual researcher. The feminist theorists allege the prevalence of gender bias in psychological research and propose the development of new guidelines and procedures to reduce this bias in research related to women's development and behaviours.

As E.G. Boring's *History of Experimental Psychology* (1950) has shown, the problem of bias in psychological research was encountered early in the discipline's history. 'Laboratory atmospheres' were repeatedly found to affect the results coming from different laboratories on the same problem, whether it concerned such issues as presence or absence of things in thought, insightful learning vs slow trial and error learning, or the accumulating research on sex difference. In his book, Boring dismissed the sex bias once and for all when evaluating the results of Francis Galton's psychological assessments on 9,337 persons at the 1884 International Health Exhibition. He declared, "No important generalizations as regards human individual differences appeared, ... [except] Galton's erroneous conclusion that women tend in all their capacities to be inferior to men".[86]

C.W. Sherif ascribes the existence of this sexist bias in psychological research to the preservation of male hierarchy in psychology.[87] She argues that male experientialists, testers and statisticians, developmentalists and social psychologists, and 'applied psychologists' dominate the academic hierarchy in major institutions and this is the reason why it has been difficult to eliminate the anti-female bias from psychological research.

Feminist theorists are making attempts to undo this bias and to develop gender-fair methods of research. These endeavours have resulted in the discovery of new 'facts' that contradict the old ones and also help in providing new insights into the experience and lives of women as well as men. Psychological research has explored the extent of similarity between a variety of stereotyped expectations and people's behaviour in real situations. Literature in this area is voluminous.[88] In particular, considerable research has focused on gender contribution in areas such as achievement, aggression, altruism, cognition, competition, cooperation, conformity, emotionality, leadership, friendliness and love. In some areas of behaviour, experimental findings only suggest slight differences between groups of women and men, but within any particular domain there are greater differences in each gender group than are between them.

For example, the stereotype that boys and men are more aggressive has been examined in hundreds of studies. The conclusions from these studies suggest that aggression is distributed across people in such a way that most of them will show some aggression in some situations, and that some people of either gender are either never or always aggressive. The differences between a stereotyped description of gender difference and a description based on statistical research findings is not always the same.[89] In reality, the distributions of aggressive tendencies overlap considerably, so that some males are found to be less aggressive than some females. In understanding and predicting any particular aggressive act, it is more important to know the situation, the characteristics of the persons involved, the amount of provocation, and the possibilities of exposure and punishment than to know the gender of the aggressor.

Similarly, throughout a great part of psychology's history, most areas of the discipline have been relatively oblivious to the question that relates to the nature of men and women and the relationships between the sexes with certain exceptions (such as the concern of child psychologists with the development of 'sex role identification'). It is not only that relatively few investigations were devoted to the topics, but even analyses of social psychological studies (published during the 1950s and 1960s) have revealed that many more men were generally employed as subjects than women. Indeed, in 1960, Carlson and Carison reported in their survey carried out between 1958 and 1960 that males were used more frequently than females as research subjects.[90]

S. Schwabacher[91] found that when the sex of the subjects was not specified in the abstract of the paper, a close examination of the original article indicated that the subjects were more likely to have been males than females. She indicates that there is a clear tendency to generalize from all male samples to humanity in general while research on women is generalized only to a female population.

Virginia O' Leary points out that sex was generally considered a "nuisance variable to be controlled, not investigated".[92] John Atkinson's[93] study of achievement motivation is a case in point. According to Mary Brown Parlee, researchers' habits of ignoring women and viewing male behaviour as the prototype of human behaviour resulted in "distorted facts and omitted problems" which, in turn, "perpetuated pseudo scientific data relevant to women".[94] Research on organizational settings has examined occupational sex typing, discrimination in the workplace, sexual harassment, and gender-based barriers to women in the development and advancement of their careers. Research on families has targeted wife battering, social isolation and stress on mothers with young children, dual career marriages, alternative child care arrangements, and power issues in child custody and visitation following divorce. Research on violence towards women focuses on rape and people's attitudes to both the rapist and the victim, on pornography and violent images of women portrayed in the media, and on sexually abused children, majority of whom were girls. Similarly, research on women's mental health and psychological well-being in general has taken a look at the disproportionately low utilization of mental health facilities by women, the power issues between women and their male therapists, and the high prevalence rates of certain psychological problems in women, such as depression, anxiety, and issues concerning eating and weight control. In respect of women of colour, research has been concerned with the high rates of suicide in young black women and the over-representation of non-white women with a psychiatric diagnosis of schizophrenia.[95] To make matters worse, women with real problems were encouraged to seek the cause in themselves. To cite just a few examples: violence against women was explained, in part, by female masochism; women's anger, by 'raging hormones'; and female under-achievement in mathematics, by genetic deficiencies.[96]

Not only this, one can also discern bias in the main techniques of psychology, specially in respect of its reliance on experiments. Evelyn Fox Keller describes how even the design and interpretation of experiments reflect the male bias. For instance, he cites the example of animal learning research in which male rats are taken as the prototype for all the species. Even the personality tests are so standardized that the male is taken as the prototype and masculine attributes are valued more than the feminine ones.

Thus, feminists are trying to evolve gender-fair methods and are delving deep into such unchartered areas of research in psychology of women as were earlier utterly ignored. More and more attention is now being paid to women's unique experiences related to their joys and sorrows. Even generally, the knowledge about both men and women has increased substantially. Researchers have extended their investigations to questions about women of colour, women in poverty, and women with non-traditional sexual orientations. Attempts are also being made to gain a deeper understanding into the lives of ignored and neglected women. It has now become clear that the psychological environments of white and black women, for example, is very different, and may well have to be understood in their separate contexts. Each new stream of researchers exploring the areas of psychology of women is likely to unearth such new truths about men and women as may change the so-called facts that underline our current understanding in this context. Each of these areas of male bias in psychological research calls for a planned intervention, community education, and social policy aimed at remedying and prevention. An example of this mandate for social change is the rise of feminist psychotherapy which aims at evolving new modes of treatment to assist women in realizing their goals.

Bias in Psychotherapy

Psychotherapy is the method of treatment used in psychoanalysis. It relies on a general theory of human psychology based on stereotyped behaviour. Because of this basic rigidity, critics of the contemporary therapy insist that the therapy given to women is closely related to the assumed (not precisely determined) causes of their illness. In relation to this, feminists argue that the contents and concerns of human psyche are not naturally given as traditional psychotherapy believed, but are rather socially constructed, and vary with changes in time, place and gender. They further contend that the historical context in which therapy is used is extremely important, for, after all, therapy is but a part of the social process surrounding ill-health. Phylis Chesler[97] declares that traditional psychotherapy is a device used by men to drive women crazy and thereby to maintain the prevailing male hegemony.

Recent studies on the prevalence of psychological disturbance show some distinct differences in the kinds of problems frequently diagnosed for women and men (see Table 3).[98]

Table 3

Diagnoses of Behavioural Disorders Assigned More Frequently to Either Women or Men

Women	*Men*
Primary degenerative dementia	Multi-infant dementia
Depression	Alcohol hallucinoses
Cyclothymic disorder	Transsexualism
Dysthymic disorder	Paraphitias
Agoraphobia	Factitious disorder
Simple phobia	Impulse control disorder
Panic disorder	Paranoid personality disorder
Somatization disorder	Antisocial personality disorder
Psychogenic pain disorder	Compulsive personality disorder
Multiple personality	
Inhibited sexual desire	
Inhibited orgasm	
Histrionic personality disorder	
Borderline personality disorder	
Dependent personality disorder	

Feminist researchers have questioned these rates of disorders and have pointed to the biased assumptions about sex-typed behaviours that are incorporated into the standard diagnostic categories.[99]

In a landmark study of the mental health professionals' existing biases towards women (in dealing with their mental health) Broverman and others[100] showed that these professionals made an unwarranted distinction between the healthy man and the healthy woman; and that visualized descriptions of the healthy man, but not of the healthy woman, were similar to those of a really healthy adult. A healthy woman was described as one who was more submissive, more emotional, less independent and less competitive. Thus, a healthy woman was generally seen more in negative terms than a healthy man. This improper pervasiveness of stereotypes has been interpreted by many as exemplifying a female's dilemma – that is a choice between being a healthy person or a really healthy woman as understood by the professionals in question.

This has necessitated a re-evaluation of women and their mental health. Literature in this field has greatly expanded.[101] Efforts are being made to develop alternative models of mental health. Feminists propose an 'androgyny model' against the traditional models which are also viewed as *congruence models*[102] or *masculinity models*.[103] The traditional model evaluates healthy personal adjustment in terms of conformity to sex role prescriptions and propose that masculine-typed traits of assertiveness, independence, and dominance will lead to more effective functioning overall, as they are more highly valued in society. Against this view, the *androgyny model*[104] proposes that only individuals with both masculine and feminine traits will be more flexible and adaptive across situations and will experience greater psychological well-being.

Thus, feminists have evolved new ways of addressing the problems of women through feminist psychotherapy which has its roots in consciousness-raising groups and in the women's movement taken generally. Feminist therapists prescribe seven essential guidelines:[105]

1. Providing an egalitarian relationship with shared responsibility between counsellor and client. The client is encouraged to trust her own judgment and to arrive at her own decisions. In contrast to many traditional counselling relationships, the client is never in a one-down position of having to accept counsellor's interpretations of her behaviour as external prescriptions for appropriate living.
2. Employing a consciousness-raising approach. Women are helped to become aware of the societal restraints on their development and opportunities. Clients are helped to differentiate between the politics of the (contrived) sexist social structure and those problems over which they have realistic personal control.

3. Helping women explore a sense of their personal power and how they can use it constructively in personal, business and political relationships.
4. Helping women to redefine themselves apart from their role relationships to men, children and home; exploring women's fears about potential role changes that may alienate spouse and children as well as co-workers and boss.
5. Helping women to get in touch with unexpressed anger in order to combat depression and to make choices about how to use their anger constructively.
6. Encouraging women to nurture themselves as well as caring for others, thereby raising self-confidence and self-esteem.
7. Encouraging multiple skill development to increase women's competence and productively. This may include assertiveness, training, economic and career skills, and negotiation skills with important others who resist change.

In addition to these guidelines, feminist therapists are concentrating on core issues related to women's lives that were earlier overlooked by traditional therapists: body image, pregnancy and childbirth, menopause and aging, incest and rape, dating wife abuse and sexual preference etc.

Towards a New Psychology of Women

The evolution of feminist approaches in the field of psychology has emerged from the combined effects of the women's movement, the increased visibility of women scholars, and the collaboration of these scholars in research and publication. Initially, feminists were concerned that little had been published in psychology concerning women. To redress this particular dearth of writing, a number of books were published including Bardwick's *Psychology of Women: A Study of Biocultural Conflicts* (1971); Sherman's *On the Psychology of Women: A Survey of Empirical Studies* (1971); Hyde and Rosenberg, *Half the Human Experience* (1975); Cox, *Female Psychology: The Emerging Self* (1976); Donnelson and Gullahorn, *Women: A Psychological Perspective* (1971); Williams, *Psychology of Women* (1977); Kopp, *Becoming Female: Perspectives on Development* (1979); and Robrbaugh, *Women: Psychology's Puzzle* (1979). These publications, followed by many more in later years, served a useful function in pointing out the inadequacy of a psychology biased against women. In order to redefine methodology, theory and research, the need to develop a 'psychology for women' seemed desirable. In doing so, psychology will naturally have to attend to the value systems within which women live their lives, and to the way in which women's lives are related to men's.[106] J.B. Rohrbaugh comments:

> Gender is inescapable. It is probably the most important determinant of any individual's life experience. For the two sexes exist in different social worlds with widely divergent pressures, rewards and expectations. In many areas of life, there is no truly human experience. There is only female experience and male experience.[107]

The extent to which these divergent worlds influence individual experience and position in relation to the dominant value system is central to the analysis of women's psychology. Feminists thus challenge psychology for dealing with predominantly male subjects and masculinity as the only subject matter. Psychologist Julia Sherman, who has reviewed the sex difference literature exhaustively, has contested all the predominant male-centric biases against women. She has categorically claimed that (a) the evidence does not support the notion that women generally are more dependent and passive than men;[108] (b) that they are generally more emotional than men;[109] and (c) that men are superior in abstract and logical thinking.[110] She concludes: "Increased research, improved conceptual models, and cultural change have revealed many sex differences to be more apparent than real".[111] Therefore, in order to create a sex-fair psychology, the feminists have suggested the following measures:

(a) Feminist must re-examine female subjects in all those researchers which had earlier been done by using predominantly male samples only.[112]
(b) They must criticize past studies of sex differences, and contest common psychological assumptions about gender that are unsupported by reliable or valid evidence.[113]
(c) They must take into account the diversity of sex differences, thereby changing the traditional, biological idea of these differences, into a more viable concept of gender differences, taking cognizance of age, experience, situation and expectations.[114]
(d) They must also try to get a more balanced picture of what established sex differences mean.[115]

Feminist psychologists have thus made important contributions to the psychology of women. Firstly, they recognize the centrality of questions about the characteristics of women's psychology, and how far women's and men's lives and behaviour are different, and why. For example, they have (a) re-analysed studies of mother-child bonding and maternal deprivation; (b) criticized conclusions drawn about good mother-child relations; and (c) have extended investigations of these relations to take into account not just maternal exclusivity and sensitivity, but also children's relationships with other adults and children, and the physical psychological and social quality of care. Feminist psychology has also tackled previously neglected areas of female experience which are relevant to its efforts to get women a better deal in men's world. These include mental disorder, abortion, sexuality, media representation, and experiences in non-traditional, male-identified employment. Secondly, feminist criticisms and research have enriched psychology by making it more scientific. It has also improved women's standing in the discipline. Thirdly, feminist scholarship has aptly demonstrated the prevalence of a male bias in the discipline. It insists on the insertion of fair values at all stages of research. This is reflected in the selection of gender-free theories, choice of topics, research methods which carefully examine gender bias and also exploration of new areas of research.[116] Lastly, and most importantly, there is the feminists' concern for change. They advocate change in the power relations between men and women.

Thus, feminist psychology has immensely contributed to the construction of a new approach to deal with the psychology of women. By reinterpreting the relations between men and women, introducing feminist values in research endeavours, offering fresh view of women's mental health etc; feminist psychology has issued a call for new ways of approaching the psychology of women.

As listed above, the various challenges posed by feminists have unravelled the ways in which the male is privileged in society. Since our society always places man above the woman, it is always the male who has a better access to resources. This results in the marginalization of women at the economic level. The following chapter concerns itself with the male bias in the sphere of economics.

Notes

1. M. Crawford and J. Marecek, "Psychology Reconstructs the Female: 1968–1988", *Psychology of Women Quarterly,* 13, 1989, p. 149.
2. Helen Thompson, "A Review of Recent Literature on the Psychology of Sex", *Psychological Bulletin,* Vol. 7, 1910, pp. 335–42. See also, R.W. Connell, *Gender and Power,* Cambridge: Polity Press, 1987, p. 30.

3. Eleanor Maccoby and Carol Jacklin, *The Psychology of Sex Differences*, Oxford: Oxford University Press, 1874.
4. Kay Deaux, "From Individual Differences to Social Categories: Analysis of Decade's Research on Gender", *American Psychologist*, Vol. 39, February, 1984, p. 107.
5. Simone de Beavuoir, *The Second Sex*, Harmondsworth: Penguin, 1972
6. Kate Millett, *Sexual Politics*, London: Rupert Hart-Davis, 1971.
7. Germaine Greer, *The Female Eunuch*, London: MacGibbon & Kee, 1970.
8. S. Firestone, *The Dialectic of Sex: The Case for Feminist Revolution*, London: Cape, 1971.
9. Naomi Weisstein, "Psychology Constructs the Female, or the Fantasy Life of the Male Psychologist", in Michele H. Garskof (ed.), *Roles Women Play: Readings towards Women's Liberation*, Belmont: Calif, 1971, pp. 68–83.
10. Ibid.
11. Josephive Donovan, *Feminist Theory*, New York: Frederich Ungar, 1985, p. 105.
12. For this distinction see Chris Beasley, *What is Feminism?* London: Sage, 1999, pp. 66–69.
13. Carol Glligan, Sara Ruddick, In this chapter we have included few of them in details: Ex: Nancy Chodrow, Dorothy Dinnerstein.
14. Chodorow argues that "shared child-rearing would have a dramatic effect on the organization of sexual oppression by undermining the current constitution of masculinity ... which is built upon disconnection from and power over others"
    - Carol Gilligan, "In a Different Voice" and Sara Ruddick, "Maternal Thinking", *Feminist Studies*, 6(2), 1980, pp. 342–67, celebrate women's fundamentally different sense of self, a 'unique female voice'. Gilligan describes a different form of moral reasoning employed by women and Ruddick refers to maternal thinking. Both writers challenge the Freudian notion of women being deficient.
15. Karen Horney, *Feminine Psychology*, London: Routledge and Kegan Paul, London, 1967, p. 6. Also see, 'The dread of women' where Horney describes the resentment harboured by all men towards women, which expresses itself in phallocentric thinking, in the devaluation of motherhood and in a misogynist civilization.
16. See J. Mitchell (ed.), *The Selected Melanie Klein*, Harmondsworth: Penguin, 1986.
17. E. Figes, *Patriarchal Attitudes*, London: Faber and Faber, 1970.
18. Simone de Beavuoir, *The Second Sex*, Harmondsworth: Penguin, 1972.
19. Betly Friedan, *The Feminine Mystique*, Harmondsworth: Penguin, 1963.
20. Kate Millett, *Sexual Politics*, London: Rupert Hart-Davis, 1971, p. 184.
21. Phyllis Chesler, *Women and Madness*, New York: Doubleday, 1972.
22. *Psychoanalysis and Feminism*, Harmondsworth: Penguin, 1974.

23. Jean Baker Miller, *Toward a New Psychology of Women,* Boston: Beacon Press, 1986.
24. Adrienne Rich, *Of Women Born*, New York: Bantam Books, 1977.
25. Nancy Chodorow, *The Reproduction of Mothering,* Berkeley: University of California Press, 1978.
26. Ibid., p. xv. See also Juliet Mitchell, *Psychoanalysis and Feminism,* New York: Vintage, 1975.
27. Like Lacan, Mitchell is selective in the parts of Freud she takes up, distinguishing between what she calls the 'Freudian Freud' – the thinker in advance of his time and the 'pre-Freudian Freud' who was unable to break away completely from the thought, concepts and terminology of his time. The Freudian Freud who interests Mitchell was concerned not with social reality but with physical reality, with mental representation of what Freud says about Feminity relates to how it is lived in the unconscious.
28. Dorothy Dinnerstein, *The Rocking of the Cradle and the Ruling of the World* (British Title of *The Mermaid and the Minotaur)*, London: Souvenir, 1978, p. 107. British Title appeared in 1978.
29. Ibid., p. 160.
30. See Jean Baker Miller, *Toward a New Psychology of Women*, Boston: Beacon Press, 1986.
31. Nancy Chodorow, *The Reproduction of Mothering,* Berkeley: University of California Press, 1978. (One of the major preoccupation of this book is Chodrow's analysis of the gender specific transmission of nurturance).
32. Object Relations theorists stress on the value of the maternal, and the crucial role that child's concrete social environment plays in the formation of its 'personality'. Feminist psychoanalysis uses object relations theory to help it develop a causal account of gender difference.
33. *The Reproduction of Mothering: Psychoanalysis and the Sociology of Gender,* Berkeley: University of California Press, 1978, p. 7.
34. Ibid., p. 209.
35. Ibid., p. 67.
36. Ibid., p. 68.
37. Jacques Lacan, *The Language of the Self: The Function of Language in Psychoanalysis,* translated by A. Wilden, Baltimore (Md): John Hopkins University Press, 1968.
38. Other names are Michile Montrelay, Sara Kofman, Engenie Lemoine Luccioni etc.
39. Phallogocentrism is a term used by Jacques Derrida. Carolyn Burke explains it as follows: 'His word weds "phallocentrism" to "logocentrism". It implies that psychoanalytical discourse is guilty of identifying the phallus with the Logos as transcendent, and therefore unexamined grounds of signification, of assigning meaning'.

40. H. Rowley and E. Grosz, "Psychoanalysis and Feminism", in Suneja Gunew (ed.), *Feminist Knowledge: Critique and Construct*, London and New York: Routledge, 1990, pp. 183–86.
41. Ibid., p. 193.
42. Ibid., pp. 192–93.
43. See J. Rose, "Introduction II", in Juliet Mitchell and J. Rose (eds.), *Feminine Sexuality: Jacques Lacan and the Ecole Freudienne*, London: MacMillan, 1982, p. 49 and pp. 53–56.
44. This stress on the positive benefits of the feminine as 'other' as a means of questioning that which is socially privileged, draws on the post structuralist thinking of Jacques Derrida. Derrida is concerned with the 'deconstruction' of forms of power with the aim of opening up alternative possibilities.
45. J.L. Orlofsky, "Relationship between Sex-Role Attitudes and Personality Traits and the Sex-Role Behaviour Scale-I: A New Measure of Masculine and Feminine Role Behaviour and Interests", *Journal of Personality and Social Psychology*, 40, 1981, pp. 127–40.
46. I.K. Broverman, D.M. Broverman, F.E. Clarkson, P.S. Rosenkrantz and S.R. Vogel, "Sex Role Stereotypes: A Current Appraisal", *Journal of Social Issues*, 28, 1972, pp. 59–78.
47. J.T. Spence, R. Helmreich and J. Stapp, "Ratings of Self and Peers on Sex-Role Attributes and their Relation to Self-Esteem and Conceptions of Masculinity and Feminity", *Journal of Personality and Social Psychology*, 32, 1975, pp. 29–39.
48. J.M. Darley and R.H. Fazio, "Expectancy Confirmation Processes Arising in the Social Interaction Sequence", *American Psychologist*, 35, 1980, pp. 867–81.
49. Seek K. Deaux, "From Individual Differences to Social Categories", *American Psychologist*, 39, 1984, pp. 105–16.
    - D. Bar Tal, "Attributional Analysis of Achievement Behaviour", *Review of Educational Research*, 48, 1978, pp. 259–71.
    - D.N. Ruble and T.L. Ruble, "Sex Stereotypes", in A.G. Miller (ed.), *In the Eye of the Beholder: Contemporary Issues in Stereotyping*, New York: Praeger, 1982.
    - J.C. Woelfel, "Women in the United States Army", *Sex Roles*, 7, 1981, pp. 785–800.
50. Judith Worell, "Images of Women in Psychology", in Mictael Paludi and Gertrude Stenernagel (eds.), *Foundations for a Feminist Restructuring of the Academic Disciplines*, New York: Hawarth Press.
51. S. Freud, "Some Psychological Consequences of the Anatomical Distinction between the Sexes", *Collected Papers*, Vol. 5, London: Hogarth, 1948. Also see *New Introductory Lectures on Psychoanalysis*, New York: Norton, 1965.

52. Quoted in Judith M. Bardivick, *Psychology of Women*, New York: Harper & Row, 1971, p. 9.
53. Quoted in ibid.
54. Sigmund Freud, "Anatomy is Destiny", in Betty Roszak and Theodre Roszak (eds.), *Masculine/Feminine*, New York: Harper and Row, 1969, p. 25.
55. Ibid., p. 22.
56. See J.A. Sherman, *On the Psychology of Women: A Survey of Empirical Studies*, Springfield, IL: C.C. Thomas, 1971.
57. See American Psychological Association, "Report of the Task Force on Sex Bias and Sex Role Stereotyping in Psychotherapeutic Practice", *American Psychologist*, 30, pp. 1165–75. Also see "Task Force on Sex Bias and Sex Women", *American Psychologist*, 1978, pp. 1122–33.
58. Erik. H. Erikson, "Inner and Outer Spaces: Reflections on Womanhood", in Robert Jay Lifton (ed.), *The Woman in America*, Boston: Beacon, 1967, p. 6.
59. Ibid., p. 5.
60. Ibid., p. 13.
61. E. Erikson, *Childhood and Society*, 2nd Edition, New York: Norton, 1963. Also see, *Identity: Youth and Crisis*, New York: Norton, 1968.
62. op. cit., 1963, p. 123.
63. Ibid., p. 123.
64. L. Kohlberg, "Stages and Sequences: The Cognitive Developmental Approach to Socialization", in D.A. Goslin (ed.), *Handbook of Socialization Theory and Research*, Chicago: Rand McNally, 1969. Also see "Moral Stages and Moralization", in T. Likonax (ed.), *Moral Development and Behavior*, New York: Holt-Rinehart, 1976.
65. L. Kohlberg and R. Kramer, "Continuities and Discontinuities in Child and Adult Moral Development", *Human Development*, 12, 1969, pp. 93–120.
66. Carol Gilligan, *In a Different Voice: Psychological Theory and Women's Development*, Cambridge: Harvard University Press, 1982.
67. See C. Blake and H. Cohen, A Meta-analysis of Sex Differences in Moral Development. Paper presented at the annual meeting of the American Psychological Association, Toronto, Canada, 1984.
68. D. Baumrind, "Sex Differences in Moral Reasoning: Responses to Walker's (1984) Conclusion that there are none", *Child Development*, 57, 1986, pp. 511–21.
69. See Judith Worell, "Images of Women in Psychology", in Michael Paludi and Gertrude Stenernagel (eds.), *Foundations for a Feminist Restructuring of Academic Disciplines*, New York: London, 1990.
70. J. Worell, "Life-Span Sex Roles: Development, Continuity and Change", in R.M. Lerner and N.A. Busch Rossanagel (eds.), *Individuals as Producers of their Development*, New York: Academic Press, 1981.

71. See A. Bandura, *Social Learning Theory*, Eaglewood, NJ: Prentice Hall, 1977. Judith Worell, "Psychological Sex Roles: Significance and Change", in J. Worell (ed.), *Psychological Development in the Elementary Years*, New York: Academic Press, 1982.
72. See Pant H. Mussen, "Early Sex-Role Development", in Nancy Reenes (ed.), *Womankind Beyond the Stereotypes*, Chicago: Aldine-Atherton, 1971, p. 399.
73. E.A. Blechman, "Behaviour Therapies", in A.M. Brodsky and R. Hare-Mustin (eds.), *Women and Psychotherapy: An Assessment of Theory and Research*, New York: Guilford Press, 1980.
74. See V.C. Flerx, D.S. Fidler and R.W. Rogers, "Sex Role Stereotypes: Developmental Aspects and Early Intervention", *Child Development*, 47, 1976, pp. 998–1007.
75. Also see, L.W. Hoffman, "Changes in Family Roles, Socialization and Sex Differences", *American Psychologist*, 32, 1977, pp. 644–57. See L.D. Eron, "Prescription for Reduction of Aggression", *American Psychologist*, 35, 1980, pp. 244–52.
76. Margaret Mead, *Sex and Temperament in Three Primitive Societies*, New York: Dell, 1968, p. 259.
77. Ibid.
78. Ibid.
79. Ibid., p. 260.
80. See S.L. Bem, "The Measurement of Psychological Androgyny", *Journal of Consulting and Clinical Psychology*, 47, 1974, pp. 155–62.
81. Androgyny, comes from the Greek words for male and female, 'andro' and 'gyne'. Its use as a psychological term has a long literary tradition. Samuel Coleridge, for example, wrote over a century ago, "The truth is, a great mind must be andro-gynous." Feminist scholars writings within the past decades (e.g., Carolyn Heilbrun in Toward a Recognition of Androgyny) have broadened its meanings to include psychological qualities.
82. S.L. Bem, "Sex Role Adaptability: One Consequence of Psychological Androgyny", *Journal of Personality and Social Psychology*, 31, 1975, pp. 634–43.
83. S.L. Bem, W. Martyn and C. Walson, "Sex Typing and Androgyny: Further Explorations of the Expressive Domain", *Journal of Personality and Social Psychology*, 34, 1976, pp. 1016–23.
84. J.A. Kelly and J. Worell, "New Formulations of Sex Roles and Androgyny: A Critical Review", *Journal of Consulting and Clinical Psychology*, 45, 1977, pp. 1101–15.
85. See S.L. Bem, "Gender Schema Theory and Its Implications for Child Development: Raising Gender Aschematic Children in a Gender Schematic Society", *Signs*, 8, 1983, pp. 598–616; "Gender Schema Theory: A Cognitive Account of Sex Typing", *Psychological Review*, 88, 1981, pp.

354–64; "Androgyny and Gender Scheme Theory: A Conceptual and Empirical Integration", in T.B. Sonderegger (ed.), *Nebraska Symposium on Motivation: Psychology and Gender*, Vol. 32, Lincoln: University of Nebraska Press, 1985, pp. 179–226.

86. E.G. Boring, *A History of Experimental Psychology*, 2nd Edition, New York: Appleton-Century-Crofts, 1950, p. 487.
87. Carolyn Wood Sherif, "Bias in Psychology", in Anne C. Herrmann and Abigail J. Stewart (eds.), *Theorizing Feminism*, Oxford: Westview Press, 1994.
88. See J.S. Hyde and M.C. Linn (eds.), *The Psychology of Gender: Advances through Meta-analysis*, Baltimore: Johns Hopkins University Press, 1986. Also see, E.E. Maccoby and C.N. Jacklin, *The Psychology of Sex Differences*, Stanford: Stanford University Press, 1974.
89. See Judith Worell, "Images of Women in Psychology", in Michael Paludi and Gertrude Steuernagel (eds.), *Foundations for a Feminist Restructuring of Academic Disciplines*, New York: London, 1990.
90. E.R. Carlson and R. Carlson, "Male and Female Subjects in Personality Research", *Journal of Abnormal and Social Psychology*, 61, 1960, pp. 482–83.
91. S. Schwabacher, "Male Versus Female Representation in Psychological Research: An Examination of the Journal of Personality and Social Psychology, 1970, 1971", *Catalogue of Selected Documents in Psychology*, 2, 1972, pp. 20–21.
92. Virginia O' Leary, *Toward Understanding Women*, Monterey, CA: Brooks Cole, 1977.
93. John Atkinson, *Motives in Fantasy, Action and Society: A Method of Assessment and Study*, New York: Van Nostrand, 1958.
94. Mary Brown Parlee, "Review Essay Psychology", *Signs: Journal of Women in Culture and Society*, 1(1), 1975, pp. 119–58.
95. D. Wilkinson, "Minority Women: Socio-Cultural Issues", in A. Brodsky and R. Hare-Mustin (eds.), *Women and Psychotherapy*, New York: Guilford, 1980.
96. Mary Roth Walsh, *Psychology of Women: Ongoing Debates*, New Haven, CT: Yale University Press, 1987.
97. Phyllis Chesler, *Women and Madness*, New York: Doubleday, 1972.
98. Judith Worell, "Image of Women in Psychology", in Michael Paludi and Gertrude Steuernagel (eds.), *Foundations for a Feminist Restructuring of Academic Disciplines*, New York: London, 1990.
99. See L.B. Rosewater, "Schizophrenia, Borderline, or Battered?" in L.B. Rosewater and L.E. Walker (eds.), *Handbook of Feminist Therapy: Women's Issues in Psychotherapy*, New York: Springer, 1985.

    J. Worell, The SDM III-R: Controversies in Gender Bias, paper presented at the annual meeting of the Association for the Advancement of Behaviour Therapy, Chicago, IL, November, 1986.

100. I.K. Broverman, D.M. Broverman, F.E. Clarkson, P.S. Rosenkrantz and S.R. Vogel, "Sex Role Stereotypes and Clinical Adjustments of Mental Health", *Journal of Consulting and Clinical Psychology*, 34, 1970, pp. 1–7.
101. Phyllis Chesler, *Women & Madness*, Palgrave Macmillan, first published, 1972.

     —, D.E. Smith and S.J. David (eds.), *Women Look at Psychiatry*, Vancouver, Canada: Press Gang, 1975.

     —, V. Franks and V. Burtle, *Women in Therapy*, New York: Brunner-Mazel, 1974.

     —, E. Rawlings and D. Carter, *Psychotherapy for Women Treatment towards Equality*, Springfield, Illinois: C.C. Thomas, 1977.
102. B.E. Whitley Jr., "Sex Role Orientation and Self Esteem: A Critical Meta-analysis Review", *Journal of Personality and Social Psychology*, 44, 1983, pp. 765–78.
103. J.A. Kelly and J. Worell, "New Formulations of Sex Roles and Androgyny: A Critical Review", *Journal of Consulting and Clinical Psychology*, 45, 1977, pp. 1101–15.
104. S.L. Bem, "The Measurement of Psychological Androgyny", *Journal of Consulting and Clinical Psychology*, 47, 1974, pp. 155–62.
105. J. Worrell, "New Directions in Counseling Women", *Personnel and Guidance Journal*, 58, 1980, pp. 477–84.
106. See W. Hollway, *Subjectivity and Method in Psychology*, London: Sage, 1989.
107. See J.B. Rohrbaugh, *Women: Psychology's Puzzle*, Reading: Abacus, 1981.
108. See Julia A. Sherman, "Some Psychological 'Facts' about Women: Will the Real Ms Please Stand Up", in Joan I. Roberts, *Beyond Intellectual Sexism*, New York: David Mckay, 1976, p. 119.
109. Ibid., p. 129.
110. Ibid., p. 130.
111. Ibid., p. 119.
112. For instance, Kohlberg's studies of moral reasoning, initially conducted with young male subjects, is being repeated with sex balanced samples, with conflicting results (See Walker, Baumrind).
113. Maccoby and Jacklin's *Psychology of Sex Differences* (1974) institutes a major reconsideration of psychological studies relevant to popular and psychological ideas of gender differences. Some of these ideas are, that girls are more 'social' and suggestible than boys; that they have lower achievement motivation and self-esteem; that they are better at rote learning and repetition, and worse at higher level cognitive tasks, etc. Maccoby and Jacklin (1974) and later works reject these hypotheses.
114. Eagly (1978) suggests that women's greater influenceability may be affected by situation factors like sex of the communicator, type of information or message, task definition, and historical period, as well as process factors, like female-male differences in verbal abilities, yielding,

and concern with personal relationships and group cooperation. Berg et al. (1981) finds that women's explanations of their success are more modest when they know they will be made public, and when a liked other has failed. See A. Eagly, "Sex Differences in Influenceability", *Psychological Bulletin*, 85, pp. 86–116. Also see Berg et al., "Attributional Modesty in Women", *Psychology of Women Quarterly*, 5, pp. 711–27.

115. Horner's (1972) study of fear of success is an early example of this. She criticized the research and theory of achievement motivation and its failure to be relevant to women. She observed that 'most women have a motive to avoid success because they expect negative consequences such as social rejection and/or feelings of being unfeminine as a result succeeding'. Similarly, Carol Gilligan's *In a Different Voice* (1982) observed that women have a different moral reasoning (discussed earlier in the chapter). See M. Horner, "Towards an Understanding of Achievement-Related Conflicts in Women", *Journal of Social Issues*, 28(2), pp. 157–76.
116. See P.B. Johnson, "Doing Psychological Research", in I.H. Frieze, J.E. Parsons, P.B. Johnson, D.N. Rublee and G. Zellman (eds.), *Women and Sex Roles: A Social Psychological Perspective*, NY: W.W. Norton, 1978.

— and B. Lott, "The Potential Enrichment of Social/Personality Psychology through Feminist Research and Vice Versa", *American Psychologist*, 40, 1985, pp. 155–64.

6

Dismantling Metanarratives

Feminist Interventions in Economics

Economics is deemed as one of the most scientific, objective and value-free social sciences. By its very definition[1] it analyses the ways in which scarce resources can be most efficiently allocated in order to maximize the welfare of society. Since the market system is the primary mechanism in the process, economists concentrate on questions pertaining to how markets for various goods and services operate. This market-oriented approach of the mainstream economics has resulted in the neglect of many economic activities in which women have traditionally been, and continue to be involved. The activities that have a market price are only counted as economic activity. To quote Waring, "The question of what entails 'economic activity' revolves around the question of value ... obvious exclusions from such activity are goods and services on which no one could put a market price because their values are spiritual, psychological, social, or political .... Women's role as socializers, as articulators of class and gender ideology, and as (too often the easy) collaborators in reproducing the conditions of their own subordination has no value."[2] Economics ignores not only the unpaid work of the reproduction of human life itself, but also its maintenance and care. Waring further invites our attention to a patent oddity:

> An infant born through the new "test tube" technology or womb implant, or a child raised in an institution, are considered "products". Those who bring the fetus to term in the laboratory or who care for the child in the orphanage or juvenile facility are seen as workers. They are

> economically activity. But a mother, daily engaged unpaid in these activities, is "just a housewife".[3]

Thus, for the most part women are taken to live their lives as 'unoccupied', 'non-productive' and 'economically inactive' majority who do not work and whose labour (both productive and reproductive) has no 'value'.[4]

Moreover, practitioners of economics have been predominantly men and hence it is not quite surprising that they have made glaring omissions in economic analysis by ignoring the domains of women's economic activity – household production and volunteer work. As a result, in all its theoretical formulations, empirical investigations and public policy implementation, economics relegates women's issues to the periphery:

> It uses theory, first of all, to decide what facts are relevant for an analysis. Only some everyday experiences are stated, recognized, and recorded by economic theory. Overwhelmingly, those experiences that are economically visible can be summarized as *what men do*.[5]

For example, GNP, which is used as a rough indicator of material well-being, is defined as the market value of all the final goods and services produced in one year. Economists and others have cautioned against using GNP figures as an indicator of well-being, since it excludes many factors that affect the welfare of women. These excluded factors pertain almost exclusively to economic activities of women designed to increase societal welfare, that is, housework, childcare, volunteer work, and unpaid work in general. Thus, statistically, a large portion of women's contribution to society is ignored.[6]

Another example of such a serious neglect is the United Nations System of National Accounts (UNSNA), which is an international system for economic measurement. Any annual report of the World Bank, the International Monetary Fund (IMF), United Nations (UN) agencies, or national governments is based on national accounts statistics. The UN uses it to assess annual contributions, and to appraise the success of regional development programmes. Aid donors use the UNSNA to identify deserving cases, 'need' being determined by 'per capita gross domestic product'. The World Bank uses these figures to identify nations that most urgently need economic assistance. To locate new areas for overseas investments, the multinational corporations use the same figures. Companies too project the markets for their goods on the basis of these national accounts projections and plan their investment, personnel, and other internal policies likewise. Further, individual countries use them for creating models or frameworks for integration of economic statistics and to analyse past and current developments in the national economy. These early national accounts were evolved to justify paying for wars. Since the institutionalization of national income accounting by United Nations, however, the motive has expanded. But whatever the change of motive, the decisions are taken predominantly by men and the values that are excluded from this determination are those of the environment, *and of women* and children.[7]

The rise of women's movement and increasing intervention of feminist scholars in the field brought to the fore various issues related to women that were earlier overlooked and may be listed as follows: unequal treatment of women in the labour market, unequal access to the means of production, inequitable work burdens, invisibility – and under-valuation of women's subsistence production in third world countries – in data systems; the link between women's unpaid work and paid work; the inequitable distribution of consumption resources within the household; absence of a focus on women in national policies; and the relevance of all these matters ton development issues.

In this regard, a meeting of women economists[8] in Athens in 1989, prior to the World Congress of the International Economists Association, proposed the principles for an alternative economic analysis "to assess the impact of theories and policies on women and development". These included:

1. An examination of all the theories and policies to determine the structural forms of discrimination, invisibility and oppression.
2. Inclusion of gender discussion in all micro and macro economic analysis.
3. The expansion of the parameters of mainstream economic and policy analysis to include those dimensions which are traditionally described as "social, cultural and political" (the 'soft' approach) from a gender perspective.

A listing of the 'main elements' determined as acceptable to all participants involved demonstrates the range of fundamental questions which feminist knowledge has brought to economics:[9]

1. A strictly economic approach does not capture the complexities of the process of development, which is determined by the interdependence of social, cultural, environmental and political dimensions. Therefore, economic theory and empirical analysis should incorporate these dimensions on a gender basis.

2. Economic science should extend its scope beyond the market to cover production of 'human welfare' and incorporate that part of the non-monetized economy, which includes production within the household, that is, housework, childcare and emotional labour (e.g., nurturing children, spouses, personal relations, etc.).
3. Economic short-term policy, programmes and projects often have negative social, environmental and political consequences, particularly for women and children. Therefore, economic research analyses and planning should have a long-term framework with long-term and medium-term policy implications and objectives.
4. The household as a unit of economic analysis does not fully represent nor measure the rights, needs and priorities of women. The unit of analysis for economic research and policy should be individual members of the household. This would facilitate assessment of intra-household relations and the distribution of resources, income and labour and bring about changes in favour of women.
5. Economists and others need to pay closer attention to the adverse effects of the debt crisis and structural adjustment policies on women in general and those in low income countries in particular.
6. The current revision of national accounts (SNA) should include the economic activity of women in the informal sector and housework.
7. The political use (and abuse) of crude indicators, such as GNP and aggregate rates of employment, leads to policy decisions which have negative impact on women's lives (e.g., employment, fiscal policies and social security schemes).
8. It is necessary to have a better understanding of quantitative and qualitative data about women in employment, their working conditions, and their pay, or, in the widest sense, their contribution to the economic life of all the countries.
9. Existing data and indicators do not take into account important aspects of women's employment, unemployment and under employment.
10. Existing techniques of data collection and analysis should be improved and internationally standardized to fully capture the conditions of work and life of women (such as unpaid family work, employment contracts, temporary and seasonal work, part-time and self-employment).

11. Macro-econometric model builders usually neglect and ignore data and information on gender difference even where it is available (such as in the employment sector). This leads to inaccurate estimates of the employment impact of public policies.
12. Social, political and cultural dimensions based on gender analysis should be better integrated in economic analyses, research and policy recommendations.
13. It should be recognized that fiscal systems discriminate against women's work and so infringe social security rights. They should not reinforce the dependent status of women. The tax system should be reformed (so as not to penalize women's work) by implementing separate assessment of women's earning).
14. Like women, nature is frequently taken for granted. It is under-valued, exploited and is being depleted for future generations. Planning for future development should include a set of indicators emphasizing the preservation of natural resources, and also encourage policies leading to sustainable development.
15. To create conditions of equity for women and sustainable development, the following research and policy steps be taken on an urgent basis: identification of distinct characteristics and conditions of three areas, namely, unpaid work in the household for production of human welfare in the households, the cultivation of renewable natural resources, and the extraction and processing of non-renewable resources; an analysis of the interplay and dynamics between these three areas in the totality of the human economy; and, the development of new methods and measures for taking these distinct components of human economy into consideration in economic policies and decisions for future development.

Following these explorations, in the past twenty years, there has been a plenty of efforts by feminists in this direction. They have prepared papers on subjects such as, equal pay, women and their invisibility in development projects, the effects of market-oriented approach on public policy and women and children, pay equity, capitalism and patriarchy, and sex role stereotyping. The more recent works of feminists[10] have challenged all the basic roles, principles, conceptual frameworks, descriptive functions and perceived outcomes of the theory, science, profession, practice and institutionalization of economics.

In this light we shall now move on to the earliest accounts of women in economics – an area of study which is thoroughly ignored in the history of economic thought.

History of Economic Thought on Women's Economic Activities

The earliest exposition of economic thought[11] on women's problems can be dated back to Mary Wollstonecraft who was the first English writer to voice a protest against the subordinate role of women in society and advocated the extension of equal rights to women. In a similar vein, John Stuart Mill[12] presented an analysis of the economic position of women and argued that the power of earning was an essential factor to women's dignity. He opposed the laws of protective labour legislation and any other law that held the male as supreme in the household. Further, he emphasized that any analysis of female behaviour within the economy should take into account the family structure, as it is very important in a woman's life.

In 1889, Charlotte Perkins Gilman[13] noted that the unique attribute of the female economic position is her economic dependence. Agreeing with Mill she contended that a woman must possess economic means outside the control of her husband in order to have an independent economic status.

The above (earlier) feminist demands were based on some kind of an 'equalitarian approach' aiming at attainment of equality through guarantees of civil liberties. It was not before the 20th century that the demand for employment became a condition for the equality of the sexes.

To begin with, Marxist thought analysed the economic status of women within the capitalist family structure. Engels[14] outlined the historical development of the family and the relations of the sexes as they were affected by the development of productive techniques. He listed three stages in the development of marriage – namely, group marriage, pairing marriage, and monogamy – and portrayed how by the third stage women became totally subjected to men thus giving way to modern capitalist family and patriarchy.

Marxist thought outlines three requirements for the liberation of women:[15]

(a) Opening up of such jobs in industrialization era as require less physical strength.
(b) Social ownership to do away with the exploitation of labour.
(c) Communicative households to liberate women from private household and their subjection to their husbands.

They further argued that since these requirements could not be met by capitalism, a new system had to come into force.

In the neo-classical economic thought too women's issues were taken up. Here, the first to draw attention were women's wages and conditions of their employment. This was necessary because even Adam Smith, the father of economics, did not devote a single page to women in his work.[16] He rationalized the gender roles and argued that men's wages should be high enough to maintain a family. While he did recognize that women work for wages, he yet emphasized that the material conditions of the families need the care of children by mother and hence reiterated the women's reproductive role in the welfare of society.

In 1859, Bodichon[17] questioned the notion that men support wives even though it is women who support them through their work in the family. She stressed the need for equal access to training skills for women so that they could also be equipped for employment and have an independent status.

These developments were followed by demand for equal pay for equal work. In this regard, Sydney Webb[18] and Beatrice Webb made a comparative study of women's wages to men and concluded that skilled women's work fetched lower pay than unskilled men's pay. They explained the cause of such wage differentials in terms of the competition between unmarried girls and single women, with married women who were just supplementing men's earnings of the family down and so could not put in as much work as those who had no family burden to bear.

This gave way to such explanations for wage differentials as the notion of women as a non-competing group in the labour market and the cognate notion of segmented labour market. Economic theories explaining differentials in relation to productivity or subsistence needs failed to explain the phenomenon of discriminatory wages for women.

Later on, economic theorists emphasized that income disparity between the sexes was an offshoot of the past subjection of women through various social and economic factors, which reproduced women's economic dependence within the family.[19] Wage differentials in the labour market continued to be voiced in terms of women's supplementary role, right up to the early decades of the last century. While men were expected to support the family, women's needs were expected to be only for their own subsistence. In these viewpoints, women's positions varied from equal rights to welfare to trade union points of view.

Another explanation regarding wage differentials came through the 'overcrowding hypothesis' which stated that it was trade union rules, employer's prejudices and social customs that denied skilled occupations to women. This caused them to overcrowd in unskilled occupations, which resulted in a decline in their general wage levels.[20] Although the hypothesis addressed the question of wage differentials, it failed to answer the crucial question as to why women crowd the way they do. The basic questions regarding denial of control over market production to women and devaluation of their housework were not asked.

Another explanation forwarded was the 'human capital' theory of Alfred Marshall.[21] It stated that women receive low wages than men because of lack of human capital; that the productivity of the workers will improve if given education by the state; and that this will in turn improve their wages.

Pigou[22] too addressed the issue of unequal wages. He argued that wages are unfair if they are below marginal productivity or if they are lower than the reward for similar labour elsewhere in the economy. Women's wages in some place or occupation may be fair relative to women's wages elsewhere, but may yet be unfair as compared to men's wages in that occupation.

Having reviewed some of the early attempts to grapple with women's economic position in society, we find that none of these early efforts ever finds a place in the teaching of the history of economic thought. To give women the rightful place in the discipline of economics, it is important that 'gender' be used as a category of economic analysis.

Gender as a Category of Economic Analysis

Scholars, social scientists and economists have made several attempts to incorporate gender in analysing the treatment of women in the realm of economics.[23] They argue that the discrimination against women in practice and the invisibility of feminist perspectives from the mainstream economics is a primary hindrance to depiction of women's reality. The first step towards redressal would be to rebuild those economic theories which have been formulated with a male-centric economic approach. Since ramifications of gender discrimination cannot be purely economic in nature, the theories suggested should also allow for non-economic or qualitative variables in economic analysis. Herein lies the limitative nature of neo-classical framework. Secondly, the theories in question should also allow for historical considerations, because, historical contexts change with time and so that what applies to one system will not be helpful in understanding another system. This indeed is why whatever holds true for economic analyses of the women of the developed countries may not hold good for those of developing countries. Thirdly, since the focus of mainstream economic theories in on *Homo economicus* or the economic man who is guided by self-interest, they do not take into account any of the following: the production for self-consumption, household as a production unit, and exchange rules based on customs and traditions that specify mutual obligations.[24] More importantly, the mainstream economic theories have been formulated on the basis of a market-oriented, industrialized and capitalized economy, and thus they fail to explain many developing economies that are not yet guided by the rules of market behaviour. Keeping all these factors in mind, women of different countries have to be understood in their separate living contexts. Fourthly, at the practical level, empirical investigations are being developed to account for gender-based discrimination. These empirical investigations have to be included while rebuilding theories. Fifthly, in order to highlight the various aspects of women's position, theories should use household as a category of analysis as it is of paramount importance to women's economic life all over the globe. This would further require the analysis of women's housework. The nature of this work should not be regarded as being entirely their burden, so that relevant measures can be adopted to overcome the problem at both levels. While measures to ease or alter the nature of housework can be immediately adopted, measures to alter the reasons for women's housework will take much more time to take effect.

Having discussed the various possibilities for including gender in economic theories, it is now necessary to raise a point about the inclusion of non-economic variables since it will make for a shift outside the accepted domain of economics. Here, Maitreyee Krishnaraj provides a solution when she observes that every economic issue can be considered at various levels. She explains, "The first level is the existence of observed reality. Within economic theory, often the existence of a situation is explained in terms of economic variables like demand and supply or factors like rewards. It is at the second level, where the causes or the explanations of a situation are to be supplied, that non-economic variables play an important part. Here, if the explanation is restricted to economic criteria, gender discrimination can never be accounted for."[25]

Krishnaraj further argues by giving the example of wage differentials and states that the economic variables involved in the issue constitute higher wages for men and lower wages for women and here if productivity is used as an explanation for a gender-specific discrimination, it would prove grossly inadequate.

Thus, we see that gender can make a lot of difference to the existing economic analysis as it leads to different economic outcomes for the sexes, measured in terms of earnings, income, hours of work and other standards used by economists to determine economic well-being. In view of the above discussion, we now turn to feminist explorations of the 'bias' in favour of men at all levels of economic inquiry, as under:
(a) Theoretical formulations
(b) Empirical investigations
(c) Public Policy implementation

Theoretical Formulations

Neo-classical Theory

The dominant paradigm in economics today is the neo-classical one which is accepted as 'mainstream' economics. Robbins defines neo-classical economics as "the study of allocation of scarce resources among different and competing ends". This paradigm underlies certain philosophical positions, namely, the impersonal working of the market in a capitalist system bringing about an efficient allocation of resources and each individual, whether producer or consumer, seeking to maximize his gain. This assumption is based on individualism and self-determination in a competitive, free enterprise market place, as factors for achieving the highest level of material well-being for society. It was derived from the *laissez faire* doctrine of the 19th century liberalism. This belief in unfettered individualism made for capitalism which underlies the positivist or 'scientifically objective' framework of neo-classical thinking. Further, the concept of equilibrium is a basic assumption in neo-classical economic analysis. These three broad assumptions of individualism, free competition and equilibrium have various ramifications for gender analysis. Ivan Illich pointed out that the central point of neo-classical economic theory is the *Homo Economicus* or the rational economic man, and that the way this theory conducts its analysis subsumes all class and gender differences and postulates a 'single universal rationality' totally out of keeping with reality, and making economic analysis 'gender neutral'.[26] To quote his words:

> The institutional identity of *Homo economicus* [that is, 'the rational economic *man*'] excludes gender. He is a *neutrum economicum*. Therefore, the loss of social gender is an integral part of the history of scarcity and of the institutions that structure it.[27]

Thus, for Illich, the individualism of neo-classical economics is 'genderless individualism'. As a result, under the neo-classical paradigm, gender is classified as non-data. Mary Daly claims that "with the immense sophistication in methodology that focuses most exclusively on quantification, relevance has been subsumed by method [,] leading to the 'tyranny of methodolatory' that classifies uncomfortable issues such as patriarchy and gender as non-data and thus, invisible".[28] In a similar vein, Krishnaraj points out that "issues which have a close connection to reality ... do not fit into model formats simply because they open the doors to 'chaos', [and that] the implications of this kind of structure that economics has attained; is drastic. Gender is one such issue".[29] Moreover, because it regarded the atomized individual as the unit of social action and behaviour, economic analysis could not but ignore (until the 1960s) the study of women as a group.

Further, neo-classical thinking bases itself on the premises of 'positivism,' 'methodological individualism' and 'motivational ascription' of rational maximizing behaviours. These attributes leave no space for the exploration of the collective aspects which pose constraints on individuals or alternately evoke altruistic or cooperative behaviour. Again, neo-classical thinking does not provide for the possibility "that things may be different from the way they seem to be". It stresses on "the way things are" and not on "the way they ought to be". What is more, such positivism addresses outcomes in an instrumental way. It suggests, for instance, that if we are not able to determine the reason of the unequal distribution of wealth and income, how it is related to power equations in all economic exchanges, and proceed to analyse things the way they are, we become apologists for the *status quo*.[30]

Similarly, in the general equilibrium theory, which is the hard core of economic theory, economists concern themselves only with the question as to how large number of 'freely' interacting individuals can produce social order and lead the economy towards a coherent disposition of resources. The rational participants of the market are assumed to react mechanically to given price signals that embody all the information they need to know and to make their choices under the assumption of perfect competition. The competitive market is yet another abstract mechanism which, given individual preference and technology, yields equilibrium prices and quantities. This established a one-to-one relationship between the individual economic agent and her (his) initial endowment. Poverty of some agents, then, is not due to any malice or power on part of others. It is just sad that some have 'low' initial endowments and preference configurations. This view is often advanced as an explanation for women's fate in the labour market.

The neo-classical welfare economics recommends taxes and subsidies by the state, to alter this initial endowment under the premise of a *pareto optimum* – situation where no one can be made better off without someone else being made worse off. There is no economic theory to tell us what kind of production arrangement will produce a fair distribution along with efficient production without an outside 'monitor' such as the state. The state, in turn, is an abstract mechanism without flesh and blood, a neutral agent waiting to oblige. The theory does not admit that there is market power in the hands of some who manipulate prices and quantities. Secondly, what is seen as voluntary free behaviours may be coerced by threats of various kinds, implicit and explicit as in the case of women. Thus, the neo-classical theory does not say anything about how power is produced in the first place and how it is reproduced in the economy. In this context, feminist theorists have challenged the neo-classical concepts of free and rational choice and independent income, and portrayed how these concepts function outside the scope of women's reality.

To begin with, let us take the neo-classical conception of rational choice. Choices within an economy are made by the one who possesses economic and political power (here patriarchy). Since women possess neither, they are not able to make choices. Their ability to make a choice is determined by their economic resource position in the existing organization of production, and by her 'home responsibilities' that are assigned to her by society, along with social and cultural conventions and sanctions imposed on her, particularly when she makes an 'unconventional choice' between 'work' and 'leisure'.

Similarly, the analysis of consumer choice is irrelevant for women most of whom lack the income to make these choices. The term 'independent income' has different connotations for men and women. For a man, independent income means inherited wealth or property income, implying that he does not have to work for a living. But for woman, the term denotes that she works and earns an income whereby she is independent of her husband's income.

Not only this, both as a 'producer' and 'consumer' woman lacks the freedom of choice allotted to a man.[31] Her economic roles consist of unpaid labour at home. Similarly, as a wife and a mother her 'feminine production function' remains concentrated in the household; and as a consumer she continues to act as the purchasing agent of the family and in effect buys the raw materials that she uses in household production.

Realizing the inadequacy of neo-classical conceptions, attempts have been made recently to include concepts of family, reproduction, etc., in the neo-classical economic analysis.

Neo-classical 'rationality' proves futile in underdeveloped and overpopulated countries where the poor find it rational to have more children who add more to the family income than they consume. This is directly opposed to the dominant micro-economic theories of fertility which equate children to 'consumer durables'[32] and more recently to 'household produced goods'.[33] These theories assume that like firms, households behave rationally in that they maximize utility in a context of scarcity and can choose to either consume commodities or produce children, subject to the usual constraints of income, prices, tastes and time. Thus, like other goods, the quantity and quality of children are a function of time and resources allocated to their production and maintenance.

In some neo-classical models of the family, children are included as a 'public good' where their welfare and consumption are incorporated in the parents' utility function, raising issues such as the potential effect of differentials in caring on household income distribution and gender-based division of household labour. These models, apart from treating children as objects, identify women's caring for children as a commitment or a responsibility or even a constraint.

According to Becker's 'rotten kid theorem' that assumes the head of the household a male, the benevolence of a compassionate head of the family reaps rich dividends. If 'he' provides generously for everyone, the most selfish beneficiary – 'the rotton kid' – in the family will be motivated to maximize family income and consumption and thereby would internalize all effect of 'his' actions on other beneficiaries. Ultimately, there will be no free riders in the family.

It is very significant to note here that the exclusion of the concept of family has important consequences regarding price theory, utility maximization and consumption theory etc. Because many of the commodities produced at home are substituted for purchased goods, what is maximized is a common utility function in which the household, and not the individual, is the unit of inquiry. This utility function is generally equated with the household head's utility function, motivated either by self-interest or the general well-being of the family. Apart from assuming that the head of the household is genderless (*neutrum economicum*), in a situation where an increasing number of households are female-headed, this assumption camouflages the different yet complementary roles of man and woman in pooling resources of time and money for the household.[34] Further, allocation of work and power relations within the family members do not share commodities and work through market transactions within the household. Here, an alternative model has been suggested, according to which, the unit of analysis is the household or family which operates on 'cooperative conflicts',[35] the bargaining problem being one of finding a particular cooperative solution, yielding a particular distribution of benefits sensitive to various parameters, including the respective powers of the different members of the family. This logically brings us to one of the most glaring lacunae in economic theory and its application, that is, the concept of work. Work in economics is generally equated with market work or paid work, i.e., labour power, which has an exchange value. The neo-classical concepts of market work, market wages and market time are not fully applicable either in underdeveloped subsistence economies or in relation to gender-based division and segmentation of labour. The relationship between patriarchy and development thus assumes significance, particularly in relation to the power relationships between men and women within the family. The family is a unit in which production and redistribution of income occur on the basis of material aspects of gender relation and division of labour resulting in conflict and change. The central instrument for maintenance of patriarchy is occupational segregation, which reinforces the traditional division of labour, resulting in lower wages for women, and so reinforcing their economic dependence on men. Simultaneously, the domestic division of labour reinforces occupational segregation by weakening women's status in the labour market.

Thus, we see that the fundamental principles of (male) economics clash with women's reality. Historian Gerda Lerner[36] argues that "women's reproductive power was the first private property amassed by men, and that domination over women provided the model for men's enslavement of other men". This is a basic challenge to what have been seen as classical and neo-classical fundamentals of 'economics'. The writings and research of women, such as Gena Corea, Maria Mies, Robyn Rowland and Renate Klein on new medical technologies (see *Issues in Reproductive and Genetic Engineering: Journal of International Feminist Analysis*) and the work of sociologists such as Mary O' Brien in her book *The Politics of*

Reproduction, are of particular significance in view of the basic absence of any feminist concept of reproduction in 'economics'. In this context, Waring foresees that "one of the key challenges feminism will offer to 'economics' in the 1990s will be the emphasis that at both theoretical and practical levels 'reproduction' is the primary exchange, and thus the primary principle of economics".[37]

Feminist theorists have also challenged the neo-classical economics of 'welfare' which equates total individual welfare with satisfaction of merely individual preferences or wants. Unlike this viewpoint, feminist welfare economics aims to establish a society in which there is sexual justice.[38] With this end in view, Frances Woolley[39] contends that Rawls' classical liberal treatise *A Theory of Justice* is of extreme importance to feminist economists, specially where Rawls articulates the values which feminists accept. This includes his emphasis on the well-being of least advantaged, his concern with poverty, and his commitment to equality and progress. To quote him:

> Social and economic inequalities are to be arranged so that they are both (a) to the greatest benefit of the least advantaged, and (b) attached to offices and positions open to all under conditions of fair equality of opportunities.[40]

There are two methodological distinctions between the feminist welfare economics and the neo-classical one,[41] namely:

(a) the notion of preference change[42] which is central to feminist economics remains at the margin of neo-classical economics; and

(b) the identification of choice with well-being,[43] which is the basis for neo-classical welfare analysis, is deeply problematic for many feminists, for the simple reason that, if only because of sheer ignorance, one does not always choose what is really conducive to one's own welfare.

Thus, feminist economics has questioned a basic dischotomy which neo-classical welfare economics quietly accepts, that is, the dichotomy posited between family altruism and market selfishness. It argues that such dichotomies are not invariably helpful for economic reasoning, as conflict is as likely to occur in families as cooperative conduct,[44] just as, in the public sphere, some pharmaceutical concerns can cooperate in pushing the sale of a newly discovered curative drug.[45] Feminist economists further point out that labour market analysis presents a similar neglect of women. It of course deals with both labour force participation and labour market segregation, and also takes both supply and demand factors into account; but in so far as a woman's participation in labour market is determined by her family situation, education and job opportunities, which may not be helpful or available to her, role in market analysis naturally gets little attention.

Further, neo-classical economic theory has concentrated more on wage differentials rather than on gender segregation, employing mainly models of perfect competition where wages are equal to the value of worker's marginal product. The conclusion of such an analysis is that women's economic situation is a result of 'tastes' and 'free choices' of women themselves, arising from individual differences and varying social relations.[46]

The two major variations of neo-classical theories based on models of perfect competition that explain wage differentials are 'overcrowding' and the 'human capital' approach. In both, a worker's wage equals his/her marginal product wage differentials existing because of their differing productivities, either due to women's lower level of accumulated human capital or to 'overcrowding' with its affiliated implications of a relatively low capital labour ratio. According to the overcrowding approach, if there is a relatively low demand for a particular type of work for which a considerable supply of labour is yet available, employment opportunities naturally become very limited.

Because receiving lower wages than men discourages women from developing their skills, they are forced into a small number of occupations in which the capital labour ratio is low and hence women have lower productivity than men. This indeed is the real cause of occupational segregation and not what it has been said to be by neo-classical theorists, that is, the employers''tastes'.[47]

As opposed to the 'overcrowding' approach, the 'human capital' approach does not assume that men and women are perfectly substitutable for one another and therefore takes it for granted that they have to compete with each other. This competitive model explains wage and productivity differentials through differences in the quality of labour between men and women. Workers, who invest in themselves through education, or job training, experience, etc., acquire a qualitative improvement in their worth as human capital. The cost of acquiring this improvement is compared with the expected 'return' on the 'investment' – obviously in terms of higher wages. This theory thus concludes that as men have invested more in themselves, they have greater value as human capital than women and so receive higher wages. Why women do not make the 'investment' in question is just not thought about by the human capital approach. The reason simply is that so many restrictions are imposed by society on woman's freedom to choose that she just does not get any chance for self-improvement.

A third (relatively less known) approach is Madden's model based on monopsony, that is, a situation in which the entire market demand for a product or service consists of only one buyer. A monopsonist gives wages lower than the value of the marginal product, the degree of divergence depending upon the strength of the monopsony elements in the labour market. The central component of this model is the relationship between wages and elasticity of supply. The less elastic the supply curve of labour, the lower will be the wage. Women receive lower wages than men because their labour supply curve is less elastic.

Marxist Theory

The Marxist school regards social structure itself as the determinant factor and the individual agent as simply conditioned by it, thus according primacy to productive forces and production relations in the analysis of economic structures and processes. Within this framework, the position of women (be it their substitution for men with some technological change, or their role in the reserve army, or in the sphere of reproduction) was always subsumed under the analysis of class relations whose main purpose was to explain the existence and evils of capitalism. Consequently, where it was at all considered, gender was regarded as a mere means to this main end. It was just not given any independent consideration.

Given the significance attached to human labour in Marxist thought, its account of women's oppression, not unexpectedly begins with the original divisions of labour in pre-class societies within a two-fold production process:

> According to the materialist conception, the determining factor in history is, in the final instance, the production and reproduction of immediate life. This, again, is of a two fold character: on the one side, the production of the means of existence, of food, clothing and shelter and the tools necessary for that production; on the other side, the production of human beings themselves, the propagation of the species.[48]

For Engels, "the first division of labour (was) that between man and woman for the propagation of children".[49] While men provided the means of subsistence, women were concerned with the production and reproduction of human life. Both contributions were seen as vital to the community, so that both sexes enjoyed equal status. Changes in the relations of production, associated with the development of agriculture and the domestication of animals, led to the production of a surplus and the accumulation of wealth and men's control over this wealth; and this led to the overthrow of mother right on which the earlier communities had been based, and laid the institutional foundations of women's subjugation, private property, monogamous marriage and patrilineal inheritance. The earliest class opposition that appears in history coincides with the development of the antagonism between man and woman in monogamous marriage, and the first class oppression coincides with that of the female sex by the male.

In later history, Engels explains, the cleavage between the production of commodities (which was shifted to the public sphere of the marketplace) and production of human life and labour (which was confined to the private sphere of the home) resulted the emergence of a generalized market economy, which is the distinguishing feature of the capitalist mode of production.

It is noteworthy here that although the works of Marx and Engels provide significant insights into the position and role of women in societies, be it their substitution for men with technological change, or their role in the reserve army, or in the sphere of reproduction, the Marxist analysis yet has quite a few limitations. It has always seen women's position as the outcome of capitalism, subsuming gender under analysis of class relations, and denying to gender the independent attention it deserves. As a distinct aspect of social structure, intra-gender relations are not accorded an autonomous position, and capitalist-commodity relations assume primacy in the fabric of society.

For the first time feminists began to note the inadequacy of the Marxist theory and pointed out how it failed to account for women's unpaid labour, sexual division of labour and the role of gender ideology. They endeavoured to revise it, first, with a view to giving due attention to the marginalization of women in the process of capital accumulation, and, secondly, to address its conceptual weaknesses. To understand the whole process of women's subordination to men, they have spread the canvass of productive work and surplus value generation to cover women's work within the household. They claim that the relationship between the worker and the capitalist is essentially antagonistic because whereas the worker, because of his productive work, generates surplus value, the capitalist merely appropriates it, and that the man-woman relationship, within the household, is more or less similar. Indeed, it is in the works of feminists that focus is, for the first time, shifted to 'domestic labour' as the first site of women's exploitation. This direct focus on sexual division of labour has been a pioneering step. The feminist theorists argued that domestic labour yielded a surplus because it saved the capitalists from paying for the full subsistence needs of the workers because women made and kept the workers fit for work without making the capitalist pay for this quiet service. The generally accepted divide between the household and the public field is but artificial. However, it was only during the new women's liberation movement of 1960s and 1970s in Western Europe and North America that various approaches were adopted to emphasize the dynamic unity of the personal and public or political spheres.[50] Quite a few attempts to trace the historical roots and contemporary complexities of the situation of women led to a rediscovery of the usefulness of Marxism. Simone de Beauvoir and Juliet Mitchell[51] examined relationships between feminism and Marxism. In the United States, Kate Millet and Shulamith Firestone used Engel's ideas to organize their viewpoints.

In her paper on women, Mitchell introduces the subject as follows:

> In advanced industrial society, *women's* work is only marginal to the total economy. Yet it is through [this] work that man changes natural conditions and thereby produces society[52] ... [So] the most elementary economic demand [for women] is not the right to work or receive equal pay for work but the right to equal *work* itself.

She further recognized the importance of the sexual division of labour in the paid work force and felt that the family as it exits is in fact incompatible with the equality of the sexes, for the whole pyramid of discrimination at work rested on 'a solid extra-economic foundation, i.e., education. Malos contradicts Mitchell's argument and sees the reason for women's selection in inferior works not due to education but sexual division of labour within the family.[53]

Margaret Benston[54] contends that the roots of the secondary status of women are in fact economic. He states that women as a group have a definite relation to the means of production that is different from men. The personal and psychological factors then follow from this special relation to production and a change in the latter will be a necessary (but not sufficient) condition for change. If this relation of women to production is accepted, the analysis of the situation of women fits naturally into a class analysis of society.

To Benston, household labour, including childcare, is pre-capitalist in a very real sense and does not constitute 'real work' in a society based on commodity production. This assignment of housework as the function of a special category of people – namely, 'women' – means that this group does stand in a different relation to production than the other group, that is, of men. Thus, Benston defines women as "that group of people who are responsible for the production of simple use values in those activities [that are] associated with home and family". "Further, they are denied an active place in the market" and "remain a very convenient and elastic part of the industrial reserve army". Mickey and John Rowntree,[55] while agreeing with Benston's analysis of women's role in the home, felt that his emphasis on women as houseworkers did not hold true for the post-Second World War period when sex compositions of labour force changed drastically. Such an emphasis minimized their role as wage labourers.

Ellen Malos is of the view that women cannot be liberated until their role in household and child rearing is done away with. She puts forward a multi-pronged strategy to tackle the problem of housework refusal and to accept the division of labour, inside or outside the house, as 'natural'. This strategy recommends the following: a study of what housework is and has been; financial recognition for women who have spent years of their lives as housewives; a fight for real equal pay; workplace demands for maternity/paternity leave etc.; campaign for the recognition of childcare as a social function and need; campaign for adequate social service and welfare benefits, especially for women bringing up their children on their own; movements to resist attempts to intensify housewives' unpaid labour by way of cuts in social services, public health care etc.; a struggle for both socialized housework and shared tasks in personal maintenance across sex lines in the home; constant fight to end the sexual division of labour and sexual discrimination in jobs outside the home; and beyond these essentially economic issues, finally, a continued fight against sexism in all the forms.

Though the focus on housework is useful, it does not answer all the questions related to women's subordination. A need is also felt to bring out its links with the processes of control over exercise of sexuality and frequency of reproduction. In this context, it is relevant to mention that reproduction indicates a dynamic process of change linked with the perpetuation of social system and so includes social as well as physical reproduction. Lourdes Beneria[56] argues that male domination develops around the need to control reproduction in its various aspects, say, the following: social reproduction (the conditions sustaining a social system); reproduction of the labour force (daily maintenance of workers and potential labour and allocation of agents to positions within the labour process); and biological reproduction or childbearing which, though it entails the reproduction of labour force, cannot be identified with the latter. Beneria delinked the control of women's reproduction activities from the institution of private property. Moreover, he admitted that conflict over reproduction would be greater in class societies than in equalitarian societies, because privileges enjoyed by some groups and not enjoyed by others affect individuals in varying degrees.

Beneria further argues that an analysis of women's role in reproduction is essential in order to understand the extent and nature not only of their participation in productive activities but also of the sexual division of labour. She looks on reproductive sphere of the household as the primary location of subordination of women. She declared that "far from viewing the household as a static unit and sexual division of labour as 'natural' or 'given', both must be viewed as being subject to change and responding to dynamic forces generated by an economy in the process of transformation".[57]

Susan Himmelweit and Simon Mohun[58] focus on analysing domestic labour and capital. Domestic labour is seen as a whole sector of production central to, but entirely outside, capitalist relations of production which produce goods and services for direct satisfaction. In his division of labour Marx has not given detailed attention to domestic labour. The only division of labour to which domestic labour is subject to is that it is divided from commodity production. An unmediated implication of such a division is that the performance of domestic labour is of no direct concern to capital. Both Himmelweit and Mohun agree with Terry Lee[59] that since productive labour is, by definition, has direct relation to capital, domestic labour cannot be regarded as productive labour in the strict sense of the term, though it cannot at the same time be called totally unproductive labour. They also explain how definitions of domestic labour can be as many as its analyses. It may well be defined as private labour, which continues to stay alongside commodity production. However, this approach suggests a question as to how exactly we can distinguish use-values (of loving and caring) produced by domestic labour from commodities which are tangible things that satisfy specific needs. Another definition of domestic labour could be that it is the labour which directly maintains and reproduces labour power. Economists like Terry Lee and J. Mincer[60] have used this approach to analyse domestic labour. Himmelweit and Mohun criticize Lee and Mincer for applying their 'commodity fetishism' to non-commodities, and, in addition, believe that it is superficial analysis since it does not penetrate the actual relations of production involved in the process of generating domestic labour.

Further, they explain how generalizations of received interpretations of value theory have led to some fundamental errors in analysis. They give special attention to two attempts that try to relate domestic labour to the system of capitalist production. Both these attempts study the effect of domestic labour on the value of labour power. One of these considers the labour time involved in the capitalist production of the wage bundle of subsistence goods and treats it as simply an additive to the labour time involved in domestic production whereby the wage bundle is transferred into directly consumable use-values. This model indicates unequal exchange, first between capitalist and worker over the purchase and sale of labour power; and second, between husband and wife over the exchange of her labour time for part of the commodities bought with the husband's wage. What is important in this analysis is the direct comparison of quantities of labour time in the production of the means of subsistence occurring in the home and in the factory; and, within the home, a comparison of the allocation of the housewife's time spent in producing use-values for herself with the time spent in producing values for her husband. This view holds that all housework could be performed according to capitalist production relations. Himmelweit and Mohun criticize this approach on the ground that the complete socialization of domestic labour requires the socialization of the very reproduction of living individuals; and, at the same time, capital would require the freedom of these individuals in the labour market. For capital to produce the living labourer it has to subvert its own relations of production; hence, it is impossible completely to incorporate domestic labour directly under capitalist relations of production.

The second attempt is made by Seacombe.[61] According to her, domestic labour creates value precisely because it is commodity production. She explains our failure to realize this truth by inviting our attention to the reproduction cycle of labour power. This is a value equilibrating process whereby wage goods from the market are transformed by the household into the labour power bound for the market. Value is neither created nor destroyed, but merely transferred in the production cycle of labour power. A housewife creates value as her contribution to the reproduction of labour power for capital and consumes equal value in the form of her own upkeep.

Institutional Approach

The institutional economic theory is a compromise between the neo-classical and Marxist schools. It attacks the premise that economic behaviour is market determined and strongly upholds the view that economic behaviour depends on the relative position of men and women in society. This approach incorporates the roles of institutions that affect economic behaviour and analyses the circumstances which provoke particular forms of behaviour. It does not perceive the individual in isolation, nor does it subscribe to the idea of a strict public-private dichotomy. What is seen as private or public varies with its immediate context and also historically. Earlier, the family was private with respect to the state; now, the market is private with respect to the state, though the production is public. The truth is that market, family and state are all interconnected social spheres. Institutional economics admits the role of power and institutional processes explicitly, but unlike the Marxist school, it goes beyond class analysis and does not give primacy to the public sphere. Unfortunately, this approach has remained a mere sideline in the discipline's hierarchy, because in the view of mainstream economics it lacks a rigorous theoretical structure. The Marxist school has rejected it for it neither exposes the evil of class conflict nor the defects of a unitary materialism.

New Household Economics

On the other hand, quite a few advances were made by feminist theorists who continued to focus on non-economic factors and took the issue of patriarchy not only beyond capitalism, but also beyond economists' narrow view of the economic worth of domestic labour by drawing upon anthropology.[62] All these efforts bore fruit and economic theorists were compelled to shift their attention to women's labour at home. They realized the need for theorizing women's unpaid labour at home. Hence, a new household economics took shape in 1960s, largely as a copy of the market model.

This economics began to determine the division of labour between husband and wife in such a way that both could specialize in their individual areas of activity and so could maximize family welfare. This further led to examination of task allocation between husband and wife and also to the study of economics of marriage, fertility and divorce.[63] However, sensible though it appears, this approach has been criticized by Dale Spender on the ground that it accepts the traditional family and the traditional division of labour between the husband and wife as rational,[64] and that in doing so it invokes the theory of 'comparative advantage' according to which the 'advantage' enjoyed by men in market work is justified by the fact that it directly encourages women's specialization in housework. But, following Spender, some feminists have criticized this attempt to justify men's superiority in market work. They contend that such a view bars even those women from entering the market who may be compelled to do so because of some contingency, such as the husband's death. How can a helpless widow with children keep herself confined to housework? Further, the view in question also (wrongly) justifies a disabled husband's refusal to do the little housework that he can when the wife has to take up a job. In this context, Bergmann contends that the new home economics has somewhat retarded the development of feminist economics by failing to preempt large areas of relevant subject matter and to tackle the issues with sophisticated methodology.[65]

Firstly, it ignores the fact that the division of labour into two rigidly fixed spheres – that is, the home where the spouses specialize and the market where husbands dominate – can easily give rise to boredom by making one to do a particular activity for too long, and that both the husband and wife might find it rewarding to share both types of works – the husband participating for a while in household work, and the wife working in the market for some time.

Secondly, this (home economics) school treats family as a stagnant and changeless economic unit. It fails to provide for a very probable situation. A wife who devotes much of her working time to the household finds the value of her work declining sharply as children grow up and require less care. At that time will she not want, and should she not be allowed, to enter the labour market?

Thirdly, it does not focus on differences in the status of the individual within the family. In a family structure where the male is the sole wage earner, the female can never enjoy an equal status. The male is naturally the decision-maker too and the female becomes totally dependent on her husband's income, thus incurring a fall in self-respect as also a lower status in the family.

Lastly, the school in question makes the quite wrong assumption that the family is a permanent, indivisible unit. Cannot a woman be left without a husband, say, because of separation, divorce or death? Such women and their dependents are frequently mired in dire poverty. The most common of such cases is that of a divorced woman, generally with children who collects little, if any, alimony or child support, and very rarely manages to re-establish her dignity as a person except through remarriage.[66] The divorced husband is also likely to incur very great inconvenience because he has no idea of housework whatsoever.

Those feminist theorists who have focused on the family refuse to accept the following key assumptions of the household economist group: (a) the unfailing benevolence of the head of the household; and (b) the belief that biological motherhood necessarily entails more responsibility of child rearing for the mother than does fatherhood for the father.

However, in spite of these shortfalls, the home economics model must be acclaimed for taking the lead in analysing household as a productive unit and for equating domestic labour in value with market labour, because, though it does not produce goods, it surely provides services. But, the problem with this model was that it never asked the question as to why women had expertise in household production only. Was it not because of the prior denial to them of training for wage/market work? And, as pointed out by a Norwegian feminist economist, Nottburga Ott,[67] will not the existing division of labour, if it is allowed to persist, lead to further attrition of women's skill for market work? It may well maximize her utility for the household, but it will also, at the same time, increase even more the value of male labour in the market, as against that of woman. Such values, however, are not rigidly fixed at any period of time. This truth is highlighted by the 'bargaining theory' developed in the late 1980s and discussed in the next section.

Bargaining Theory

According to this theory, the exchange between economic agents is a process of bargaining. The competitive economy was hitherto conceptualized as an abstract mechanism where individual economic agents were seen to react to given prices. In this scheme prices are unique and exogenous to the actors, and here there is no room for strategic or conflictual behaviour. This was reformulated so that an economic transaction was now seen as an interaction between identifiable agents, who are like players in a chess game, able to anticipate possible sequence of moves and counter-moves, and to plan a strategy for dealing with the reaction of other agents. This approach, known as the 'bargaining theory', caught the attention of feminist economists because it facilitated understanding of what happens outside the household.

What is more, this model (of 'bargaining') can be used for analysing not only the gender relations both inside and outside the household but also the worker-employee relation. The object of bargaining can be the determination of the household division of labour, or of the duration of time and services or distribution of consumption goods. At the workplace, it can also be the nature of work, its intensity and wages and peripheral benefits. Bargaining between the worker and the employer may also be done with an eye to securing such conditions as may ensure their maximum well-being even after their relation comes to an end. The object here will be a comfortable 'fall back' position. The emphasis of this model is on regulating the external structural factors that provide some stimulus for increase in efficiency and devotion to work. In a way, it combines the neo-classical concern for efficiency with the Marxist concern for reduction of conflictual possibilities.

Talking of conflicts, Amartya Sen distinguishes conflicts of interest between men and women from other class conflicts. The former arise between those who have to live together, if only because of sexual complementarity. So, their conflicts have to be viewed against the background of a pervasively cooperative behaviour. There is indeed eminent sense in the following words of Sen:

> While serious conflicts of interest may, in fact, be involved, the nature of family organization requires these conflicts to be moulded into a general form of cooperation, with conflicts treated as aberrations and deviant behaviours.[68]

Household partnership is at once cooperative and conflictual. It is cooperative because each member gains more from the common pool than she or he could expect in solitary existence. At the same time, however, conflicts can easily arise because differences in tastes, age levels and temperaments may call for a patient and meticulous determination of how much may be given to each member of the family. Sen further acknowledges that, in so far as sexual difference produces different needs – such as the need of the female's physical protection by the male – 'bargaining' in the family cannot proceed in the impersonal way of the market. A female may have to be saved from her own tendency to belittle her personnel interests too much for the welfare of the whole family. The truth indeed is that the model of bargaining cannot be accepted as valid in utter isolation from the context of life, persons and traditions.

As Elizabeth Katz[69] points out, not all bargaining is voluntary. It may be quietly determined by tradition. The assignment of childcaring to the mother, as against that of earning a living to the father, is not the result of any voluntary bargaining but is simply an acquiescence in traditional practice. No amount of bargaining can relieve a mother from her obligation to look after the newly born. Nor can a husband be relieved of his obligation to protect his wife from threats of molestation by the most skilful kind of bargaining. So, despite its advantages over the earlier unitary model of household, a formalized model like the 'bargaining' one, has its own limitations. No model can be used without qualitative, specific data to answer such questions as what is bargained over, and what are the prescribed rules for bargaining. Further, qualities of character have also to be taken into account. The contribution of (a puny) earning made by a husband may be of far less value to the family's welfare than the services rendered by his wife, but if he is domineering by nature – and she quite docile – he may well be able to exercise greater decision-making power. So, some feminists have contested the concept of a common household pool from which the husband and the wife are equally free to draw facilities and conveniences. The concept is indeed not a fit model for the third world.[70] Yet, in many ways, the bargaining model was an advance over the earlier one of home economics. To quote Krishnaraj, "The home economics model defines tastes and preferences in a joint household function. The bargaining model disaggregates tastes and preferences by household members and shows how the individual's influence over the expenditure of household income varies according to the bargaining power of the members."

Empirical Investigations

Now, all such thinking highlights two basic facts. First, the issues that the economists take up and the questions they address are motivated by the kind of society they live in; and, secondly, the theories they formulate to explain human behaviour are validated or invalidated on the basis of real word data. Unfortunately, however, this data is collected and interpreted by economists in a way which is male-dominated and androcentric. The male here is valued over the female and issues related to patriarchy and gender are classified as non-data. This distorted concern with the real world has profound implications for empirical investigations into the economic position of women. For example, the data that is made available for study relates to the market activity of men and not to the household activity of women, and whereas market transactions that determine prices, wages and costs lend themselves to tabulation, household economic activity, say, of spending and saving money which does not result in goods and services being bought and sold, does not admit of similar determination.

Most of the time, the process of collection of data is not completely objective and value-free; on the other hand, in many instances, it reflects cultural norms and stereotypes.[71] These limitations of data pose problems in analysing the economic activity of women. Recognizing such limitations, attempts have been made by international agencies like the United Nations to compile the most relevant and reliable information that the actual situation of women may be brought to light. The International Research and Training Institute for the Advancement of Women (INSTRAW) takes into account the nature, scope and limitations of the basic national sources of data. Based on the statistics compiled by various international data collecting bodies, it identifies relevant concepts and methods most widely used in ongoing general data collection programmes from the point of view of their suitability of women.[72] Yet, at times, even international concepts and definitions fail to completely cover the role of women's economic contribution. So, in the light of such inadequacies of macro-data, micro-studies have been undertaken to try out other methods for generating alternative data. Time use methods have been tried to get a detailed picture of the various kinds of work that women do, and analyses have been attempted to derive principles of allocation of time between work and leisure.

Public Policy Implementation

The importance of having adequate data, which may reflect the position of women in the economy, is highlighted by the close linkage of data with resulting policy measures. Where the macro-data already collected are biased, the policies framed thereon are also biased.

Government plays a crucial role in all economics and its policies exert considerable influence both on the labour force participation of women and their economic status in the labour market. Its policies are obviously not formulated in a vacuum; if there are biases against women in society in general, or if specific theories are based on assumptions that are not really objective, then the economic policy will naturally reflect the biases. Further, even though the government policy can be used as an instrument of social change, in the realm of economic policy, it is often the case that policy changes lag behind changes in attitudes, and in economic and social institutions. Indeed, an economic policy, which was once well suited to an earlier time, may now have an adverse effect upon women if there has been a significant change in their economic behaviour.

Be that as it may, instances of bias and outmoded assumptions in government policy can be easily given from the situations of women in the US. Two areas of government policy that affect virtually all members of society are the income tax system and social security system, and both affect women adversely because of their outdated (and middle-class) biased concept of the family.[73]

To begin with the income tax system, its effect on women is not favourable because of two reasons: first, the unit of taxation is the family; and second, the tax system is progressive in the senses that it taxes a large percentage of the income from higher income families. Though woman's employment and income are both secondary in the family unit, she has yet to pay taxes at the highest rate that apply to her husband's income. Since labour force participation decisions are motivated in part by wage rates, and the high tax rates effectively reduce wages, the system constitutes a potentially serious disincentive for married women to participate in the labour force.[74]

What is more, since the tax system is progressive, two individuals who marry and continue working may find that their tax liability increases simply as a result of marriage. This so-called marriage tax can be substantial in some cases – up to a several thousand dollars a year for high income couples. Moreover, the more severe the penalty, the greater is the dent in wife's income too.[75] Luckily, however, the increasing importance of the two-earner family led to a sympathetic policy response in 1981. A legislation was passed to provide for a two-earner deduction and it was to become fully effective by 1983.[76] The legislation was intended to respond to claims of unfair tax treatment of married working couples by reducing their tax liability; but while the change in policy did provide some relief, it did not eliminate the marriage penalty.

Apart from their disincentive effects on women's labour force participation in the market, these two programmes have implications for the non-market sphere as well. They perpetuate the traditional sexual diversion of labour. The programmes as they currently operate result in a systematic undervaluation of women's contributions to the market. Government's welfare policy for women in poverty too had an adverse effect on them as here again the policy was based on the traditional notion of ideal family structure.[77]

To undo the harmful effects of these government policies based on outdated values and stereotypes, one needs to reformulate policies in such a manner that they could become a force for constructive change. This can be done by developing new tools for a critical analysis of the theories, and also by improving the existing methods of testing policies.

It is noteworthy that the impact of social security system on women is also inequitable. This is so largely because of our model view of the family. The retirement benefits received under social security plan are based on the concept of dependence or spouse benefits.[78] Thus, a woman, even if she has not worked outside the home, may collect benefits on her husband's record. This feature of the system was appended by some as a recognition of the homemaker's economic contribution to the family. Yet, in one respect, this system is problematic for those women who work outside the home. On retirement they could avail of spouse benefits or benefits based on their own earning records, but not both.[79] This creates disincentive effects for women as they realize that their wages will be reduced by social security taxes, for which they will receive little compensation in the future.

Similarly, it has also been found that the impact of government payment to families is likely to have very great impact on women's participation in the labour force.[80] Government can also influence women's participation in labour force by providing, or subsidizing services for the household; and it is only proper that, in this context, there has been a considerable focus on day care centres.[81]

Before 1960, in development literature, there were very few reflections on women's specific problems and contributions. Earlier, economists (mostly males) assumed that modernization would break sex inequality by replacing inscriptive bases of social organization with achieved ones. This assumption was ruled out with the publication of Ester Boserup's *Women's Role in Economic Development* (1970). It encompassed information from all the regions of the world and pointed out that the transition from a traditional to modern economy presented both a threat and some promise to the status of women.[82] Boserup's contributions influenced the work of scholars and also had a great impact on the policies of the countries and international agencies that provide aids and loans to developing economies.[83]

Towards a Feminist Economics

To sum up, so far, we have tried to explore how a focus on women's experience may transform the ways in which we theorize in the field of economics, challenging its conventional paradigms and understandings. The attempts of feminist theorists to bring in women's perspectives through their critique not only of prevalent theories but of empirical investigations, and the public policy making techniques, have made economics more open to the concerns of women.

The rebirth of women's movement in the 1960s increased the visibility of women – and made them more audible – in public. This development naturally suggested questions regarding the very scope of economics, which had hitherto neglected women as they remained confined to their private domains.

There was a perceptible shift in the nature of the discipline in question by the end of the 1970s. Martha Griffith stated in hearings before the joint economic committee of the US Congress in 1973 that the policy developed on the basis of economic analysis had not met the social concerns of the nation in respect of women as women themselves saw these concerns against them, and that it had been determined only by the male view of these concerns. As we have seen, in the 1960s, the new home economics emerged, focusing on allocation of time and other resources within the household. An exclusive literature sprang up dealing with determinants of labour force participation, and examining occupational segregation and indicating earning differentials between men and women. The effect of governmental policies and legislation on the economic status of women was also studied. Further, special attention was paid to the role of women in economic development.

Thus, we see that feminist theory has highlighted the concerns erupting across the various paradigms of economics where gender has been a secondary concern. The formation of feminist economics as a defined field is a far cry from the early "add women and stir" approach. The recent attempts by feminist theorists have altered the neo-classical framework with varying degrees of success.[84]

To cite instances, whereas Howkerworth exposed the persistence of 'androcentrism' in the allegedly 'neutral' and 'scientific' discipline that economics was thought to be, Wooley challenged its dominant analytical paradigm. She drew up a feminist economics agenda involving the well-being of both men and women, advocating policies to promote equity and for conducting such research as steered clear of the andocentric bias.

Recognizing the multiplicity of voices that constitute feminist economics taken generally, Grapard outlines its difference from other heterodox approaches to questions about human nature, assumptions and methodologies of Western science and definitions of the proper domain of economic investigations. Apart from this, developments such as the creation of International Association for Feminist Economics in 1992 and the publication of the journal, *Feminist Economics* (Routledge) since 1955, have highlighted the newly gendered nature of the discipline, its assumptions, methods, domains and category of analysis.

Further, in Ferber and Nelson's book, which was the first anthology of feminist economic writings to appear, writers have provided the theoretical underpinnings for a neo-classical critique and a reorientation of economic thinking towards a new paradigm, thus striving to pave the way of reformation and re-creation of a more self-critical economics. Nelson[85] draws on feminist theories from many disciplines to present a critique of contemporary economics. She evaluates the abstract core models of neo-classical economics by exploring their relationship with cultural conceptions of gender and value, and presents a tool called 'gender-value compass' to analyse the theory of the family, income tax policy and macro-economics.

Providing a critique that is distinctively feminist, she discusses perspectives in labour economics, statistical surveys, the history of national accounting, special problems of poverty in developing nations and environmental issues among others, and shows her concern for the problem of lack of official measurement of household production, consumption and bias in imputed labour income.

Ferber undertook to explain how the costs of caring for children and other dependants are distributed in societies over time. She proposed a theory which combined the aspects of neo-classical, institutional and Marxist economics with insights from feminist thought. Similarly, Gardiner explored the history of neglect of household as the basic unit of care and revived attention to household economic relations and gender dimensions since the mid-1960s. In a similar vein, Mewitson made an attempt at theorizing post-structuralist feminist economics.

Having glanced over some of the recent attempts (which appear to be endless), we may state that feminist theorists have opened up the discipline which did not even have a 'fringe field' devoted to women earlier. These feminist economists feel that a radical solution to women's disadvantageous position would be a truly equal sharing of domestic responsibilities between men and women. Applauding these feminist attempts, Barbara Bergmann writes:

> The task that feminist economists have set for themselves is to produces the design for a more equitable future. What really distinguishes feminist economists is their view that the present assignment of economic duties based on sex is unfair and should be eliminated.[86] Though the feminists have done a lot in this regard, it can be treated as just a beginning to their journey from the margins to the center.

The economic and social deprivation of women has strong implications for the power relations that exist between the male and the female in both public and private spheres. Until and unless the gap between these two spheres is bridged, women shall remain powerless for ever. The chapter that follows is an attempt in this direction.

Notes

1. Economics has been defined as "the systematic study of the production, distribution and use of scarce resources of a society so as to satisfy the maximum number of wants. It is the study of choices among alternatives in a situation of scarcity" (W.E. Peterson, *Elements of Economics*, New York: Norton, 1973).
2. Marilyn J. Waring, "Economics", in Cheris Kramrae and Dale Spender (eds.), *The Knowledge Explosion*, New York: Harvester Wheatsheaf, 1993, p. 306.
3. Ibid.
4. Ibid.
5. Marilyn J. Waring, "Economics", op. cit.
6. W.D. Nordhaus and James Tobin, "Is growth obsolete?" in Economic Growth, Fiftieth Anniversary Colloquium V.N.7, National Bureau of Economic, Res: 1972.

   Also see Tibor Scitovsky's *The Joyless Economy*, New York: Oxford University Press, 1976.
7. See Marilyn J. Waring, "Economics", op. cit., pp. 307–8.
8. This workshop involved women from 14 countries and was empowered by Mediterranean Women's Studies Institute and the International Research and Training Institute for Advancement of Women (INSTRAW).
9. As quoted by Waring, "Economics", op. cit., p. 307.
10. Some of them are cited below:

    Marilyn J. Waring, *If Women Counted*, San Francisco: Harper and Row, 1989.

Gerda Lerner, *The Creation of Patriarchy*, New York: Oxford University Press, 1986.

Barbara Bergmann, *The Economic Emergence of Women*, New York: Basic Books, 1986.

C. Faulker, "The Feminist Challenge to Economics", *Frontiers*, 8, pp. 55–61.

C. Lloyd and B. Niemi, *The Economics of Sex Differentials*, New York: Columbia University Press, 1979.

I.V. Swahill, "Economic Perspectives on the Family", *Daedalus*, 106, pp. 115–26.

M.A. Warren, *The Nature of Women*, Inverness, CA: Edge Press, 1980.

T.G. Tullock and R. McKenzie, *The New World of Economics*, Homewood, IL: Irwin, 1984.

P. England, "The Failure of Human Capital Theory to Explain Occupational Segregation", *Journal of Human Resources*, 28, pp. 538–70.

Dale Spender (ed.), *Men's Studies Modified*, New York: Pergamon Press, 1981.

Jessie Bernard, *The Female World*, New York: Free Press, 1981.

Ester Boserup, *Women's Role in Economic Development*, New York: St. Martin's Press, 1970.

11. Mary Wollstonecraft, *A Vindication of the Rights of Women*, London: J. Johnson, 1976.
12. John Stuart Mill, *The Subjection of Women*, London: Longmans, Green, Reader and Dyer, 1869.
13. Charlotts Parkins Gillman, *Women and Economics*, Boston, Small: Baynard and Co., 1898.
14. Fredrich Engels, *The Origin of the Family, Private Property, and the State*, London: Lawrence and Wishart, 1972, p. 71.
15. J. Madden, "A Two Century Review of Economic Thought", in Maitreyee Krishnaraj and Joy Deshmukh (eds.), *Gender in Economics: Theory and Practice*, New Delhi: Ajanta Publishers, 1993.
16. A. Smith, *An Inquiry into the Nature and Courses of the Wealth of Nations*, Oxford: Claremont Press, 1776.
17. B.L.S. Bodichon, *Women and Work*, London: Bosworth and Harrison, 1857.
18. Sydney Webb, "The Alleged Differences in the Wages Paid to Men and Women for Similar Work", *Economic Journal*, 1(4), 1891.
19. See Matheson E. Cadbury, M. Cecile and Shann George, *Women's Work and Wages: A Phase of Life in an Industrial City*, Chicago: Chicago University Press, 1907.
20. M. Faucett, "Equal Pay for Equal Work", *Economic Journal*, March, 1918. Also see F.Y. Edgeworth, "Equal Pay to Men and Women for Equal Work", *Economic Journal*, December, 1922.

21. Alfred Marshall, "The Social Possibilities of Economic Chivalry", *Economic Journal*, 17 March 1907, pp. 7–29.
22. A.C. Pigou, "Men's and Women's Wages", reprinted in *Essays in Economics*, London: Macmillan, 1952.
23. See here, the following: Gary Becker, *The Economics of Discrimination*, Chicago: Chicago University Press, 1971.

    —, "A Theory of Marriage", *Journal of Political Economy*, 81, 1973.

    —, *A Treatise on the Family*, Cambridge: Harvard University Press, 1981.

    —, "An Economic Way of Looking at Behaviours", *Journal of Political Economy*, Vol. 101, July-August, 1993.

    Lourdes Beneria, "Reproduction, Production and Sexual Division of Labour", *Cambridge Journal of Economics*, 3, 1979.

    Lorraine Corner, "Women, Men and Economics: The Gender-Differentiated Impact of Macroeconomics: with special reference to Asia and the Pacific", UNIFEM, 1996"

    Eva Kaluzynska, "Wiping the Floor with Theory: A Survey of Writings on Housework", *Feminist Review*, No. 6, July-August, 1980.

    Amartya Sen, "Gender Inequality and Theories of Justice", in Martha Nussbaum and Jonathan Glover (eds.), *Women, Culture and Development*, Oxford: Clarendon Press, 1995.

    These are just a few of the numerous relevant works.
24. Maitreyee Krishnaraj and Joy Deshmukh (eds.), op. cit.
25. Ibid.
26. See Ivan Illich, *Gender*, New York: Pantheon Books, 1982.
27. Ibid.
28. See Mary Daly, *Beyond God the Father*, Boston: Beacon Press, 1973.
29. Maitreyee Krishnaraj and Joy Deshmukh (eds.), op. cit., p. 1.
30. See Maitreyi Krishnaraj, "Gender in Economic Theorizing and Philosophy", *Economic and Political Weekly*, April 28, 2001. Also see, Ritu Dewan, "Gender in Neoclassical Economics", *Economic and Political Weekly*, April 29, 1995.
31. Carolyn Shall Bell, "Economics, Sex and Gender", in Nona Glazer and Helen Y. Wahrer (eds.), *Women in a Man-made World*, Chicago: Rand McNally, 1977.
32. Richard Easterlin, "An Economic Framework for Fertility Analyses", *Studies in Family Planning*, No. 6, 1975.
33. T. Paul Schultz, *Economics of Population*, Reading, MA: Addison-Wesley, 1981.
34. A. Mitra, "A Note on Proposed Research on Women's Role in the Social Organization of Production". All India Conference on Women Studies, Trivandrum.

35. Amartya Sen, "Economics and the Family", *Asian Development Review,* Vol. 1, No. 2, 1983.
36. Gerda Lerner, *The Creation of Patriarchy,* New York: Oxford University Press, 1986.
37. Marilyn J. Waring, "Economics", in Cheris Kramarae and Dale Spender (eds.), *The Knowledge Explosion,* New York: Harvester Wheatsheaf, 1993.
38. Janet R. Richards, *The Sceptical Feminist,* Harmondsworth, Middlesex: Penguin Books, 1980.
39. Frances Woolley, "Degrees of Connection: A Critique of Rawls's Theory of Mutual Disinterest", *Feminist Economics,* 6(2), 2000, pp. 1–21.
40. John Rawls, *A Theory of Justice,* Oxford: Oxford University Press, 1971, p. 83.
41. Frances Woolley, "The Feminist Challenge to Neoclassical Economics", *Cambridge Journal of Economics,* 17, 1993, pp. 485–500.
42. Feminist models of preference change differ fundamentally from neo-classical models of endogenous preference, mainly as follows:
    (a) Feminist economics looks to a broad range of influences, including language, culture and politics, as well as economic variables such as prices and incomes.
    (b) They see preference change as resulting in part from dissatisfaction or internal conflict with internalized social norms, and not as the rational choice of fully informed individuals.
    (c) Feminist models of preference change are not deterministic. There can be individual or collective action in transforming respective wants and values.
    (d) Feminists attack the existence of 'a stable, underlying, meta preference order', and maintain that there can be no universal man and woman who could be understood apart from a set of social institutions which constitute them as subjects and agents. So, for feminists, the concept of 'individual preference' is meaningless.
43. Feminists argue that the economic view of choice, where choice simply involves maximization of utility, subject to some constraints, is deterministic.
44. See Bina Agarwal, *A Field of One's Own: Gender and Land Rights in South Asia,* Cambridge, UK: Cambridge University Press, 1994. Also see, Amartya Sen, "Gender and Cooperative Conflicts", in Irene Tinker (ed.), *Persistent Inequalities: Women and World Development,* New York: Oxford University Press, 1990; and Frances Woolley, "Getting the Better of Becker", *Feminist Economics,* 2(1), 1996, pp. 114–20.
45. Nancy Folbre, *Who Pays for the Kid? Gender and the Structure of Constraint,* London: Routledge, 1994.
46. Helen Y. Wahrer, "An Economic Perspective", in Nona Glazer and Helen Y. Wahrer (eds.), op. cit.
47. Francine D. Blau and Carol Jusenuis, "Sex Segregation in the Labour Market", in Nona Glazer and Helen Y, Wahrer (eds.), op. cit.

48. Fredrich Engels, op. cit.
49. Ibid., p. 129.
50. See Pat Mainardi, *The Politics of Housework;* Susan Gail, *The Housewife;* Jan Williams, Hazal Twort and Ann Bachelli, *Women and the Family.*
51. Feminists have used conjugal metaphors to describe the relationship between Feminism and Marxism, Weinbaum calls it 'Curious Courtship' and Hartmam 'Unhappy Marriage'.
52. Juliet Mitchell, "Women: The Longest Revolution", *New Left Review,* December, 1966.
53. Ellen Malos, *Housework and the Politics of Women's Liberation,* London: Alison and Busby, 1980.
54. Margaret Benston, "A Political Economy of Women's Liberation", *Monthly Review,* 21(4), September 1969 reprinted in Edith Altback (ed.), *From Feminism to Liberation,* Cambridge, Massachusetts: Shenkman, 1971.
55. "More on the Political Economy of Women's Liberation", *Monthly Review,* Vol. 21, January 1970.
56. Loudres Beneria, "Reproduction, Production and the Sexual Division of Labour", *Cambridge Journal of Economics,* 3, 1979.
57. Ibid.
58. Susan Himmelweit and Simon Mohun, "Domestic Labour and Capital", *Cambridge Journal of Economics,* 1, 1977, pp. 15–31.
59. Terry Lee, "Domestic Labour: An Analysis of Housework and its Relation to the Production Process", *Review of Radical Political Economy,* 8(1).
60. J. Mincer, "Labour Force Participation of Married Women", *Aspects of Labour Economics,* 1962.
61. W. Seacombe, "The Housewife and the Labour under Capitalism", *New Left Review,* 83, 1974. Also see, W. Seacombe, "Domestic Labour: Reply to Critics", *New Left Review,* 94, 1975.
62. S. Coontz and R. Henderson, *Women's Work, Men's Property: The Origin of Gender and Class,* UK: Verso Press, 1986. Also see R. Hirschon (ed.), *Women and Property: Women as Property,* London: Groom Helm, 1984.
63. See G.S. Becker, "A Theory of the Allocation of Time", *Economic Journal,* Vol. 75, No. 299, September 1965.

    —, "A Theory of Marriage, Part I and II", *Journal of Political Economy,* Vol. 81, No. 4, July-August, 1973 and Vol. 82, No. 4, July-August, 1974.

    —, "An Economic Analysis of Marital Instability", *Journal of Political Economy,* Vol. 85, No. 4, July-August, 1979; A Volume of related works in T.W. Schultz (ed.), *Economics of the Family: Marriage, Children and the Human Capital,* Chicago: University of Chicago Press, 1974.
64. M. Feber and M. Teiman, "The Oldest, the Most Established, the Most Quantitative of the Social Sciences and the most Dominated by Men: The Impact of Feminism on Economics", in Dale Spender (ed.), *Men's Studies Modified,* London: Pergamon Press, 1981, pp. 125–39.

65. Barbara R. Bergmann, "Feminism in Economics", *Women's Studies Quarterly*, Vol. XVIII, Nos. 3 and 4, (Fall/Winter 1990), pp. 68–73.
66. According to Census Bureau Report, Divorce, Child Custody and Child Support, series, p. 23, the amount of child support paid to most women is small; two fifths received less than $1,000 during 1975 and three-fifths less than $ 1,500 (US).
67. Nottburga Ott, "Women in Neoclassical Theory", in Siv Gustaffson, *Out of the Margin*, Amsterdam: University of Amsterdam, 1992.
68. Amartya K. Sen, "Women, Technology and Sexual Division", *Trade and Development UNCTAD Review*, 6, New York, UN, 1985.
69. Elizabeth Katz, "Breaking the Myth of Harmony: Theoretical and Methodological Guidelines to the Study of Rural Third World Households", *Review of Radical Political Economics*, Vol. 23, Nos. 3 and 4, 1991.
70. Eleanor Fopehonda, "The Non-pooling Household: A Challenge to Theory", in Daisy Dwyer and Judith Bruce (eds.), *Home Divided: Women and Income in the Third World*, Stanford: Stanford University Press, 1988.
71. Two examples from the US will illustrate this point:
    (a) Until a welcome change that took place in the 1980 Census of Population, if a household comprised a husband and a wife, the husband was designated as the head of the household, even if responses to census questionaries indicated otherwise.
    (b) The way in which data are classified by Census bureau suggests that some traditional value judgements are built into the categorization process. Data on labour force status, for example, have a heading for "employed persons" followed by a subheading for "employed females".

    See Babara S. Burnell, "Images of Women: An Economic Perspective", in M. Paludi and G. Steuernagel (eds.), *Foundations for a Feminist Restructuring of the Discipline*, New York and London: Routledge, 1990.
72. UN-INSTRAW. Improving concepts and methods for statistics and indication on the situation of women, Santa Domingo, 1988.
73. Both programmes assume a 'traditional' family with a wage-earning husband, homemaker wife, and dependent children. This is no longer a correct portrayal the American household.
74. Empirical analysis has supported the hypothesis that the tax system results in a significant disincentive effect for married women. See, for example, J. Leuthold, "The Effect of Taxation on the Housework Done by Married Women", *Industrial and Labour Relations Review*, 31, 1976, pp. 520–26.
75. See N.M. Gordon, "Institutional Responses: The Federal Income Tax System", in R. Smith (ed.), *The Subtle Revolution: Women at Work*, Washington: Urban Institute Press, 1979, pp. 201–22.

76. The law allowed a tax deduction of tax per cent of the lower-earning spouse up to a maximum of $3.000. Unfortunately, in the new tax reform legislation, the two earner deduction has been discontinued, the rationale given being that under the new tax system tax rates are not as progressive; and that therefore the marriage penalty is less severe.
77. It is widely acknowledged that the poverty problem in US has become increasingly a women's problem. In 1985, there were 33.1 million people living below the poverty line in the US, out of these 7.8 million were white children; 4.1 were black children; out of 16.4 million people, almost half were children and almost half they told households were headed by women (*Statistical Abstract*, 1986).
78. A retired couple collects benefits based upon a worker's payment into the system plus 50 per cent of the worker's benefits.
79. Given the fact that women earn significantly less than men, and that, historically, their labour force participation has not been continuous, it is often the case that a woman's own benefits are not significantly better, and sometimes even worse, than her dependent benefits. This means that a married woman paying into the system receives little, if anything, back for those payments.
80. G.G. Cain and H.W. Watts (eds.), *Income Maintenance and Labour Supply: Econometric Studies*, Chicago: Rand McNally, 1973. Also see, J.F. Cagan, Negative Income Taxation and Labour Supply: New Evidence for the New Jersey-Pennsylvania Experiment, Report R-2155–HEW, Santa Monica, California, Rand Corporation, 1978.
    - J.A. Pechman and P.M. Tipane (eds.). *Work Incentives and Income Guarantees: The New Jersey Negative Income Tax Experiment*, Washington, DC: Brookings Institution, 1975.
81. See R.D. Husby, "Day Care for Families on Public Assistance: Workplace versus Welfare", *Industrial and Labour Relations Review*, Vol. 27, No. 4, July, 1974.
82. The disintegration of traditional division of labour deprives women of their productive functions, thus retarding their growth. On the other hand, educational and training programs enhance the productive functions of women in the underdeveloped countries so that they can contribute more to economic development.
83. See Ester Boserup and Christina Liljenkratz, *Integration of Women in Development: Why, When, How*, New York: UN Development Programme, 1975.

    N.S. Chinchilla, "Industrialization, Monopoly, Capitalism and Women's Work in Guatemala", *Signs*, Vol. 3, No. 1, Autumn, 1977.

    Achola Pala, "Definition of Women and Development: An African Perspective", *Signs*, Vol. 3, No. 1, Autumn, 1977.

    Hanna Papanek, "Development Planning for Women", *Signs*, Vol. 3, No. 1, Autumn, 1977.

Irene Tinker, "The Adverse Impact of Development on Women", in Frene Tinber and M.B. Bramsen (eds.), *Women and World Development*, Overseas World Development Council, 1976.

N.H. Youssef, "Women and Work in Developing Societies", Population Monographs Series, No. 15, Berkeley: University of California, 1974.

84. See Marianne Ferber and Julie. A. Nelson (eds.), *Beyond Economic Man: Feminist Theory and Economics*, Chicago: Chicago University Press, 1993.

Nancy Folbre, *Who Pays for the Kids? Gender and the Structures of Constraint*, London and New York: Routledge, 1994.

Jean Gardiner, *Gender, Care and Economics*, Basingstoke: Macmillan, 1997.

Ulla Grrapard, "Feminist Economics: Let me Count the Ways", in Fred. E. Foldvary (ed.), *Beyond Neoclassical Economics: Heterodox Approaches to Economic Theory*, Cheltenham, Gloucestershire: Elgar, 1996.

J. Gillian Hewitson, *Feminist Economics: Interrogating the Masculinity of Rational Economic Man*, Cheltenham, Gloucestershire: Elgar, 1999.

Jane Humphries (ed.), *Gender and Economics*, Aldershot, Hampshire: Elgar, 1995.

Edith Kuiper and Jolande Sap (eds.), *Out of the Margin: Feminist Perspective on Economics*, London and New York: Routledge, 1995.

Frances. R. Woolley, op. cit., 1993.

85. Julie A. Nelson, *Feminism, Objectivity and Economics*, New York and London: Routledge, 1996.

86. Barbara Bergman, "Feminism in Economics", *Women Studies Quarterly*, Vol. XVIII, Nos. 3 and 4 (Fall/Winter 1990), p. 73.

7

Bridging the Public-Private Gap

Feminist Voices in Political Science

Throughout history, women have been marginalized in the study and practice of politics. Here, indeed, one sees many a deep-seated prejudice against women. Since at least the 5th century BCE, Western political thought has been finding it difficult to recognize woman as citizen or regard as one who is eligible for participation in public affairs. Moreover, women have never been treated as primary initiators or even as significant subjects of political discourse. Not only this, they have rarely been regarded as capable of commenting on political topics or as commanding a suitable perspective for political judgments or political activities.[1] Even after the Greek period and right up to the 19th century women have always been accorded an inferior status. While males are projected as 'productive', 'political', 'public' and 'rational', women have been portrayed as 'non-political', 'non-productive', 'private' and 'emotional'. Since traditional political science operates with the help of such rigidly opposed concepts, women have always remained at the outermost margins of this academic discipline. In Sapiro's words:

> Women do not appear in political life as much as men do, in part because they are not valued and encouraged in politics as much as men are; they do not 'fit' into politics as comfortably. Women and women's issues do not appear in political research and teaching as much as do men and the issue they consider important, in part because they are not valued as much as men are; they do not 'fit' into the concerns of political science as comfortably.[2]

It is indeed a patent irony that political space has always been occupied by men. Virtually, all offices entrusted with the responsibility of carrying out decisions that affect society as a whole have been male-dominated. Women have seldom exercised authority over groups containing men of equivalent age and social class. Anthropologists confirm the universality of this ugly truth in different kinds of societies. As Michelle Rosaldo puts it:

> Women may have ritual powers of considerable significance to themselves as well as men, but women never dominate in rites requiring the participation of the community as a whole .... I know of no case where men are required to serve as an obligatory *audience to female ritual* of political performance.[3]

Feminists scholars have given many reasons for this neglect of women in politics. The most important among them was the monopolization of jural/executive, military and other 'coercive' offices by males in almost all societies. If but indirectly, this has led to the exclusion of women from politics by denying them occasions for gaining status in public arena. Even women like Elizabeth and Deborah, Catherine and Cleopatra, Boadicea and Joan of Arc, whose contributions to politics are legendary, have been ignored in politics as an academic discipline. What is more, the very idea of women exercising power has always been viewed with fear and suspicion. The few scholars who were struck by the presence of women in power in the past have been concerned more about warning against the "monstrous regimen of women" – or about speculating in respect of the problems faced (say,) by a female prince in disposing her sexual favours without disturbing the equilibrium of the kingdom – than about providing a fair account of feminine rulership.[4] Nor have scholars in political theory ever taken pains to show how a woman's way of exercising authority differs from that of a man. Generally, they pay attention only to those arenas in which men are found in authoritative roles and utterly neglect those where women play a significant part, such as corporations, convents, harems, universities, families, nursery schools and even as prison officers. By restricting its focus narrowly to the formal business of the state and failing to take into account the exercise of women's authority in areas as listed above, the study of politics has systematically neglected those fields in which men have hardly made any impact at all.

Further, as the feminists have pointed out, traditional taboos play a significant part in keeping women out of public life. The common taboo associated with women is that femininity is essentially modest, and that "women should not speak". One common way of highlighting these taboos is by using the language of speaking and silence,[5] mainly because vocal eloquence has been acclaimed as essentially a male excellence right since the Greek period. Women, on the other hand, have always been credited with the capacity for quiet forbearance. This naturally puts them in a subordinate position because from Plato's creation of a "city in speech" in the *Republic,* through the power of the Hobbesian sovereign as the power of taming and controlling worlds, to Hannah Arendt's contemporary characterization of speech as the central activity in a fully human life, and Albert Hirsehman's metaphors of *exit, voice* and *loyalty,* vocal power has been a central force in human public life. Woman, we repeat, has been admired for abstention from eloquence. Thus, Aristotle quotes Sophocles approvingly: "A modest silence is a woman's crown."[6] It is indeed a general norm in different cultures not only that women should be silent, but also that they should not be regarded by men as important subjects of discussion. In olden days, if a woman ever became an object of male discourse, it was only because she had become a *public* woman in the sense ascribed to the word by Rousseau, that is, as a loose woman or a prostitute.[7] The great "Funeral Oration" of Pericles as reconstructed by Thucydides, crystallizes this demeaning attitude to women. At the very end, just before the benediction, Pericels remarks:

> ... if I must say anything on the subject of female excellence to those of you who will now be in widowhood, it will be all comprised in this brief exhortation: Great will be your glory in ... [being] least talked of among the men, whether for good or for bad.[8]

Here, for projecting the oddity of this attitude to women, it is essential to point out that there surely were quite a few Greek women who were fairly eloquent, of course, without getting public notice. One of the most prominent among them was Aspasia, Pericles' own mistress. All this makes it clear that one signal task that faces a feminist political theory is to highlight the value of the voices of "the silenced majority".[9]

Feminist Contributions

Luckily, by the early 1970s, various efforts were made by feminist scholars to restore women to their rightful place in politics. To this end they tried to reveal the rampant sexism in the classic texts of political philosophy. Further, they also attempted to fill in the gaps in such studies and correct the misconceptions that vitiated them by highlighting the need and value of the feminist perspectives in existing literature of political philosophy. More recently, they have tried to show how the inclusion of women's experience could fairly challenge the conventional understanding and paradigms in works on political science.

To speak quite generally, feminist scholarship on women in politics reflects three major trends: one that explores the presence of women as political actors;[10] second, that which addresses women as objects of policy;[11] and the third that examines women's relationship with the welfare state.[12] This entire triple effort calls for some extra comment by going into details.

It was not before the early 1970s that feminist voice began to be heard in the domain of political science, and it was revealed that, in its traditional form, the discipline was definitely sexist in nature. It was discovered that the concepts and categories used in the discipline were inadequate to map the experiences of women all over the globe. In Europe, the first feminist challenge came from Kirsten Amundsen's work, *The Silenced Majority* in 1971. The author here argued that if women were politically invisible, as indeed they were so far, it was essentially because of their economic dependence on men. She also uncovered the hidden but patently 'coercive patterns' of institutional sexism. Then, in 1974, Bourque and Grosshotlz isolated the sexist bias in empirical studies taken generally. They identified four ways in which female experience was understood and recorded wrongly: 'fudging in the footnotes', that is, generalizing without adequate documentation; glib 'assumption of male dominance' in every field of thought and action; undiscriminating promotion of a masculine ideal of political behaviour; and evocation of the ideal of the 'eternally feminine' or soft and subservient as the only suitable norm for women.

The first, that is, 'fudging in the footnotes' comprised "those statements of female political characteristics, attitudes or behaviour which were not substantiated [by any reliable evidence] in the manual cited or in the source".[13] The second distortion, that is, uncritical 'assumption of male dominance' prevented objective assessment of frequent bungling in political matters by male agents, as also of occasional, but striking female achievements in the same field of activity. As for the third distortion, it was clearly there in the unwarranted assumption that the masculine characteristics of aggressiveness and pragmatism are ideal equipment for the right kind of political behaviour. Altogether these three distortions made a very powerful check on women's entry into politics.[14] Nor was the cause of women in any way helped by the dogma of the eternally feminine that dogged empirical studies generally – a dogma which merely assumed that women's present weak political position is necessary and functional,[15] because it is only by limiting their active participation in politics that women can be given sufficient time for functions that are essential for preservation of the human race.

Such revelations of defects in the discipline of political science encouraged further work in the direction in subsequent years. In late 1974, three articles appeared simultaneously calling attention to this selfsame set of flaws,[16] to which we have already referred. Pursuing the trend, in the same year, two important books on women in politics were published.[17] Similar studies followed a little later.[18] To illustrate, in 1980, a journal, specifically titled as *Women and Politics,* appeared for the first time in the United States. It included some challenging essays by Susan Borque, Jean Grosshotlz, Jean Bethke Elshtain, Lynn Iglitzen, and Jane Jacquette.[19] They all contended that the delimitation of politics to issues of war and power alone was ruinous for mankind as a whole, and not merely an unwelcome preventive against women's entry into politics. Another political theorist, S. Welch[20] contested the widely accepted notion that women are suitable only for passive roles, as against active politics. After examining a vast amount of empirical data, Welch concluded "that the stereotype of the politically passive woman is simply untrue". Further, she contended that women have lower levels of participation in politics than men not because they are intrinsically unsuited to active, vigorous work but simply because they are not as likely as men to be found among groups who do participate in politics, namely, the employed and the highly educated.

The feminist challenge to the traditional manner of political science has indeed been various. Thus, in her essay "The Politics of Male-Female Relations: The Functions of Feminist Scholarship," Kay Boals argued for a shift in political theory from its obsessive concern with the concept of competition for power "toward conceptions that are oriented to shared values and interpersonal relationships". Developing her view, Boals maintains that feminist scholarship should perform the following three functions: "the expansion of empirical knowledge, the critique of existing theory, and the reconceptualization of core concepts."[21] Similarly, Andersen and Cook insist on a watchful and renewed empirical investigation of women's adult political socialization. The emphasis is warranted, for much of the conventional wisdom of political science assumes a connection between infantile political beliefs and their adult equivalents, but provides very little data in support of this interpretation.[22]

The male bias in politics was also challenged by Shabad and Andersen in their reflections on "Candidate Evaluations by Men and Women". Here, they attacked the widely accepted generalization that "women tend to personalize politics and politicians", or that they pay more attention to candidates' personal attributes than to their views on major political issues. Shabad and Andersen pleaded for a removal of this myth.[23] In a similar study, "Political Implications of Gender Roles: A Review of the Literature", Krauss emphasized that women's political behaviour was of a piece with their broader sex roles; that, therefore, there was nothing unnatural about women's entry into politics; that if their political behaviour was not so aggressive as that of men, it was simply because of their greater natural passivity. Krauss added that women would participate more actively in politics if their broader gender roles were expanded to include the male domain of politics.[24] In contrast to Krauss, many feminists have noted that the image of women as politically passive is as closely linked to a faulty understanding of politics as to a wrong view of actual female behaviour exhibited by women in politics.

Current feminist correctives to political science appear in the form of reasoned invitations to rethink the very definitions of politics and political behaviour. Recently, feminists have argued that, because of their very nature and life experience, women have different ways of conceptualizing political thought and exercising political power, and that therefore their entry into political life may well be expected to replace violence with tolerant and cooperative attitudes. Radical feminists in America and a large number of French writers are exploring those typical metaphors, which are vitiating the very language of political science with thoughts of male dominance and perpetuating a 'phallogocentric' image of our world. They also claim that a female-centred language and literature would give more prominence to the ideals of embracing, enfolding, blending and sheltering diverse cultures, faiths and attitudes in a richly unified political theory, and so promote the welfare of humanity.

Bias in Political Theory

So far, however, our discussion of feminist challenges to political science as it has so far prevailed has been rather diffuse. To make oneself understood, we may now put the matter in an organized form. Criticisms of the mainstream political theories have been, in the main, three-fold. The first one focuses on that discrimination against women which ignores their needs, aspirations, capacities, and value sense as a distinct sex; the second one seeks to expose the falsity of the rigid way in which the public is distinguished from, or even opposed to the, private; and the third one alleges that a male bias vitiates the very concept and dispensation of justice. The three protests are now given some individual attention in the following paragraphs:

Critique of Baised Gender Account of Sexual Differences

Feminist scholars have made it clear that the existing concepts and values of political theory are not gender-neutral but biased against women, and so of limited relevance. To illustrate, the concepts of liberty and equality simply leave out the significance of interdependence, both physical and emotional, say, between husband and wife, or between parents and children. Equality can be as much an attribute of mutual dependence as of individual rights. Are not the tiny tots and grandfathers in a family mutually dependent, and equally necessarily, for their everyday happiness? And, as Catherine Mackinnon[25] contends, is the mere accident of being born a female taken into account in framing and imposing 'sex equality laws'. Are women given an extra measure of physical security that they need and the requisite measure of minimal respect and dignity that they deserve as human beings, in spite of being physically weaker than men? Feminists are surely right in protesting that all sex equality laws are sex-blind because they ignore gender inequalities. Are not jobs and the related working conditions so structured that they suit only men who have no childcare responsibilities.[26] Unfortunately, discrimination on the basis of gender is evident in the very concept of citizenship. Here, woman finds herself hedged in the Wollstone-craft dilemma.[27] The two 'horns' of this dilemma are as follows: on the one hand, in virtue of being a citizen very much as men are, women feel entitled to press for equal rights with men. But this may be taken to mean that women must become (like) men. On the other hand, as some contemporary feminists rightly insist, women's distinctive attributes and capacities call for a different kind of concern. How can the two sides of this situation be reconciled? If, as Jane Flax rightly points out, "women must cease being feminine to be citizens, to speak of women's political emancipation would be an oxymoron since they would already be similar to, and not lower than men",[28] and so not in need of any emancipation. What is therefore needed is such a feminist reconstruction of political science that, instead of being regarded as simply a matter of rights, equality may be construed in a wider sense, that is, as equality of concern and consideration. This alone is the way to put women on an equal footing with men and yet also to provide for their distinctive, feminine needs.

Be that as it may, feminist theorists have shown how correct political constructions of what it means to be a man or a woman are central to the conception of a well-ordered polity. The emphasis is warranted by the unfortunate fact that women have always been thought to naturally lack the characteristics required for participation in political life; and, accordingly, citizenship has been conceived after the male image[29] of assertiveness, power-seeking and political machinations, and not on the model of quiet, selfless servicing that distinguishes women in their roles in the family. The unfortunate truth rather is that such an important phase in a woman's life as motherhood, which is so essential for the very continuance of humanity, has been taken as a kind of permanent barrier against taking to active politics, little realizing that motherhood is an automatic training in self-effacing service which political life so sorely needs. Feminist scholars like bell hooks and Jean Bethke Elshtain are surely justified in insisting that mothering is a strength rather than a weakness of women. Elshtain has argued that women as mothers should be the starting-point of any feminist political analysis, and that this alone can provide a new political ethic in place of the individual utilitarianism of liberal democracies. Her following words rightly fix the way feminist thinkers should challenge the attitude of established political theory to women:

> … to affirm the protection of fragile and vulnerable human existence as the basis of a mode of political discourse, and to create the terms for its flourishing as a worthy political activity; for women to stand firm against the cries of 'emotional' or 'sentimental' even as they refuse to lapse into a sentimental rendering of the values and language which flow from 'mothering' would signal a force of great reconstructive potential.

hooks voices a more or less similar view:

> Had black women voiced their [own] views on motherhood, it would not have been named a serious obstacle to our freedom as women.

And, Michelle Rosaldo thus insists on the wider significance of woman's diverse roles in the family:

> Woman's [real] place in human social life is not in any direct sense a product of the things she does (or even less, a function of what, biologically, she is) but the meaning her activities [of serving and caring] acquire [by serving as a model for] concrete social interactions.[30]

The fact that women mother in a variety of societies is not as significant as the value that is everywhere attached to this humane activity. The distinction between the natural act of mothering and the value that has to be attached to it is indeed an important one – one that needs to be stated and analysed contextually. Is not a woman's quiet efficiency as a wife vitally (if invisibly) related to man's overt effectiveness in public life and on the battlefield?

The trouble with political theory is that, as Jean Elshtain points out, it is a bit too occupied with the public world, and so utterly ignores what really sustains the basic unit of the social structure.[31] And, as Ruddick suggests, feminists would do well to insist on such a reshaping of the "theory of justice that it may incorporate maternal thinking",[32] say, by tempering the concept of punishment with that of loving and persuasive reform. What is really needed is a concerted effort to bring the feminine perspectives of nurturing into the public arena.[33] Politics, on the other hand (until very recent times), has always been shy of what is distinctively feminine. Her very femininity, so manifest and helpful in the private realm of family, has been used as an excuse to kept her out of the public domain of politics. Luckily, feminists today are revolting, with reason, against this absolute severance of the public from the private.

Critique of Public-Private Dichotomy

Political scientists have all along tended to regard the distinction between 'public' and 'private' spheres of life as an absolute one. The 'public' or formal/legal area of human life is normally associated with males, and the 'private' – family and domestic life – mainly with females. But this distinction, in spite of the obvious (spatial) opposition it involves – between 'outside' and 'inside' the home – is a mere abstraction from the intricate web of human life. The quality of a man's life in the family is directly related (as a means) to his ability to work in public, and it is impossible to determine the point where one could be separated from the other. Why should the political theorists forget that the public realm of politics is possible only because the messy content of the body, its very emergence and basic needs are taken care of elsewhere, that is, in the family? It is indeed proper that, as a protest against the general neglect of the private realm, some feminists have given explicit attention to it. Their main contention is that if 'the political' be regarded as a complex web of human interrelationships, the private realm of the family may well be regarded as eminently 'political' because the relationships are much more immediate than in the public realm. Working together for the goal of common welfare is (in principle) as much a feature of family life as of a settled state. There is no natural divide between the private and the public. It has only been assumed by political scientists, most of whom are male and therefore more or less indifferent to the field where women are an important, if silent, source of common welfare. Therefore, the discipline of political science must incorporate the range of concerns that relate to women. This is the cry of quite a few feminists today. They all alike hold the following basic views:

1. The public and private domains are integrally, if not directly related, even where a public figure's image camouflages what he really is at home.
2. The distinction between the public and the private is itself a political one, in so far as what it opposes is groups of people, not mere individuals.
3. Yet, in both spheres, human relations have to be nurtured; and so both may be said to be political. Neither a family nor a state is a mere aggregate of people.

In her article 'Feminist Critiques of Public/Private Dichotomy', Carole Pateman argues that abolition of the "dichotomy between the public and the private ... is, ultimately, what the feminist movement is all about". The neglect of the family has been generally present in political theory essentially because the public sphere has been taken as the opposite of the private one, and because equality has therefore been regarded as a relation between individuals who are essentially independent rather[34] than as equality of interdependence that distinguishes a family truly so called. What is worse, the glorification of the public sphere has gone hand in hand with the neglect – nay, even exploitation – of the private sphere. Unless the myth of the private as opposed to the public sphere is destroyed, public life would continue to be regarded as the exclusive work area of men. Pateman has aptly remarked:

> In popular (and academic) consciousness, the duality of male and female often serves to encapsulate or represent the series (or circle) of literal separations and oppositions, [say, between] female ... personal, emotional, love, private, intuition ... particular, subjection; and male ... political, reason, public, philosophy, achievement, universal freedom.[35]

Such a spurious opposition of the female as 'subject' and the male as essentially 'free' is wholly put to nought by some new researches on women's community activism which reveal that, both historically and in the contemporary period, women have been involved in resistance movements in close areas and communities against the conventional notion of women as passive members of polity, content with living their lives in the cloistered, non-political, 'private sphere of the home'.[36] Studies on women's participation have also made it clear that, as caretakers of communities and households, women have a special sensitivity to 'quality of life' issues, such as those that relate to uninterrupted water and power supply as against the policy of multiplying things which only dazzle the eye (say, flyovers and imposing, but expensive shopping complexes) that this not only justifies but necessitate their engagement in collective action; and that, as Cockburn points out, the factitious split between the public and the private disappears the moment we pay due attention to women's community activities. Poor and 'coloured' women are freely seen crossing the household boundaries in the very process of carrying out their domestic duties more efficiently than they could if they remained confined to their homes. They come out to negotiate with landlords, market leaders and such agents of the state as health care providers and welfare officers.[37] In view of all this, feminist political theory concludes that the 20th century politics requires a basic reconstruction of the so far quietly accepted and exaggerated distinction between the public and the private for the sake of saner political thinking.[38]

Critique of Theory of Justice

This is specially necessary because the liberal political theories in contemporary West have produced very partial concepts of reason, subjectivity and justice. Feminist psychoanalytic and postmodernist theories have questioned not only the definition of reason in essentially transcendental terms, but also the claim that liberation, stable meaning, insight, self-understanding and justice all depend essentially on the primacy of reason and intelligence. They assert that there are many other factors on which the development of subjectivity, self-understanding and justice depend. These 'other' factors may be listed as follows: the actual character of political practice; the absence of such kinds of domination as are based on racial or gender discrimination; empathy; feelings, or creative imagination.

Feminist criticisms of the traditional framework of justice have come from the development of what has been called, 'an ethic of care', as opposed to a thoroughly impersonal application of laws.

What goes by the name of 'an ethic of care' examines the moral issues, values and problems discernible in specific human relationships, especially as they obtain in the family and between friends, and, more importantly, as women look at, and are involved in them. To speak quite generally, the feminist criticisms that we have in mind look at justice not as something that has to be meted out to persons regarded as isolated individuals, but as it affects members of a network of human relationships. And, this widening of outlook only seems justified. If one man having many young dependants is awarded a death sentence for the murder he has admittedly committed, is it not virtually an act of condemning the whole family to death, say, by starvation? Such a mechanical dispensation of justice surely does not meet the demands of an adequate morality.[39]

However, advocates of 'an ethic of care' sometimes see the morality of rights and justice as inherently masculine and are not only neglectful of women's experience but actually hostile to the handling of moral problems as women interpret them. Carol Gilligan[40] argues that justice and rights have always structured male moral norms, values and virtues. She has contended that "a morality of rights and non-interference may appear frightening to women in its potential justification of indifference and unconcern". Surely, in the case of a murderer that we have visualized, if the highest authority of the state – say, its President – abstains from interfering in a mechanical application of law by refusing to grant, say, the wife's petition for mercy, it would be a patent case of indifference and unconcern for that 'to be widowed' wife who has not committed any crime. It is no wonder, therefore, that Neb Noddings emphasizes "the destructive role of rules and principles", where they are followed quite in isolation from 'the ethic of care'. As Carol Gilligan points out, an ethic of care proceeds by keeping the following distinctions in mind: the capacity to understand moral principles and their application to specific situations, for the absence of which young children cannot be punished; the proper way to apply a universal moral principle to a particular case – a wife just widowed cannot be accused of disturbing the peace of neighbourhood with her loud lamentations; and no one can be excused for only pressing for rights in the very midst of ignoring his (or her) responsibilities.

Towards a Feminist Political Science

Guided by such watchful thinking, the development of a feminist consciousness amongst academic women has transformed the traditional discipline of political science by questioning its earlier paradigms and paving the way for a woman-friendly and more visibly humane political science. As a result, male political theorists of today have been compelled to acknowledge the inadequacy of the following: a dominantly masculine view of rationality; excessive sharpness of the disjunction between reason and feeling; and equating the rational with the impersonal, justice with abstract impartiality, and equality with mechanical uniformity.

A feminist reconstruction of political science not only requires a proper understanding of differences between men and women but also between women themselves, say, between destitute widows and professionally qualified divorced women. Feminist theorists have argued that it is necessary to transform both political institutions and idioms of speech,[41] and to incorporate in our thinking new ways of relating thought with emotion, and reason with experience. A signal wisdom of contemporary feminist scholarship has been its exposition of the error of ignoring the importance of sheer bodily necessities to which ancient Greece was so clearly alive. The emphasis today rightly is on discovering ways to create cultural and political institutions that may sensibly live with, rather than flee from the contingencies of the body.[42]

A variety of different feminist discourses converge in addressing this set of concerns. Thus ecofeminists[43] question those ideologies of control that manifest themselves in attempts to control not only women but the earth itself, and they suggest alternatively the need for developing a better new understanding of the relationship between human communities and the environment in which they are located. Many feminists have questioned the ways in which the liberal political paradigms seem to necessarily include an acceptance of the need for domination and subordination. What is more, they suggest, alternatively, the value of building on cooperative networks and sustaining communities. Still others advocate a rethinking of our understandings of the state and of women's relationship to it so that we could develop political communities that nurture rather than dominate[44] or in which women can truly become full citizens.[45] And, there are still others who press for looking anew even at the feminist language of "the right to one's body," suggesting that, while it poses important challenges to men's undue power over women and clearly articulates the value of female subjectivity, it too is subject to the error of instrumental rationalism, say, as seen in the argument that a woman is free to use her body in any way.

Anyway, through all these various endeavours feminists have laid the foundations for a woman-friendly political science which would account for the differences among women, as also from men; relieve her of the suffocating public-private dichotomy; and develop a notion of justice based on an ethic of care.

However, all the challenges posed by feminists (we have so far discussed) to the various disciplines discussed, i.e., philosophy, history, sociology, psychology, economics and political science, only cover the Western perspectives, to the utter neglect of the third world realities. It is precisely this lacuna which the next chapter seeks to redeem.

Notes

1. Barbara J. Nelson, "Women and Knowledge in Political Science: Texts, Histories, and Epistemologies", *Women and Politics*, 9(2), 1989, p. 2.
2. V. Sapiro, *The Political Integration of Women*, Urbana: University of Illinois Press, 1983, p. 3. Italics added.
3. Michelle Rosaldo, "The Use and Abuse of Anthropology: Reflections on Feminism and Cross-Cultural Understandings", *Signs*, Vol. 3 (Spring 1980), p. 395. Italics added.
4. John Knox's First Blast of the Trumpet against the Monstrous Regiment of Women, and Jean Bodin's Speculations about the Sexual Favors of a Female Prince, are both discussed in Keohane's paper, "Female Citizenship", presented at the Annual Meeting of the Conference for the Study of Political Thought in April 1979.
5. Nanneri. O. Keshane, "Speaking from Silence: Women and the Science of Politics", in Elizabeth Langland and Walter Gove (eds.), *A Feminist Perspective in the Academy: The Difference it Makes*, Chicago: The University of Chicago Press, 1983, p. 91.
6. Aristotle, *Politics*, Book I (1260a).
7. See, for example, Emile, Book IV; in the Pleiade Edition of *Rosseau's Oeuvres Completes*, Paris: Gallimard, 1969, Vol. IV, p. 518.
8. The Peloponnesian War, II: 7, in the Modern Library Edition of *The Complete Writings of Thucydides*, New York: Random House, 1951, p. 109.
9. Kirsten Amundsen, *A New Look at Silenced Majority: Women and American Democracy*, New Jersey: Prentice Hall, 1977. Italics added.
10. Irene Diamond, *Sex Roles in the State House*, New Haven: Yale University Press, 1977.

    J.A. Flammang, *Political Women: Current Roles in State and Local Government*, Newburg Park: Sage, 1984.

    S. Carroll, *Women as Candidates in American Politics*, Bloomington: Indiana University Press, 1985.

    A. Miller, "Gender and the Vote: 1984", in C. Mueller (ed.), *The Politics of the Gender Gap*, Newbury Park, CA: Sage, 1987.

J.A. Mansbridge, "Myth and Reality: The ERA and the Gender Gap in the 1980 Election", *Public Opinion Quarterly*, 49(2), 1985, pp. 164–78.

E. Klein, *Gender Politics*, Cambridge, MA: Harvard University Press, 1984.

11. J.K. Boals, *The Politics of the Equal Rights Amendment*, New York: Longman, 1979.

    C.T. Adams and K.T. Winston, *Women at Work: Public Policy in the United States, Sweden and China*, New York: Longmans, 1980.

    J. Steilim, *Bring Me Men and Women*, Berkeley: University of California Press, 1981.

    Irene Diamond, *Families, Politics and Public Policies*, New York: Longmans, 1983.

12. Theda Skocpol, "Bringing the State Back In: Strategies of Analysis in Current Research", in P.B. Evans et al. (eds.), *Bringing the State Back In*, Cambridge: Cambridge University Press, 1985, pp. 3–37.

    Diana Pearce, "Women, Work and Welfare: The Feminization of Poverty", in K.W. Feinstein (ed.), *Working Women and Families*, Newbury Park, CA: Sage, 1979, pp. 103–24.

    Z. Eisenstein, *Feminism and Sexual Equality: Crisis in Liberal America*, New York: Monthly Review Press, 1984.

    K.E. Ferguson, *The Feminist Case against Bureaucracy*, Philadelphia: Temple University Press, 1984.

13. S.C. Bourque and J. Grossholtz, "Politics an Unnatural Practice: Political Science Looks at Female Participation", *Politics and Society* (Winter 1974), p. 229.
14. Ibid., p. 229.
15. Ibid. Italics added.
16. Mary L. Stanley and Victoria Schuck, "In Search of Political Women", *Social Science Quarterly*, LV: 3, December 1974, p. 642.

    Susan Bourque and Jean Grossholtz, "Politics an Unnatural Practice: Political Science Looks at Female Participation", *Politics and Society*, IV, (Winter 1974), pp. 225–65.

    Wilma Rule Krauss, "Political Implications of Gender Roles: A Review of Literature", *American Political Science Review*, LX VIII, December 1974, pp. 706–23.

17. Jane Jaquette (ed.), *Women in Politics*, New York: John Wiley; Jeane Kirpatrick, *Political Woman*, New York: Basic Books.
18. *American Politics Quarterly*, V: 3, July, 1977; *Journal of Politics*, XL1: 2, May, 1979; *Western Political Quarterly* and *American Political Science Review* and many others.
19. Jane S. Jacquette, "Political Science: Whose Common Good?" in Chris Kramarae and Dale Spender (eds.), *The Knowledge Explosion*, New York: Harvester, Wheatsheaf, 1998, p. 141.

20. S. Welch, "Women as Political Animals", *American Journal of Political Science*, 21, 1977, pp. 711–30.
21. See K. Boals, "The Politics of Male-Female Relations: The Functions of Feminist Scholarship", *Signs*, 1, 1975, pp. 161–74.
22. K. Andersen and E.A. Cook, "Women, Work and Political Attitude", *American Journal of Political Science*, 29, 1985, pp. 606–25.
23. See G. Shabad and K. Andersen, "Candidate Evaluations by Men and Women", *Public Opinion Quarterly*, 43, 1979, pp. 18–35.
24. W.R. Krauss, "Political Implications of Gender Roles: A Review of the Literature", *American Political Science Review*, 68, 1974, pp. 1706–23.
25. Catherine MacKinnon, *Feminism Unmodified: Discourses on Life and Law*, Cambridge: Harvard University Press, 1987, p. 23.
26. Ibid.
27. See Carole Pateman, "Equality, Difference, Subordination: The Politics of Motherhood and Women's Citizenship", in Gisela Bock and Susan James (eds.), *Beyond Equality and Difference*, London: Routledge, 1992, pp. 18–31.
28. Jane Flax, "Beyond Equality: Gender, Justice and Difference", in Gisela Bock and Susan James (eds.), *Beyond Equality and Difference*, London: Routledge, 1992, p. 195.
29. See Carole Pateman's *The Sexual Contract*, Cambridge: Polity Press, 1988.
30. M.A. Rosaldo, "The Case and Abuse of Anthropology: Reflections on Feminism and Cross-Cultural Understandings", *Signs*, 53, 1980, p. 400. Here, only the second bracketing is original.
31. Cited in M. Dietz, "Citizenship with a Feminist Face: The Problem with Maternal Thinking", *Political Theory*, 13(1), 1985, p. 23.
32. S. Ruddick, "Maternal Thinking", in *Feminist Studies*, Beacon Press, 1995, p. 226.
33. See S. Ruddick's essay "Maternal Thinking", in *Feminist Studies*, 6(2), Beacon Press, pp. 342–67.
34. See S. Evans, *Personal Politics: The Roots of Women's Liberation in the Civil Rights Movement and the New Left*, New York: Vintage Books, 1979.
35. Carole Pateman, *The Disorder of Women*, California: Stanford University Press, 1989, pp. 123–24.
36. See Ida Susser, *Norman Street: Poverty and Politics in an Urban Neighborhood*, New York: OUP, 1982. Also see Cynthia Cockburn, *The Local State*, London: Pluto Press, 1977.
37. Ibid.
38. See J. Elshtain, "Public Man, Private Woman: Women in Social and Political Thought", Princeton, New Jersey, Princeton University Press, 1981.
39. See A. Baier, *Moral Prejudices: Essays on Ethics*, Cambridge, MA: Harvard University Press, 1994.

40. Also see, Virguna Held, *Feminist Morality: Transforming Culture, Society, and Politics*, Chicago, IL: University of Chicago Press, 1993.
41. See K.E. Ferguson, *The Feminist Case against Bureaucracy*, Philadelphia: Temple University Press, 1984, p. 155.
42. See I. Diamond and L. Quinby, "American Feminism in the Age of the Body", *Signs*, 10(2), 1986, pp. 119–25.
43. Two well-known ecofeminists are Susan Griffin and Y. King.
44. See Jean Elshtain, "Reclaiming the Socialist Feminist Citizen", *Socialist Review*, 74, 1984, pp. 21–27.
45. See Carole Pateman, Feminism and Participatory Democracy: Some Reflections on Sexual Difference and Citizenship (unpublished manuscript), 1986.

8

Deconstructing Western Feminist Theory

Authorizing Third World Women's Voices

It should be clear by now that Western feminist discourse has done a good deal by way of pleading for women's welfare. Yet, in recent times, it has been contested by both third world scholars and some select scholars from the West. The third world scholars have argued that the Western understanding of notions such as 'culture', 'tradition' and 'national identity' is very faulty and needs to be radically amended. Their call for a transnational and global feminism presses for a thorough re-articulation of many of the settled conceptual categories and definitions, for the simple reason that a very distorted picture of 'third world traditions' has been presented by Western feminists simply because of writings like Daly's critique of just one obnoxious ritual of *sati*. Nor has the presentation been impartial. The forms of violence against the third world women, such as 'dowry murders', get represented as instances of 'death by culture', while analogous forms of violence in Western contexts, such as domestic brutality and murders, have been regarded as merely episodic. Unless a historically attentive and politically astute understanding of the 19th century colonial constructions of Western and third world cultures is secured, we cannot avoid acquiescing in a summary, undiscriminating picture of third world cultures. Luckily, there are quite few third world feminists too who are active, and whose concerns and analyses are rooted in and responsive to the problems women actually face and whose writings are not simple-minded emulations of Western feminist political works.

Third world feminism is surely not a mindless mimicking of 'Western agendas' in one clear and simple way.[1] Western culture, which projects itself as staunchly committed to values like equality and liberty – a commitment that was often upheld as its distinguishing feature and as a mark of its superiority – conveniently forgets the fact that it is Western powers only who have (in the past) been engaged in imposing slavery and resorting to colonization, and that they had resisted granting political and civil rights to a large number of Western subjects, including women. Anyway, as Rosy Braidotti insists:

> No discussion of the feminist international perspective is complete unless it rests on a lucid analysis of one's own national roots, of one's own inscription in the network of power and signification that make up one's culture .... Feminists cannot avoid confrontation with our national ties, our location within a specific national framework. Unless this kind of feminist analysis gets elaborated, women run the risk of waving the international flag as an empty rhetorical gesture, slipping into a fantasy world, ... a no (wo)man's land. Proposing an international perspective without critical scrutiny of our roles in our cultural, national contexts would be only a form of supernationalism, that is, ultimately, a form of planetary exile.[2]

However, it is not only the national ties and a specific national framework which have to be taken into account, but also the impact of increasing transnational economic forces which adversely affect the lives of many different groups of people scattered over a multiplicity of third world nations. It is therefore only proper for Inder Paul Grewal and Caren Kaplan to speak thus:

> We know that there is an imperative need to address the concerns of women around the world in the historicized particularly of their relationship to multiple patriarchies as well as to international economic hegemonies .... We need to articulate the relationship of gender to scattering hegemonies ... global economic structures, patriarchal nationalism, 'authentic' forms of tradition, local structures of domination, and legal-juridical oppression on multiple levels.[3]

Authorizing Voices of Third World Women

The dominant Western feminist discourse has always taken its own specific perspective as a norm to analyse women's issues universally. Such an approach has resulted in wrong portrayals of other cultures that differ from the Western one. So, the third world scholars plead for two strategies as discussed below for undoing the flaw:

(i) The Need to Contest Colonialist Representation of the Third World by both Western and Third World Scholars

Colonialist (mis-)representation of the third world has been done by both Western and third world scholars. As Rey Chow points out, orientalists are not only white but can also be new Westerners "who conform behaviourally in every respect with the elitism of their social origins ... [and] who nonetheless proclaim dedication to 'vindicating the subalterns'."[4] Similarly, Marnia Lazreg discovered that writings on Algeria by both Northerners and indigenous scholars generally reflected Northern stereotypes about Arab peoples and culture, particularly the primacy of Islam, which is seen as a self-contained and flawed belief system impervious to change. Such (mis-)representations pose an obstacle for feminists to form such communities of resistance as transcend boundaries of class, race, ethnicity and national background. Thus, Lazreg calls for a new approach – one that may challenge prevailing (Western) paradigms while also revealing third world women's lives "as meaningful, coherent and understandable, instead of being infused by us with doom and sorrow."[5]

(ii) Confronting the Anthropological Perspective

This approach, however, needs a supplement, that is, challenging the anthropological perspective of cultures. This way of looking rests on an analysis of cultures on the basis of outward modes of living such as dress and food habits, etc., and it is precisely this perspective which shapes most of the feminist approaches to the third world today. Now, in spite of its popularity, this way of looking at the matter has faced severe criticisms from third world scholars, mainly on two grounds:

(a) In speaking of culture in general, Western culture either totally excludes or marginalizes third world culture.

(b) It is unsympathetic to other cultures as it has always based its understanding of these cultures not on what they really are but only on their mere representations which have often been replete with unduly negative stereotypes and imputations of cultural inferiority.

As a reaction against such an attitude, Trinh T. Minh-ha has pointed out that such a view only fails to be sympathetic to cultural differences and so tends to prescribe a kind of apartheid policy of separate development which may be put thus: "keep your way of life and ethnic values *within the borders of your homelands.*"[6] Trinh also criticizes the white feminists. On the one hand, they prefer to adopt, condescendingly, a benevolent attitude by taking 'special care' to insist that third world women be represented in feminist writing.[7] On the other hand, they exhibit a strong tendency to visualize all women merely on the basis of the feminine figure and other merely external features, ignoring the unseen but essential differences of value-sense and cultural traditions.

Against this background, let us analyse how and in what different ways the third world scholars have challenged the basic assumptions of Western feminist thought. They have been most influenced by Edward Said's *Orientalism,* which was instrumental in showing how superficial and often biased perceptions of the orient became a means of controlling the regions and people so perceived. Orientalism is a Western style for dominating, intellectual restructuring, and having authority over the orient. Said's critique has been taken up by historians like Gyan Prakash who condemns Orientalism for, "first, its [assumed] authoritative status; second, its fabrication of the orient in terms of founding essences invulnerable to historical change and prior to their representation in knowledge; and third, its incestuous relationship with the Western exercise of power over what we call the third world."[8]

Third World Feminist Challenges to Western Feminist Discourse

Feminist thinkers from the third world therefore argue that if their women are to be liberated, they have to raise their voice against the following:

(a) essentialist construction of the third world woman;
(b) universalist assumptions of sexist oppression across different cultures; and
(c) binary constructions of modernity vs tradition.

Dismantling the Essentialist Construction of the Third World Woman

Western feminist scholars have, so to say, colonized the third world women by ignoring the material and historical heterogeneity of their lives and by glibly imposing on feminist writing the image of a singular, 'third world woman' – an image which is arbitrarily constructed, but which nevertheless carries with it the authorizing signature of Western feminist discourse which holds the field today. To quote Aihwa Ong:

> [Western] feminist voices in the social sciences unconsciously echo [the] masculinist will to power in its relation to non-western societies. Thus, for feminists looking overseas, the non-feminist other is not so much patriarchy as the non-western woman. Western feminists seek to establish *their* authority on the backs of non-western women, determining for them the meanings and goals of their lives.[9]

In the 1980s, some feminists began to criticize what they regarded as the ethnocentric assumptions of mainstream feminist theory and Western social science, which (they maintained) were inappropriate to the study of third world peoples.[10] To begin with, they attacked it for portraying the third world women as a homogenous, 'powerless', 'backward' group that could well be regarded simply as the victim of particular socio-economic systems. Since the dominant discourse today uses Western women as the parameter to judge in every case and utterly ignore the third world women, it fails to represent them as they are. As a result, in the various texts, third world women are defined as victims of male violence;[11] victims of the colonial process;[12] victims of the Islamic Code[13], that is, victims and nothing else. In the postcolonial discourse we discover three distorted images of Southern women. The first image is that of *Zenãnã,* whereby the 'veiled' third world women are looked upon as simply the mindless and merely physical members of a *harem,* preoccupied with petty domestic rivalries, rather than with artistic and political affairs of their times.[14] In this representation, the third world women are deemed as inferior to Western women just because they remain confined to the private sphere and do not play any part in public affairs. They are monolithically represented as oblivious to the 'real' world and as utterly dominated in their lives by male-dominated traditions.

The second image of the third world woman is that of a mere sex object. This image is found in Malek Alloula's exposure of the *Colonial Harem* (1986). Here, the women of South are portrayed as eroticised and unclothed and, therefore needed to be 'civilized' through their contact with the colonizers. It is noteworthy that whereas in the first image the women of South are criticized for being fully clothed, in the second they are berated for being half naked. In both cases, however, the third world women are represented as inferior to and subjugated by men and also as mere objects of sexual desire. G.C. Spivak says that in both images the third world women are "not allowed to speak" and are always shown, as "deeply in shadow".[15] I.C. Schick alleges that such a colonization is then justified as a 'mission civilisatrice' of the benign and paternalistic colonizer, instead of being acknowledged as a "subjugating and exploitative practice which it really is".[16]

In the third image women of the third world are portrayed simply as victims. The feminists who create and hold on to such images claim that they base their analyses on that widespread oppression of women which is due to their very gender. Proceeding in this general way, they homogenize the experiences and conditions of Western women, without caring for their individualing differences, and then apply this undiscriminating view to women all over the world. As a result, the varied lives and interests of women of South are not only misrepresented but given less value and attention. The multiple realities of third world women are either wholly ignored or trifled with.[17]

In all the three images distinguished above the implicit assumption is that all the third world women are traditional and non-liberated and need to be civilized and developed in the manner of Western women. In addition to this summary way of portraying the state of third world women, the very way of modernist discourse proceeds according to the typically Western dichotomy of modern and traditional, or liberated and non-liberated, suggesting that the third world can be emancipated only by dismantling its traditions totally, and by making it adopt the path of modern Western economic rationality.

The ethnocentric approach, which (we have seen) is clearly superficial, has been critiqued by various scholars. Their common complaint is that any theory of femininity, any definition of woman in general, any description that abstracts from the particular, historical, cultural, ethnic and class positions of particular women, verges perilously close to essentialism. This is, in fact, the main point in Toril Moi's critique of Irigray's notion of woman or the feminine:

> any attempt to formulate a general theory of femininity will be metaphysical. This is precisely Irigray's dilemma: having shown that so far femininity has been presented exclusively in relation to the logic of the same, she falls for the temptation to produce her own positive theory of femininity. But, as we have seen, to define 'woman' is necessarily to essentialize her.[18]

Gayatri Spivak speaks in a somewhat similar vein when she declares that concepts and theoretical principles should be used not as guidelines, rules, principles, or blueprints for struggle, but as tools and weapons of struggle:

> You pick up the universal that will give you the power to fight against the other side and what you are throwing away by doing that is your theoretical purity .... The great custodians of the anti-universal are obliged, therefore, simply to act in the interest of a great narrative, the narrative of exploitation, while they keep themselves clean by not committing themselves to anything ... [common and] by repudiating essentialism.[19]

In challenging the domination of patriarchal models, which rely on essentialism, naturalism, biologism or universalism – all such conceptual tools as are oblivious of differences and possibilities of change – feminists have pointed to the crucial role these assumptions play in making change difficult to conceive or undertake. To quote Spivak:

> I think it is absolutely on target to get a stand against the discourses of essentialism, universalism as it comes to terms with the universal of classical German philosophy or the universal as the white upper class male ... etc. But *strategically* we cannot. Even as we talk about *feminist* practice, or privileging practice over theory, we are universalizing. Since the moment of essentializing, universalizing, saying yes to the onto-phenomenological question, is irreducible, let us at the moment ... become vigilant about our own practice and use it as much as we can rather than make the totally counter-productive gesture of repudiating it.[20]

In other words, though in the act of theorizing we cannot wholly avoid the tendency to generalize – and so to ignore differences and changes – in actual practice we have to keep mindful of the pitfall.

Anyway, as Valerie Amos and Pratibha Parmar insist,

> feminist theories which examine our [that is, third world women's] cultural practices as 'feudal residues' or label us 'traditional', also portray us as politically immature women who need to be versed and schooled in the ethos of western Feminism ... [such theories] need to be continually challenged ...[21]

Luckily, there is some feminist writing which is self-critical. Thus, Adrienne Rich's work, *On Lies, Secrets and Silence: Selected Prose,* represents a milestone in the acknowledgment by the women's movement of its own racist blindspots.[22] It cautions that whereas academic white women are indeed capable of comprehending the intellectual theories of racism, they find it more difficult to acknowledge and to identify the material reality of racism, not only in the lives of others but, more particularly, in the fabric of their own lives. Women, Rich adds, have always been asked to identify themselves with male models, and to ignore their own specific oppression, as appears to have been the case in the black movement, at least until recently. While not wishing to indulge in the game of visualizing 'hierarchies of oppression', Rich does emphasize that white feminists need to explore these issues, particularly in their most insidious form, say, as of 'colour blindness' because of which the particularities of *non*-white women's experiences are not so much actively opposed as rendered completely invisible.

Universalist Assumptions of Oppression

A more general consequence of the Western feminist universalist approach is the assumption that wholly by itself, gender constitutes a superordinate category which can organize social relations across the most diverse cultures. The result is that, in any given piece of Western feminist analysis, women are characterized, pretty glibly, as a singular group on the basis of shared oppression. Here, when the talk turns to the third world, no attention is paid to historical and cultural specificity in matters of reproduction, sexual division of labour, family, marriage, household and patriarchy. Fran Hosken, for example, quietly equates *purdah* in Muslim societies with rape, forced prostitution and beating of girls. She thus confines herself to the sex-regulating function of *purdah* and completely ignores the historical and cultural determinants of this mode of dressing. Likewise, Mary Daly misrepresents the *sati prathã*. To turn to *purdah,* again, Mohanty provides some interesting information regarding the transformation of its meaning. During the 1979 revolution, we are told, the Iranian middle class women voluntarily veiled themselves to express their solidarity with their working class sisters. In present-day Iran, on the other hand, it is some mandatory laws that compel women to veil themselves.

It is precisely such distinctions that are either merely ignored or glossed over by many Western feminist writers; and in so far as they seek to impose their own (mis-)interpretation of third world women on feminist thought, these (third world) women have been dubbed as 'the last colony'.[23] This is also borne out by the evidence of practice. As Werlhof points out, the relationship of the third world subsistence workers of both genders to first world multinationals closely resembles the iniquitous relationship between men and women worldwide. Women, as mere colonies (so to say), are both low wage and non-wage producers; they share structural subordination and are overwhelmingly poor. Here, it is noteworthy that, for the third world women, gender represents a compounding factor of their oppression, just as race or ethnicity does for racial ethnic women living in first world countries. The concept of women as a last colony thus becomes a compelling metaphor of liberation and should be an integral part of any liberation struggle. Moreover, even if (for purposes of theory) one accepts a universal mode of oppression, our understanding of third world women's actual condition, everyday oppression will remain quite inadequate unless we make an extra effort to look at the situation as it really is. Mohanty is indeed right in arguing that the glib assumption of a selfsame universal oppression

> limits theoretical analysis as well as reinforces western cultural imperialism. For in the context of a first/third world balance of power, feminist analyses which perpetrate and sustain the hegemony of the idea of the superiority of the West, produce a corresponding set of universal images of the 'third world woman', images such as the veiled woman, the powerful mother, the Chaste Virgin, the obedient wife, etc. These images exist in universal, a-historical splendor, setting in motion a colonialist discourse which exercises a very specific power in defining, coding, and maintaining existing first/third world connections.

Indeed, the trouble is that even when notice is taken of what the non-Western woman says, it is wrenched out of the context of her society and presented in the idiom of Western feminist discourse. Further, howsoever admirable be their attitude in exposing the oppression of third world women, the ideal state that is visualized for these women by the Western feminist scholars is simply a likeness to women in the West. It is the state of these (Western) women which is taken as the norm; and so, if incidentally, all the third world women are regarded as inferior to Western women. Western standards and feelings all along take precedence over those of their third world subjects.

Deconstructing the Tradition-Modern Dichotomy

There is yet another questionable feature of the Western feminist discourse. It functions on the basis of an exaggerated distinction between tradition and modernity, and whereas the third world women are summarily regarded as merely traditional and non-liberated, modernity is equated with westernization, industrialization and the resulting superiority.[24] It is precisely in this context that Ester Boserup's pioneering work, *Women's Role in Economic Development*, which appeared in the 1970s, acquires a special significance. It rightly asserted that modernization had marginalized women and their contributions in the third world. Chandra Mohanty also questions the Western approach, quite sensibly, as follows:

> Is it possible to refer to the sexual division of labour [quite generally] when the content of this division changes radically from one environment to the next, from one historical juncture to another? At its most abstract level ... concepts such as the sexual division of labour can be useful only if they are generated through local, contextual analyses. If such concepts are assumed to be universally applicable, the resultant homogenization of class, race, religion, and daily material practices of women in the third world can create a false sense of the commonality of oppressions, interests, and struggles between and among women globally.[25]

Another feminist thinker, A. Ong, speaks more or less similarly:

> By using a traditional/modernity framework, these [western] feminists view the destruction of 'traditional customs' as either a decline of women's status in a romanticized 'natural' economy, or as their liberation by western economic rationality. This either/or argument reveals a kind of magical thinking about modernity which has proliferated in third world governments, while confusing and obscuring the social meanings of change for people caught up in it.[26]

In such a binary (tradition-modernity) analytic discourse the assumption all along is that women can be emancipated only through Western economic rationality. Mohanty therefore rightly argues that such theoretical excesses need to be continually challenged. The following note of protest, sounded by G. Sen and C. Crown, is noteworthy:

> Feminism cannot be *monolithic* in its issues, goals and strategies, since it constitutes the political expression of the concerns of women from *different* regions, classes, nationalities, and ethnic backgrounds. There is and must be a diversity of feminism, responsive to the different needs and concerns of different women, and defined by them for themselves.[27]

Such a protest, we may note, is surely quite warranted, for, as W.W. Rostow[28] has shown, most of the literature in developmental studies falls within the framework of the so-called modernization school. Each generation of scholars has reworked this model which opposes Western modernity to third world traditionalism. In the 1960s, Raphael Patai in *Women in the Changing World*, accounted for gender inequalities in terms of the degree to which age-old, custom-determining roles were being broken down by 'westernization' – a process which was seen to favour women's access to wage work and higher social status.[29] Happily, this position was challenged by Laura Bossen, who argued that westernization had caused women to lose highly variable roles in traditional economy. By placing structural limits on women's access to new production activities, the modernization process had reduced women's status in comparison to men's in the third world.

A recent revival of the modernization theory is seen in Linda Lim's paper[30] on the dilemma of the third world women workers in multinational factories. She maintains that in societies "where capitalist relations are least developed ... *traditional* patriarchy is sufficiently strong to maintain women in an *inferior* labor market position".[31] Building on this logic, she maintains that by providing these women with paid employment, transnational companies contribute to their emancipation. Moreover, patriarchal power is reconstituted in the factory setting, inducing the attitudes of both challenge and self-control on the part of women workers.[32] By using the tradition-modernity opposition, these feminists view the destruction of traditional customs as either a decline of women's status in a romanticized 'natural' economy, or as their liberation by Western economic rationality. This either/or argument reveals a kind of magical thinking about modernity which has proliferated in third world governments, while confusing and obscuring the social meanings of change for people caught up in it.

Basically, there have been two dominant points of view. One of these is that women have been marginalized in the course of development and that it is necessary to integrate them in the process. This may be called the 'women-in-development' (WID) school, which grew out of a critical reaction to the belief that growth would automatically trickle down to the lowest level of society, which did not actually happen. The other school of thought questioned the very nature of development and the structural context within which development takes place in which marginalization becomes an inevitable fact, and in which integration is not possible without altering the structural context that causes it. Studies carried out from the integrationist point of view are innumerable, and they are policy-oriented. They examine the effects of a policy on women and suggest ways whereby, within a specific context, the benefits of a policy could reach women more effectively.

Many others felt that such integration was neither possible nor fruitful. So they began to focus on the structure itself and its potential for integrated growth. The Dawn Report[33] provides one of the clearest examples of this approach. What it says may be noted bit by bit:

(a) "Existing economic and political structures which are highly unequal between nations, classes, genders and ethnic groups are often the historical legacy of colonial domination. Postcolonial development process and strategies have often exacerbated these inequities and in some instances even worsened the levels of absolute poverty. In the case of women it has been further reinforced by systems of male domination that on the one hand deny or limit their access to economic resources and political participation, and on the other hand, impose sexual divisions of labour that allocate to them the most onerous, labour intensive, poorly rewarded tasks inside the home, as well as the longest hours of work ..."

(b) "The almost uniform conclusion of the decade's research is that, with a few exceptions, women's relative access to economic resources, income and employment has worsened, their burden of work has increased and their relative and even absolute health, nutritional and educational status has declined. The causes for these have to be sought in the larger development process that effect women."

(c) "... the failure of growth to trickle down to the poor led, in the 1970s to a significant shift in the stated orientation of multilateral development strategies in favour of 'basic human needs' which stressed the importance in nutrition, health, water, sanitation, housing and education. The implications and the effects of commercialization in the context of structural inequality are questionable. The new anti-poverty programmes are striking for their singular silence on structural changes."

(d) "The problems of women are thus inextricably caught up in the overall development process that acknowledges and builds on women's responsibilities in producing goods and reproducing human beings, [and can yet] avoid the crises of reproduction ... afflicting a large majority of the poor in the third world."

In their critique of Ester Boserup, Lourdes Beneria and Gita Sen offer a 'capital accumulation' model to discuss the "specific ways in which women are affected by the hierarchical and exploitative structure of production associated with capitalism's penetration in the third world."[34] Capitalism is personified and differentiated in terms of its varied effects on 'domestic work', production and reproduction, population control and birth control. Women in Africa, Latin America and Asia are differentiated only in terms of their status as wives and workers in reproduction (i.e., the production of use values in the household) and production (of commodities). Beneia and Sen's claim to "a richly textured understanding" may well be accepted in respect of "tensions between gender and class"[35] but their representation of "women in the third world", taken generally, is hardly adequate.

It should be clear by now that by portraying women in non-Western societies as all of the same kind, and more exploited than women in the dominant capitalist societies, Western feminists encode a belief in their own cultural superiority. On the one hand, they operate on a set of Western standards to evaluate the degree of patriarchal oppression inflicted on women as wives, mothers and workers in the third world. On the other hand, they have a tendency to treat gender and sexuality as categories that are value-free and so measurable, and to ignore indigenous meanings which may relate them (gender and sexuality) inseparably to moral values.

Feminist approaches which purport to understand indigenous traditions and meanings that have persisted even during the course of modernization often appear to suggest that non-Western women are simply out of tune with the West,[36] and that even if they (third world women) may be said to be approaching modernity, they are still lagging behind western women who are already in tune with postmodernism. No thought is paid to the question if it is at all proper to expect third world to toe the line of the West.

Towards a Third World-Friendly Social Science

Luckily, quite a few scholars have questioned the propriety of such an expectation. Thus, see the following piece from C. Mohanty:

> ... Feminist analyses which perpetrate and sustain the hegemony of the idea of superiority of the western women produce a corresponding set of universal images of the third world women, images such as the veiled women, the powerful mother, the chaste virgin, the obedient wife etc. These images exist in a universal historical splendor, setting in motion a colonialist discourse which exercises a very specific power in defining, coding and maintaining [and vitiating] existing first/third world connections.[37]

Added point to such protests is provided by the following succinct remark of Homi Bhabha:

> [Colonial discourse is] an apparatus of power .... An apparatus that turns on the recognition and [yet] disavowal of racial/cultural/historical differences.[38]

What is implicit in the above remark is a protest against the application of the essentialist categories of modernism to third world women. However, a mere emphasis on anti-essentialism will not do. It may simply lead to the proliferation of the numerous religious taboos that plague the third world society. What is really needed is the creation of a bridge between essentialism and awareness of local, contextual differences. This alone can cater for the common interests of the third world women and also for the variety of interests that distinguish different sections of these women. The general and the particular are not necessarily opposed to each other. An excerpt from M. Nussbaum may be cited with advantage:

> [Even in the past] essentialism and particular perception were not opposed: they were complementary aspects of a single process of deliberation. Had the women not been seen as human beings who shared with other women a common humanity, the local women could not have told their story they did, nor could development workers have brought their own experiences of feminism into participatory dialogue as if they had some relevance for the local women. The very structure of the dialogue presupposed the recognition of common humanity, and it was only with this basis securely established that they could fruitfully explore the concrete circumstances in which they were trying, in the one case, to live, and in the other case, to promote flourishing lives.[39]

If we continue to theorize without putting due emphasis on essentialism and universalism, women's experiences in the third world will never be intelligible to Western feminists as women themselves. We will not be able to understand the dynamics of such resistance movements in widely removed parts of the world as *chipko movement* in the hills of India, the struggle of working women in Trinidad and Tobago against the economic policies of development, and the struggle of women of Caribbean countries against USAID etc. These are all cases of women fighting as one, in spite of their differences as individuals. It is only through deconstruction of the specific-general opposition that we can really construct a new paradigm whereby women of both North and South can be liberated in true sense of the term. Although feminists share a universal struggle against gender subordination and for egalitarian relations, the experiences of third world women, with their compounding layers of oppression, will continue to generate a wide variety of feminist movements. They represent articulated responses from women of all classes, races, ethnicities and nationalities, who, in the midst of their economic and social dilemmas, are carrying the struggle for liberation and equality forward on a variety of fronts, in their homes and families, against whole governments, and for international peace, human rights, and a healthy environment.

We may close this chapter by suggesting that, with a view to creating a social science that is duly friendly to third world women, the discipline has to be relieved of the deep-seated androcentric and Eurocentric paradigms, and the glibly essentialist thinking that have plagued it so far.

The concluding chapter that follows should make the point clearer.

Notes

1. Uma Narayan, *Dislocating Culture,* New York: Routledge, 1997, p. 13.
2. Rosy Braidotti, "The Exile, the Nomad and the Vagrant: Reflections on International Feminism", *Women's Studies International Forum,* 15(1), 1992, pp. 7–8.
3. Inderpal Grewal and Caren Kaplan, "Introduction: Transnational Feminist Practices and Questions of Postmodernity", in *Scattered Hegemonies,* Minneapolis: University of Minnesota Press, 1996, p. 17.
4. See Ray Chow, *Writing Diaspora,* Bloomington: Indiana University Press, 1993, p. 14.
5. M. Lazreg, "Feminism and Difference: The Perils of Writing as a Woman on Women in Algeria", *Feminist Studies,* 14(1), 1998, pp. 81–107.
6. Trinh T. Minh-ha, *Woman, Native, Other: Writing Post Coloniality and Feminism,* Bloomington: Indiana University Press, 1989, p. 80.
7. Ibid., pp. 100–4.
8. Gyan Prakash, "Writing Post Orientalist Histories of the Third World: Perspectives from Indian Historiography", *Comparative Studies in Society and History,* 32(2), 1990, p. 384.
9. See Aihwa Ong, "Colonialism and Modernity: Feminist Representations of Women in Non-western Societies", in Anne C. Herrmann and Abigail. J. Stewart (eds.), *Theorizing Feminism,* Oxford: Westview Press, 1994, pp. 372–81.
10. Michele Barrett and Mary Mcintosh, "Ethnocentrism and Socialist Feminist Theory", *Feminist Review,* No. 20, pp. 23–47.
11. Fran Hosken, "Female Genital Mutilation and Human Rights", *Feminist Issues,* 1(3), 1981.
12. Maria Rose Cutrufelli, *Women of Africa Roots of Oppression,* London: Zed Press, 1983.

    Also See; Juliette Minces, *The House of Obedience: Women in Arab Society,* London: Zed Press, 1980.

Beverly Lindsay (ed.), *Comparative Perspectives of Third World Women: The Impact of Race, Sex and Class*, New York: Praeger, 1983.

13. Patricia Jeffery, *Frogs in a Well: Indian Women in Purdah*, London: Zed Press, 1979.
14. C. Enloe, *Bananas, Beaches and Bases: Making Feminist Sense of International Politics*, Berkeley: University of California Press, 1991, p. 4.
15. G.C. Spivak, *In Other Worlds: Essays in Cultural Politics*, New York: Routledge, 1988, p. 287.
16. I.C. Schick, "Representing Middle Eastern Women: Feminism and Colonial Discourse", *Feminist Studies*, 16(2), 1990, p. 347.
17. A.M. Goetz, "Feminism and the Limits of the Claim to Know: Contradictions in the Feminist Approach to Women in Development", in R. Grant and K. Newland (eds.), *Gender and International Relations*, Bloomington: Indiana University Press, 1991, p. 143.
18. Toril Moi, *Sexual/Textual Politics: Feminist Literary Theory*, London: Methuen, 1985, p. 139.
19. G.C. Spivak, "Criticism, Feminism and the Institution", *Thesis Eleven*, 10/11, 1984, p. 184.
20. Ibid.
21. Valerie Amos and Pratibha Parmar, "Challenging Imperial Feminism", *Feminist Review*, 17, 1984, pp. 3–19.
22. Adrienne Rich, *On Lies, Secrets and Silence: Selected Prose, 1966–78*, New York: W.W. Norton, pp. 275–310.
23. See Maria Mies, Veronika Bennholdt Thomson, and Claudia Von Werlhof, *Women: The Last Colony*, London: Zed, 1988.
24. Geeta Chowdhry, "Engendering Development", in Marianne H. Marchand and Jane L. Parpart (eds.), *Feminism: Postmodernism Development*, London: Routledge, 1995.
25. Chandra Mohanty, "Cartographies of Struggle: Third World Women and the Politics of Feminism", in C. Mohanty, A. Russo and L. Torres (eds.), *Third World Women and the Politics of Feminism*, Bloomington: Indiana University Press, 1991, pp. 67–68.
26. A. Ong, "Colonialism and Modernity: Feminist Representations of Women in Non-Western Societies", *Inscriptions*, 3/4, 1988, p. 83.
27. G. Sen and C. Crown, *Development Crises and Alternative Visions: Third World Women's Perspectives*, New York: Monthly Review Press, 1987, pp. 18–19.
28. W.W. Rostow, *Stages of Economic Growth: A Non-Communist Manifesto*, New York: Free Press, 1960.
29. Raphael Patai, *Women in the Changing World*, New York: Free Press, 1967.
30. Linda Lim, "Capitalism, Imperialism and Patriarchy: The Dilemma of Third World Women Workers in Multinational Factories", in June Nash and Maria Patricia Fernandez Kelly (eds.), *Women, Men and International Division of Labor*, Albany: State University of New York Press, 1983.

31. Ibid., p. 79.
32. Aihwa Ong, *Spirits of Resistance and Capitalist Discipline: Factory Women in Malaysia*, New York: State University of New York, 1987.
33. Gita Sen and Caren Grown, *Development, Crises and Alternative Vision: Third World Women's Perspective*, Norway: A.S. Verbum, 1985.
34. Lourdes Beneria and Gita Sen, "Accumulation, Reproduction and Women's Role in Economic Development: Boserup Revisited", *Signs*, 7, 1981, pp. 279–98.
35. Ibid., p. 156.
36. See Johannes Fabian, *Time and the Other: How Anthropology Makes its Object*, New York: Columbia University Press, 1983.
37. C. Mohanty, A. Russo and L. Torres (eds.), op. cit., p. 73.
38. Homi Bhabha, "The Other Question: The Stereotype and Colonial Discourse", *Screen*, 24(6), 1983, p. 23.
39. M. Nussbaum, "Human Functionary and Social Justice: In Defense of Aristotelian Essentialism", *Political Theory*, 20(2), 1992, pp. 236–37.

9

Conclusion

As we now approach the end of this work, a little retrospection may be done by way of highlighting its key emphasis and gathering its diverse threads of enquiry.

One thing is patently clear. Throughout the course of history woman has been subject to many inequities not only in life, but in almost all those academic disciplines that relate to humanity. She has been kept largely quiet and subservient not only in family life, but also in social and cultural institutions, as well as trade and industry. Men alone have held the reins of power, defined official memory and controlled public archives. In the Greek period, woman was mostly regarded as inferior to man. She enjoyed little freedom outside the home. Aristotle treated her as mere matter waiting to be 'formed' by the active male principle. In Roman times, her position deteriorated further. Here, woman was treated as inferior to man at every level – be it personal, familial, national or international. The degradation continued even in the middle ages when it was fuelled by the curious Biblical thesis that woman is the root cause of the fall of humanity. Even Renaissance, which was a kind of break from medieval thought, reverted to the Graeco-Roman view that reason is supreme in the conduct of life, and that, therefore, the male is superior to the female because whereas the former is guided in his actions by reason, the latter is a creature of mere feeling and impulse.

Luckily, however, from the late 15th century onwards, some scholars started talking about the rights of the fair sex. In her magnum opus, *Vindication of Rights of Women* (1792), Mary Wollstonecraft was the first to contend that the liberal ideas of the Enlightenment could be applied to women as well. She argued that if properly performed, domestic duties were also a kind of political duties, and that therefore they should be regarded as conducive to public good rather than as merely a source of private satisfaction. In fact, what is called 'public' is merely an overall view of individual household. Many more thinkers, like John Stuart Mill, Harriet Taylor and Betty Friedan, followed the trailblazer and pleaded with both passion and reason for provision of equal opportunities and maximum autonomy for women.

This liberal trend, however, was not destined to continue quite as it began. The Marxists saw the salvation of women only in a classless society. Engels argued that the subordination of women began with the institution of private property, and that, with the advent of the capitalist mode of production, they lost a good deal of control even in the home being economically dependent on men. She became the slave of his lust and a mere instrument for the production of his children.

But this Marxian interpretation of women's lot was contested by some socialist feminists like Charlone Perkins Gilman who argued that human freedom will come not through class conflict and revolution but gradually by means of persuasive and peaceful methods. Emma Goldman contended that peace or harmony between the sexes and individuals does not necessarily depend on a superficial equalization of human beings, say, by giving them equal rights, and that a desirable state of co-existence can be attained only when woman comes to realize, through patient examination of her own being that its basic needs for love and amity can be met only through peaceable communion with fellow beings. Thus alone, we are told, the vacancy and estrangement of feminine life can be replaced with a feeling of blissful fulfilment.

However, though they cannot be dismissed as being quite in significant, the basic assumptions of all these three approaches – liberal, Marxist and socialist – were not accepted by the radical feminists. They argued that all the three positions, as discussed above, had not quite realized the ubiquity of male power, which held sway not only in the public worlds of economic and political activity, but even in the world of private relationships; and that the state, the family and the economic system are all alike vitiated by the presence of patriarchal structures that oppress women. The feminist challenge, however, did not end here. The third world feminist scholars have pushed it further. Their contention is that all these approaches reflect only the experiences of white middle class women and ignore or obscure the problems faced by black and third world women. Agreeing with this protest of third world scholars, the postmodernists have called for a recognition and celebration of differences. Any universal, simplistic definition of social phenomena, they assert, cannot but fail to reveal the complexity of life as lived experience.

This is clearly true. Yet, we repeat, all these approaches have made the feminist challenge prismatic, contributing richly to the emancipation of women in all walks of life. Attempts have been made in different disciplines of humanities and social sciences to incorporate women's point of view in the mainstream theories; and there is, today, an exciting awareness of the fact that feminist perspective has for long been missing in different areas of knowledge. Philosophy, for instance, has never focused on the family. It has all along identified culture with the ways of man, essentially because, as against woman, he alone is guided by reason. Further, until the emergence of phenomenology and existentialism, philosophy has tended to shut over the personal, the concrete and the specific. Feminists are therefore justified in pressing for the construction of a new methodology which could do justice to the value of the private, the emotional and the intimate. What they emphasize is a radical raise of collective and sympathetic awareness of woman's being, life and experience. How is it proper, they ask, to slight the value of emotions categorically? Is it not the sentiment of love that alone can hold us truly as one, as against the external commandments of religious heads or the state? And, whatever be the task that we undertake, is not a passionate commitment in every case necessary? So, there is a need to create a theory of knowledge which will give due value to emotions and sentiments, and insist on intimate experience too as the ground for verifying truths which are essentially subjective. A feminist epistemology may well be expected to provide for all this.

In this context, it is important to note a crucial contribution of feminist philosophers towards a proper understanding of the contents of human consciousness, that is, their emphasis on the concept of self as essentially relational, that is, the self as involved in and constituted by its connectedness with others. Intersubjectivity has been projected as basic, and individual subjectivity as merely secondary. As a consequence of this, the hierarchical models of dominance and subordination have appeared as deeply flawed. To speak quite generally, feminist philosophy insists that in the fabric of knowledge the subject and the object make an indivisible continuity. There is no case of actual awareness in respect of which we could clearly mark where exactly the subject's contribution ends and the object's own impact begins. Above all, feminist philosophy advises men to avoid being guided by the dehumanizing interpretations of masculinity, and pleads for eradication of patriarchal domination, deepening of mutual compassion, and overgrowing commitment to breakdown barriers that divide peoples and nations, and men from women.

Nor has the discipline of history been ignored by feminist challenges. They begin by heightening all that has vitiated history so far. Most of the events, institutions and documents of the past have been recorded and written by and, so to say, on behalf of men only. Great value was accorded to male activities and, in spite of their obvious value, the female activities of childbearing and child rearing were completely ignored. A female became a part of history only when she appeared to possess some male virtues. In other words, history was written primarily from the authoritarian, male point of view.

Even during the 1950s when, with the rise of social history, the experiences of the powerless and inarticulate began to be taken into account, it was only the powerless male whose presence was taken cognizance of. Similarly, in the sphere of labour history, gender was not considered as a category of historical analysis. Nor did the situation show any improvement with the dawn of Marxist history. This history sure professed to emphasize the need to begin by paying attention to the lowest level of society, but it yet failed to map the experiences of working class women. Even in the sphere of family history woman was given scanty attention. What is worse, unmarried and widowed women were almost utterly excluded from historical accounts of the institution of family, as if such women did not exist. Writing, here, concentrated only on the relationship of fathers and sons, and on property arrangements between them alone, completely ignoring the relationships of fathers with their daughters and of a mother with her children. Not only this, no notice was taken even of the vital contribution of daughters in supporting their brothers' education, and in providing every possible comfort to their aged parents. Nor was any notice taken of woman's role in preserving religious traditions. The very periodization of history was done by giving prominence to wars, conquests and revolutions which, it is obvious, are mainly male activities. It is all this that has prompted quite a few scholarly women to so reconstruct history that it could give due prominence to the life and work of women. This, in turn, pointed to the need to study personal diaries and autobiographies, as also to pay attention to oral traditions. There was no other way to do what the current history had been so indifferent about.

Every possible source of information had to be tapped, for not only the philosophers and historians, but even the great champions of social equality and protagonists of radical sociological theories had been indifferent to the life, needs and experiences of women. Surprisingly, even Marx and Engels did not say anything against the relevant division of labour between men and women. Max Weber, the father of modern sociology, considered the mother-child relation as just a natural, if important one, and regarded father as the one who had to civilize, so to say, this readymade kinship of raw nature. Emile Durkheim thought of ideal society as a neatly integrated functioning whole in which everyone had their place, with women playing their part only in the home. It is only in the writings of George Simmel that one sees a touch of sensitivity towards the female gender. However, it was mainly with the emergence of a few learned feminist scholars that the focus appeared to shift towards women, in respect of both social stratification and research.

Here, we may note one important reason because of which there has been so much of scholarly indifference towards women. An important distinction has for long been missed, namely, the difference between sex and gender. Sex is a physical fact; gender, on the other hand, is an intellectual construction. In respect of sex (as a bodily part) all women may be said to be similar, but the moment we speak of all women as being feminine in respect of gender, we run the risk of glibness regarding all women as similar, and are therefore tempted to attribute to them such common, essential qualities as modesty, subservience and gentility. It is precisely this difference which was built on by Margaret Mead in her writings, and so she very boldly questioned the naturalistic assumptions about sex differences. Her study of three New Guinea societies proved that gender is always a constructed category, not a natural one, and also that the fact of being feminine in gender does not make an inexorable limit to her capacity for growth and work in different areas. Another feminist scholar, Cynthia Fuchs Epstein, made it clear by her writings that women changed radically when they began pursuing a professional career, and that they changed even more noticeably if they were successful in their careers. Further, the traditional theories of political socialization were challenged on the ground that they attributed stereotyped motivations to women's behaviour, ignoring numberless women who got actively engaged in unbeaten tracks like that of politics. The stratification model has also been subjected to severe criticism for its male-centric biases and unequal treatment of women. Women's contribution to the sphere of economic well-being in the home, say by regulating expenses, by working on farms and even in offices has been totally ignored. However, quite a few bold feminists have challenged all this, and effectively tried to fight the many biases against women.

Nor have they hesitated to challenge the psychologists' bias against women. In both theory and practice, great scholars, including Sigmund Freud, have denigrated women and her qualities noticeably. Luckily, however, psychoanalysts like Karen Horney, Melanie Klein and Ernest Jones argued against the Freudian notions of masculinity and femininity. Horny argued that women's capacity to reproduce constituted an undeniable psychological superiority, say, in respect of suffering pain for the very continuance of mankind. Klein also attached great value to maternal functions. Simone de Beauvoir argued that the theory of psychoanalysis needed to be viewed in a historical and philosophical context, and that the intrinsic weakness of psychoanalytic theory was its male-centred character. She criticized Freud for setting up a masculine model of individual development, for equating human with man and for regarding woman as merely the 'other'. Some other scholars joined her in challenging such stereotyped conceptions of women's roles as simply 'feminine' (e.g., emotional and passive), as contrasted with the 'masculine' (e.g., rational and active) – conceptions which always implied that man was superior to woman. All these scholars projected the ugly truth that masculine traits have always received more positive evaluation than the feminine ones, and that the underrating of women's competence has all along resulted in biased evaluations and created artificial barriers to their achievement. It is indeed noteworthy that in contemporary psychological and psychoanalytical researches almost every prejudice against women has been duly uncovered, and that the great value of questions about the positive characteristics of women's psychology has been amply recognized. Today, female experience has become an important part of all psychological researches. Contemporary psychology has indeed contributed to the rise of a new approach to deal with the psychology of women.

To turn now to economics, we have already shown how women have all along been subject to such inequities as unequal treatment in the labour market and access to the means of production, inequitable work burdens and undervaluation of their subsistence production. It was only in 1989 in Athens that a meeting of women economists formulated some definite principles for an alternative method of economic analysis, which aimed at securing proper attention to the cause of women. They insisted that economic science had to extend its scope beyond the market and include unpaid household work, childcare, and 'emotional' labour, that is, taking pains to bring up children and in providing everyday comforts to husbands. Emphasis was also laid on the need to include the economic activity of women (in informal sector and in the family) in estimating national accounts. The meeting in question also resolved that proper research and policy steps had to be undertaken for a better understanding of, and improvement in, the following three areas: unpaid work in the household as a vital means to promoting human welfare, cultivation of renewable natural resources, and the extraction and processing of non-renewable resources. It was emphasized that such a widening of concern would make the science of economics more helpful not only to human welfare generally, but also to the interests of women in particular, which had been grossly neglected so far.

However, it is not only economics which has needed such changes in its ways of working. Politics too is in need of some basic improvements, for this discipline has been as averse towards the interests of women as any other. Here, indeed, women have never been treated as primary actors or even as subjects of political discourse. On the other hand, males have been projected all along as 'productive', 'political', 'public' and 'rational', as against women, who have been spoken of as 'non-political', 'non-productive', 'private' and 'emotional'. Women have seldom exercised authority over groups containing men of equivalent age and social class. Researches carried out by anthropologists have confirmed that such a derogatory attitude towards women has prevailed in widely different societies. Therefore, in the early 1970s, various efforts were made by feminist scholars to restore women to their rightful place in politics. As incidental to such efforts, great pains were taken to reveal the sexism prevalent in the classic texts of political philosophy, and in the empirical studies of political participation and citizenship. Further, the gender-neutral account of sexual discrimination, exaggerated emphasis on the public-private distinction, and theories of justice which only pleaded for equality of distribution and neglected equality of interdependence – all were subjected to a critical scrutiny. Protests were also made against the sharp disjunction often posited between reason and feeling. It is in these diverse ways that feminists have given a well-reasoned call for a women-friendly political science, which would account for differences not only between men and women, but among women themselves, relieve women of the ill-effects of the public-private dichotomy, and promote a notion of justice based on an ethic of care.

It is noteworthy that such a call has also come from some select Western feminist scholars, and that they all seem to echo similar sentiments. However, some third world scholars have opposed the monolithic tenor of the entire (Western) feminist discourse. They contend that discourse distorts the multiple realities of the third world women, and has ignored indigenous knowledge and local expertise. Moreover, it always operates on the basis of Western values and merely ignores the world views and values of the third world societies. Emphasis on various *vratas*, for instance, is common among Indian women, but, in the West, it is practically unknown, and so is the language relating to such abstinence. It is therefore only proper that scholars like Gayatri Spivak issue the following call for balancing theory with practice:

> I think it is absolutely on target to take a stand against the discourses of essentialism, universalism as it comes to terms with the universal – of classical German philosophy or the universal as the white upper class male ... etc. But *strategically* we cannot. Even as we talk about *feminist* practice, or privileging practice over *theory*, we are universalizing [because we here speak of *practice* and theory quite generally]. Since the moment of essentialising, universalizing, saying yes to the onto-phenomenological question, is irreducible, let us at least situate it at the moment; let us become vigilant about our own practice and use it as much as we can, rather than make the totally counter-productive gesture of repudiating it.

The greatest contribution of this third world perspective has been to emphasize that every analysis and interpretation must take cognizance of the particular, the historical, and the cultural context. As Rosy Braidotli contends, no discussion of the feminist perspective is complete unless it rests on a lucid analysis of women's own national and cultural roots. Unless this kind of feminist analysis is resorted to in a sustained way, women feminists will only be waving the international flag as an empty rhetorical gesture, slipping into a fantasy world and in a no women's land.

This is why, the third world scholars have contested the following in particular: colonial representations of the third world, merely anthropological views of culture, essentialist constructions of the third world, universalist concepts of oppression, and the overdrawn opposition of tradition and modernity. What they ultimately emphasize is the need to create a space not only for the white women, but also for the women belonging to minority class in the West on one hand, and women of the third world, on the other.

Here, however, a question may be put. Is there no meeting point between the first world and the third world feminism? Are terms and conditions of women's liberation entirely different in the context of these two worlds? A soul-searching exercise and candid analysis into the multilayered realities and complexities of both the worlds reveals that they have been alike insensitive to the female gender; that both have devalued women's contribution in all spheres of life; and that both have equally created a monolithic structure where women have little space to breath freely and to project their own identity. Yet, the nature of oppression, historical mutilation, and process of constructing knowledge systems have been very different in the two worlds. The basic assumptions of a predominantly liberal world view cannot be applied to the women of third world. Nor can the ideals of a free, independent individual can be beneficial to these women. Their happy survival depends on leading a collective and interdependent life at all levels, and this can be possible only when there is a consistent effort to remove all those aberrations which have posited women as a second class citizens.

The need of the hour is not to imitate the West or to adopt their world view, but to reclaim our own identity, first, as women, and then as women of the third world. Similarly, the fate of first world women does not lie in blindly imitating the path shown by liberal philosophy but in reasserting and reclaiming many of the rich Western traditions. They have already shown immense courage in overthrowing the androcentric and ethnocentric assumptions of social science disciplines and now they can well take a lead in creating a just and happy social order for themselves.

References

Books

Acker, S. and D.W. Piper (eds.), *Is Higher Education Fair to Women?* Guildford: SRHE and NFER-Nelson, 1984.

Ackerly, Brooke A., *Political Theory and Feminist Social Criticism*, Cambridge: Cambridge University Press, 2000.

Agrawal, C.M. (ed.), *Dimensions of Indian Womanhood*, 3 Volumes, Almora, Shri Almora Book Depot, 1993.

Alcoff, Linda and Elizabeth Potter (eds.), *Feminist Epistemologies*, London: Routledge, 1993.

Alexander, M. Jacqui and Chandra Talpade Mohanty (eds.), *Feminist Genealogies, Colonial Legacies, Democratic Futures*, London: Routledge, 1997.

Amico, Eleanor B. (ed.), *Reader's Guide to Women's Studies*, Chicago and London: Fitzroy Dearborn Publishers, 1998.

Arneil, Barbara, *Politics and Feminism*, Oxford: Blackwell Publishers, 1999.

Bader, Clarisse, *Women in Ancient India*, Delhi: Anmol Publications, 1986.

Battersby, Christine, *The Phenomenal Woman: Feminist Metaphysics and the Patterns of Identity*, New York: Routledge, 1998.

Beasley, Chris, *What is Feminism? An Introduction to Feminist Theory*, London: Sage, 1999.

Beddoe, Dierdre, *Discovering Women's History*, London and New York: Longman, 1998.

Benhabib, Seyla and D. Cornell (eds.), *Feminism as Critique*, Oxford: Polity Press, 1987.

Bergmann, Barbara, *The Economic Emergence of Women*, New York: Basic Books, 1986.

Bhasin, Kamla and N.S. Khan, *Some Questions on Feminism and Its Relevance in South Asia*, New Delhi: Kali for Women, 1986.

Bock, Gisela and Susan James (eds.), *Beyond Equality and Difference*, London: Routledge, 1992.

Bologh, Roslyn W., *Love or Greatness: Max Weber and Masculine Thinking: A Feminist Inquiry*, London: Unwin Hyman, 1990.

Bowles, Gloria and Renate Klein (eds.), *Theories of Women's Studies*, London: Routledge, 1983.

Braidotti, Rosi, Ewa Charkiewicz, Sabine Hausler and Saskia Wieringa, *Women, the Environment and Sustainable Development: Towards a Theoretical Synthesis*, UK: (Zed Books in association with INSTRAW) first published, 1994.

Bryson, Valerie, *Feminist Political Theory: An Introduction*, London: MacMillan Press, 1994.

——, *Feminist Debates*, London: MacMillan, 1999.

Buchan, Marog, *Women in Plato's Political Theory*, New York: Routledge, 1999.

Burman, Erica (ed.), *Feminists and Psychological Practice*, Delhi: Sage Publications, 1982.

Butler, Judith, *Bodies That Matter*, New York: Routledge, 1993.

——, *Gender Trouble*, New York: Routledge, 1990.

Caine, Barbara, E.A. Grosz and Marie De Lepervanche (eds.), *Crossing Boundaries: Feminism and the Critique of Knowledges*, Sydney: Allen and Unwin, 1988.

Campbell, Kate (ed.), *Critical Feminism: Argument in the Disciplines*, Buckingham: Open University Press, 1992.

Cantor, Dorothy W., *Women as Therapists*, London: Jason Aronson Inc., 1990.

Carroll, Berenice A. (ed.), *Liberating Women's History: Theoretical and Critical Essays*, Urbana: University of Illinois Press, 1976.

Charlton, Sue Ellen M., *Women in Third World Development*, Boulder and London: Westview Press, 1984.

Chodorow, Nancy, *Feminism and Psychoanalytic Theory*, Cambridge: Polity Press, 1989.

——, *The Reproduction of Mothering: Psychoanalysis and the Sociology of Gender*, Berkeley: University of California Press, 1978.

Clough, Patricia Ticineto, *Feminist Thought*, Oxford: Blackwell, 1994.

Cole, Eve Browning, *Philosophy and Feminist Criticism: An Introduction*, New York: Paragon House, 1992.

Collins, Patricia Hill, *Black Feminist Thought*, London: Unwin Hyman, 1990.

Coole, Diana H., *Women in Political Theory*, Sussex: Wheatsheaf Books, 1988.

Curthoys, Jean, *Feminist Amnesia: The Wake of Women's Liberation*, London and New York: Routledge, 1997.

de Beauvoir, Simone, *The Second Sex*, trans. H.M. Parshley, Harmondsworth: Penguin, 1972.

Demos, Vasilikie and Marcia Texler Segal (eds.), *An International Feminist Challenge to Theory*, London: JAI, 2001 (Five Volumes).

Dinnerstein, Dorothy, *The Mermaid and the Minotaur*, New York: Harper and Row, 1976.

Durkheim, Emile, *The Division of Labor in Society*, New York: Free Press, 1964.

Elshtain, Jean Bethke, *Public Man, Private Woman: Women in Social and Political Thought*, Princeton: Princeton University Press, 1981.

Evans, Judith and Others, *Feminism and Political Theory*, London: Sage Publications, 1986.

Flax, Jane, *Disputed Subjects: Essays on Psychoanalysis, Politics and Philosophy*, London: Routledge, 1993.

Frazer, Elizabeth, Jennifer Hornsby and Sabina Lovibond, *Ethics: A Feminist Reader*, Oxford: Blackwell Publishers, 1994.

Freedman, Jane, *Feminism*, Buckingham: Open University Press, 2001.

Fricker, Miranda and Jennifer Hornsby (eds.), *The Cambridge Companion to Feminism in Philosophy*, Cambridge: Cambridge University Press, 2000.

Gandhi, Nandita and Nandita Shah, *The Issues at Stake: Theory and Practice in the Contemporary Women's Movement in India*, New Delhi: Kali for Women, 1991.

Gatens, Moira, *Feminism and Philosophy: Perspectives on Difference and Equality*, Cambridge: Polity Press, 1991.

Gilligan, Carol, *In a Different Voice*, Cambridge, Massachusetts: Harvard University Press, 1982.

Gould, Carol C. (ed.), *Gender: Key Concepts in Critical Theory*, New Jersey: Humanities Press, 1997.

Grant, Judith, *Fundamental Feminism*, London: Routledge, 1993.

Gunew, Sneja (ed.), *Feminist Knowledge: Critique and Construct*, London: Routledge, 1990.

Harding, Sandra and M.B. Hintikka (eds.), *Discovering Reality: Feminist Perspectives on Epistemology, Metaphysics, Methodology and Philosophy of Science*, Dordrecht: Reidel, 1983.

Hartsock, Nancy, *The Feminist Standpoint Revisited and Other Essays*, Colorado: Westview Press, 1998.

Heller, Frank (ed.), *The Use and Abuse of Social Science*, New Delhi: Sage Publications, 1986.

Hess, Beth B. and M.M. Ferree (eds.), *Analyzing Gender: A Handbook of Social Science Research*, New Delhi: Sage Publications, 1987.

Holland, Nancy J., *Is Women's Philosophy Possible?*, USA: Rowman and Littlefield Publishers, 1990.

hooks, bell, *Ain't I a Woman*, London: Pluto Press, 1982.

——, *Feminist Theory: From Margin to Center*, Boston: South End Press, 1984.

Humm, Maggie, *The Dictionary of Feminist Theory*, New York: Harvester Wheatsheaf, 1989.

Jackson, Stevi and Jackie Jones (eds.), *Contemporary Feminist Theories*, Edinburgh: Edinburgh University Press, 1998.

Jackson, Stevi, Deirdre Beddoe et al. (eds.), *Women's Studies: A Reader*, London and New York: Harvester Wheatsheaf, 1993.

Jacobsen, Joyce P., *The Economics of Gender*, UK: Blackwell Publishers, 1994.

Jaggar, Alison M. and Iris Marion Young (eds.), *A Companion to Feminist Philosophy*, Oxford: Blackwell Publishers, 1998.

Jaggar, Alison, *Feminist Politics and Human Nature*, New Jersey: Rowman and Allanheld Publishers, 1983.

Janapathy, Varalakshmi, *Indian Women through the Ages*, New Delhi: Gyan Publishing House, 2002.

John, Mary E., *Discrepant Dislocations: Feminism, Theory and Post Colonial Histories*, New Delhi: Oxford University Press, 1996.

Kabeer, Naila, *Reversed Realities: Gender Hierarchies in Development Thought*, New Delhi: Kali for Women, 1995.

Kelkar, Meena, *Subordination of Women*, New Delhi: Discovery Publishing House, 1995.

Kemp, Sandra and Judith Squires (eds.), *Feminisms*, New York: Oxford University Press, 1997.

Kramarae, Cheris and Dale Spender (eds.), *The Knowledge Explosion*, New York: Harvester Wheatsheaf, 1992.

Krishnaraj, Maithreyi (ed.), *Women's Studies in India: Some Perspectives*, Bombay: Popular Prakshan, 1986.

Krishnaraj, Maithreyi and Joy Deshmukh, *Gender in Economics: Theory and Practice*, Delhi: Ajanta Press, 1993.

Kuiper, Edith and Jolande Sap (eds.), *Out of the Margin: Feminist Perspectives on Economics*, London: Routledge, 1995.

Kumar, Nita (ed.), *Women as Subjects: South Asian Histories*, Delhi: Stree, 1994.

Kuper, Adam and Jessica Kuper (eds.), *The Social Science Encyclopedia*, London, Boston and Henley: Routledge and Kegan Paul, 1985.

Langland, E. and W. Gove (eds.), *A Feminist Perspective in the Academy: The Difference it Makes*, Chicago: The University of Chicago Press, 1983.

Laslett, Barbara et al. (eds.), *History and Theory: Feminist Research, Debates, Contestations*, Chicago: University of Chicago Press, 1997.

Ledger, Sally, Josephine McDonagh and Jane Spencer (eds.), *Political Gender*, London: Harvester Wheatsheaf, 1994.

Lerner, Gerda, *The Creation of Patriarchy*, Oxford and New York: Oxford University Press, 1986.

——, *The Majority Finds its Past: Placing Women in History*, New York: Oxford University Press, 1979.

——, *Teaching Women's History,* Washington: American Historical Association, 1981.

Lindsey, Linda L. and Sandra Christy, *Gender Roles: A Sociological Perspective,* New Jersey: Upper Saddle River, 1997.

MacKinnon, Catharine A., *Feminism Unmodified: Discourses on Life and Law,* London: Harvard University Press, 1987.

——, *Toward a Feminist Theory of the State,* London: Harvard University Press, 1989.

Marx, Karl, *Capital,* Harmondsworth: Penguin, 1976.

Mead, Margaret, *Sex and Temperament in Three Primitive Societies,* London: Routledge, 1935.

Michie, Jonathan, *Encyclopedia of Social Sciences,* London: Fitzroy Dearborn Publishers, 2001.

Mies, Maria, *Indian Women and Patriarchy,* New Delhi: Vikas, 1980.

Mill, J.S., *The Subjection of Women,* London: Virago, 1969.

Millett, Kate, *Sexual Politics,* London: Virago, 1985.

Minh-ha, Trinh T., *Woman, Native, Other: Writing Postcoloniality and Feminism,* Bloomington: Indiana University Press, 1989.

Mitchell, Juliet, *Women: The Longest Revolution,* London: Virago, 1984.

Mohanty, Chandra et al. (eds.), *Third World Women and the Politics of Feminism,* Bloomington: Indiana University Press, 1991.

Moraga, C. and G. Anzaldua (eds.), *This Bridge Called My Back: Writings by Radical Women of Color,* New York: Women of Color Press, 1983.

Nelson, Barbara and Najma Chowdhury (eds.), *Women and Politics Worldwide,* Delhi: Oxford University Press, 1997.

Nelson, C. and L. Grossberg (eds.), *Marxism and Interpretation of Culture,* Urbana: University of Illinois Press, 1988.

Nielsen, Joyce McCarl (ed.), *Feminist Research Methods: Exemplary Readings in the Social Sciences,* Boulder: Westview Press, 1990.

Oakley, Ann, *Experiments in Knowing: Gender and Method in the Social Sciences,* UK: Polity Press, 2000.

Offen, Karen, Ruth Roach Pierson and Jane Rendall (eds.), *Writing Women's History,* London: MacMillan, 1991.

Okin, Susan Moller and Jane Mansbridge (eds.), *Feminism,* Vols. 1 and 2, England: Edward Elgar, 1994.

Okin, Susan Moller, *Women in Western Political Thought,* London: Virago, 1980.

Padia, Chandrakala (ed.), *Feminism, Tradition and Modernity,* Shimla: Indian Institute of Advanced Study, 2002.

Paludi, Michele and Gertrude A. Steuernagel (eds.), *Foundations for a Feminist Restructuring of the Academic Disciplines,* New York: London, 1990.

Pandit, S.K., *Women in Society*, Delhi: Rajat Publications, 1998.

Parsons, Talcott, *Societies: Evolutionary and Comparative Perspectives*, New Jersey: Prentice-Hall, 1966.

Pateman, Carole and E. Gross (eds.), *Feminist Challenges: Social and Political Theory*, Boston: Northeastern University Press, 1987.

Pateman, Carole, *The Sexual Contract*, Cambridge: Polity Press, 1988.

——, *The Disorder of Women: Democracy, Feminism and Political Theory*, Cambridge: Cambridge University Press, 1989.

Phadnis, Urmila and Indira Malani (eds.), *Women of the World: Illusion and Reality*, New Delhi: Vikas Publishing House, 1978.

Purvis, June, *Hard Lessons*, UK: Polity Press, 1989.

Raj, Sebasti L., *Quest for Gender Justice: A Critique of the Status of Women in India*, Madras: T.R. Publications, 1991.

Ray, Bharati and Aparna Basu (eds.), *From Independence towards Freedom*, Delhi: Oxford University Press, 1999.

Ray, Rajat Kanta, *Exploring Emotional History: Gender, Mentality and Literature in the Indian Awakening*, New Delhi: Oxford University Press, 2001.

Riencourt, Amaury De, *Woman and Power in History*, New Delhi: Sterling Publishing House, 1989.

Robinson, Victoria and Diane Richardson (eds.), *Introducing Women's Studies*, London: MacMillan, 1997.

Rowbotham, Sheila, *Hidden from History*, London: Pluto Press, 1974.

Roy, Kumkum (ed.), *Women in Early Indian Societies*, New Delhi: Manohar Publishers, 1999.

Sangari, Kumkum and Sudesh Vaid (eds.), *Recasting Women: Essays in Indian Colonial History*, New Delhi: Kali for Women, 1989.

Sayers, Janet, *Biological Politics: Feminist and Anti-Feminist Perspectives*, London and New York: Tavistock Publications, 1982.

——, *Sexual Contradictions: Psychology, Psychoanalysis and Feminism*, London: Tavistock Publications, 1985.

Schneir, Miriam (ed.), *Feminism: The Essential Historical Writings*, New York: Random House, 1972.

Scott, J.W., *Feminism and History*, Oxford: Oxford University Press, 1996.

Segal, Lynne, *Is the Future Female? Troubled Thoughts on Contemporary Feminism*, London: Virago, 1987.

Sen, Illina (ed.), A *Space Within the Struggle: Women's Participation in People's Movements*, Delhi: Kali for Women, 1990.

Sherman, Julie and Evelyn T. Beck (eds.), *The Prism of Sex: Essays in the Sociology of Knowledge*, Madison: University of Wisconsin Press, 1979.

Shoemaker, Robert and Mary Vincent (eds.), *Gender and History in Western Europe*, London: Arnold, 1998.

Singh, Shanta Serbjeet and Jyoti Sabharwal (eds.), *The Fiftieth Milestone: A Feminine Critique*, New Delhi: Sterling Publishers, 1998.

Smith, Bonnie G., *The Gender of History: Men, Women and Historical Practice*, London: Harvard University Press, 1998.

Spender, Dale, *Men's Studies Modified*, London: Pergamon Press, 1981.

Spivak, Gayatri C., *In Other Worlds: Essays in Cultural Politics*, New York: Routledge, 1988.

Squire, Corrine, *Significant Differences: Feminism in Psychology*, London and New York: Routledge, 1989.

Squires, Judith, *Gender in Political Theory*, UK: Polity Press, 1999.

Stanford, Michael, *A Companion to the Study of History*, Oxford: Blackwell Publishers, 1994.

Stanley, Liz (ed.), *Feminist Praxis: Research, Theory and Epistemology in Feminist Sociology*, London: Routledge, 1990.

——, *Knowing Feminisms: On Academic Borders, Territories and Tribes*, London: Sage Publications, 1997.

Stearns, Peter N., *Gender in World History*, London: Routledge, 2000.

Stewart, Abigail J. and Anne E. Herrmann (eds.), *Theorizing Feminism: Parallel Trends in the Humanities and Social Sciences*, Boulder: Westview Press, 1994.

Suryaumari, A. (ed.), *Women's Studies: An Emerging Discipline*, New Delhi: Gyan Publishing House, 1993.

Sutherland, Sally J. (ed.), *Bridging Worlds*, Delhi: Oxford University Press, 1992.

Tanesini, Alessandra, *An Introduction to Feminist Epistemologies*, UK: Blackwell Publishers, 1999.

Wallace, Ruth A. (ed.), *Feminism and Sociological Theory*, Newbury Park: Sage Publications, 1989.

Wallace, Ruth A. and Alison Wolf, *Contemporary Sociological Theory*, Woodcliff: Prentice-Hall, 1980.

Wallerstein, Immanuel et al., *Open the Social Sciences: Report of the Gulbenkian Commission on the Restructuring of the Social Sciences*, New Delhi: Vistaar Publications, 1997.

Waring, Marilyn J., *If Women Counted*, San Francisco: Harper and Row, 1989.

Zalk, Sue Rosenberg and Janice Gordon-Kelter, *Revolutions in Knowledge: Feminism in the Social Sciences*, Boulder: Westview Press, 1992.

Articles

Agnihotri, Indu, "Re-reading Histories", *Seminar*, No. 505, September, 2001, pp. 16–25.

——, "Women and Historical Studies", *Samya Shakti*, Vol. 1, No. 1, July, 1983, pp. 63–67.

Agnihotri, S.B., "Missing Females: A Disaggregated Analysis", *Economic and Political Weekly*, Vol. 30, No. 33, August 19, 1995, pp. 2074–84.

Beechey, Veronica, "On Patriarchy", *Feminist Review*, No. 3, 1979, pp. 66–82.

Benston, Margaret, "The Political Economy of Women's Liberation", *Monthly Review*, Vol. 21, September, 1969, pp. 13–27.

Bergmann, Barbara, "Feminism and Economics", *Women's Studies Quarterly*, Vol. XVIII, Nos. 3 and 4, Fall/Winter 1990, pp. 68–74.

Chafetz, Janet Saltzman, "Feminist Theory and Sociology", *Annual Review of Sociology*, Vol. 23, No. 120, 1997, pp. 97–120.

Chanda, Geetanjali Singh and Norman G. Owen, "Tainted Goods? Western Feminism and the Asian Experience", *Asian Journal of Women's Studies*, Vol. 7, No. 4, 2001, pp. 90–105.

Coulson, Margaret, Branka Magas and Hilary Wainwright, "The Housewife and her Labour under Capitalism: A Critique", *New Left Review*, No. 89, January-February, 1975, pp. 59–71.

Deshpande, Satish, "The Crisis in Sociology: A Tired Discipline?", *Economic and Political Weekly*, Vol. 29, No. 10, March 5, 1994, pp. 575–76.

Dewan, Ritu, "Gender in Neoclassical Economics: Conceptual Overview", Vol. 30, No. 17, April 29, 1995, pp. WS46–WS48.

Doeuff, Michele Le, "Harsh Times", *New Left Review*, No. 199, May-June, 1993, pp. 127–42.

Epstein, Barbara, "What Happened to the Women's Movement?", *Signs*, Vol. 12, No. 4, 1987, pp. 1–13.

Faulkner, C., "The Feminist Challenge to Economics", *Frontiers*, Vol. 8, 1986, pp. 55–61.

Flax, Jane, "Post Modernism and Gender Relations in Feminist Theory", *Signs*, Vol. 12, No. 4, Summer 1987, pp. 621–43.

Fox-Genovese, Elizabeth, "Placing Women's History in History", *New Left Review*, No. 133, May/June, 1982, pp. 5–29.

Gardiner, Judith, "Self Psychology as Feminist Theory", *Signs*, Vol. 12, No. 4, Summer 1987, pp. 761–80.

Gupta, Dipankar, "Feminification of Theory", *Economic and Political Weekly*, March 25, 1995, pp. 617–20.

Haider, Saraswati, "Once More to Feminification of Theory", *Economic and Political Weekly*, Vol. 30, No. 36, September 9, 1995, pp. 2272–76.

Harding, Sandra, "The Instability of the Analytical Categories of Feminist Theory", *Signs*, Vol. 11, No. 4, Summer 1986, pp. 645–64.

Hartmann, H. et al., "Bringing Together Feminist Theory and Practice: A Collective Interview", *Signs*, Vol. 21, No. 4, 1996, pp. 917–51.

Hartsock, Nancy, "Comment on Hekman's "Truth and Method: Feminist Standpoint Theory Revisited: Truth or Justice?", *Signs*, Vol. 22, No. 2, Winter 1997, pp. 367–74.

Hawkesworth, Mary E., "Knowers, Knowing, Known: Feminist Theory and Claims of Truth", *Signs*, Vol. 14, No. 3, Spring 1989, pp. 533–57.

——, "Confounding Gender", *Signs*, Vol. 22, No. 3, Spring 1997, pp. 649–85.

Heinen, Jacqueline, "Kollontai and the History of Women's Oppression", *New Left Review,* No. 110, July-August, 1978, pp. 43–63.

Hekman, Susan, "Truth and Method: Feminist Standpoint Theory Revisited", *Signs,* Vol. 22, No. 2, Winter 1997, pp. 341–65.

Henley, Nancy M., "Psychology and Gender", *Signs,* Vol. 11, No. 1, Autumn 1985, pp. 101–19.

Herbold, Sarah, "Well-Placed Reflections: (Post)modern Woman as Symptom of (Post)modern Man", *Signs,* Vol. 21, No. 1, Autumn 1995, pp. 83–115.

Hirschmann, Nancy J., "Toward a Feminist Theory of Freedom", *Political Theory,* Vol. 24, No. 1, February, 1996, pp. 46–67.

Huilgol, Glynn, "Manu and Mother-Right: Social Transformation in Antiquity", *Journal of South Asian Studies,* Vol. 4, No. 1, June, 1981, pp. 22–34.

Jackson, Cecile, "Radical Environment Myths: A Gender Perspective", *New Left Review,* No. 210, 1995, pp. 124–40.

Jenson, Jane, "Different but not Exceptional: The Feminism of Permeable Fordism", *New Left Review,* No. 184, November-December, 1990, pp. 58–68.

John, Mary E., "The Encounter of Sociology and Women's Studies: Questions from the Borders", *Contributions to Indian Sociology,* Vol. 35, No. 2, June, 2001, pp. 237–58.

Kachuk, Beatrice, "Feminist Social Theories: Themes and Variations", *Sociological Bulletin,* Vol. 44, No. 2, September, 1995, pp. 169–93.

Kaluzynska, Eva, "Wiping the Floor with Theory: A Survey of Writings on Housework", *Feminist Review,* Vol. 6, No. 2, 2000, pp. 1–21.

Kelly-Gadol, Joan, "The Social Relation of The Sexes: Methodological Implications of Women's History", *Signs,* Vol. 1, No. 4, Summer 1976, pp. 809–24.

Kishwar, Madhu, "Why I do not call myself a Feminist", *Manushi,* No. 61, November-December, 1990, pp. 2–8.

Krishnaraj, Maithreyi, "How Gender Figures in Economic Theorising and Philosophy", *Economic and Political Weekly,* Vol. 36, No. 17, April, 2001, pp. 1425–34.

——, "Androgyny: An Alternative to Gender Polarity?", *Economic and Political Weekly,* Vol. 31, No. 16/17, April 20–27, 1996, pp. WS9–WS14.

Lama-Rewal, Stephanie Tawa, "Fluctuating, Ambivalent Legitimacy of Gender as a Political Category", *Economic and Political Weekly,* Vol. 36, No. 17, April 28, 2001, pp. 1435–40.

Lokaneeta, Jineeta, "Alexandra Kollontai and Marxist Feminism", *Economic and Political Weekly,* Vol. 36, No. 17, April 28, 2001, pp. 1405–12.

Loomba, Ania, "The Indian Women's Movement", *Women,* Vol. 1, April, 1990, pp. 29–34.

Lovibond, Sabina, "Feminism and Postmodernism", *New Left Review*, No. 178, November-December, 1989, pp. 5–28.

——, "Feminism and the Crisis of Rationality", *New Left Review*, No. 207, September-October, 1994, pp. 72–86.

——, "Meaning What We Say: Feminist Ethics and the Critique of Humanism", *New Left Review*, No. 220, November-December, 1996, pp. 98–115.

MacKinnon, Catharine, "Feminism, Marxism, Method, and the State: An Agenda for Theory", *Signs*, Vol. 7, No. 3, 1982, pp. 515–44.

Martin, Jane Roland, "Methodological Essentialism, False Difference, and Other Dangerous Traps", *Signs*, Vol. 19, No. 3, Spring 1994, pp. 630–57.

Minault, Gail, "Women and History: Some Theoretical Considerations", *Samya Shakti*, Vol. 1, No. 1, July, 1983, pp. 59–62.

Moghadam, Valentine, "Women in Societies", *International Social Science Journal*, No. 139, February, 1994, pp. 95–115.

Mohanram, Radhika, "Indian Feminism in an International Frame", *Indian Journal of Gender Studies*, Vol. 3, No. 2, September, 1996, pp. 283–300.

Moss, P. and Martha McMahon, "Between a Flake and a Strident Bitch", *Resources for Feminist Research*, Vol. 28, Nos. 1–2, Spring/Summer 2000, pp. 15–32.

Natarajan, Kanchana, "Gendering of Early Indian Philosophy: A Study of Samkhyakarika", *Economic and Political Weekly*, Vol. 36, No. 17, April 28, 2001, pp. 1398–1404.

Niranjana, Seemathini, "Off the Body: Further Considerations on Women, Sexuality and Agency", *Indian Journal of Gender Studies*, Vol. 6, No. 1, 1999, pp. 1–19.

O' Brien, Mary, "Feminist Theory and Dialectical Logic", *Signs*, Vol. 7, No. 1, Autumn 1981, pp. 144–57.

——, "Feminist Theory and Dialectical Logic", *Signs*, Vol. 7, No. 1, 1981, pp. 144–57.

Okin, Susan Moller, "Feminism and Multiculturalism: Some Tensions", *Ethics*, Vol. 108, No. 4, July, 1998, pp. 661–84.

Padia, Chandrakala, "Authorising Women's Voices: A Study in Modernity and Postmodernity", in Abha Avasthi and A.K. Srivastava (eds.), *Modernity, Feminism and Women Empowerment*, Jaipur and New Delhi: Rawat Publications, 2001, pp. 25–32.

——, "Demystifying Gender: A Step to Social Equity", in Niroj Sinha (ed.), *Women in Indian Politics*, New Delhi: Gyan Publishing House, 2000, pp. 29–40.

——, "Environment, Gender and Development", in *Kashi, Ganga and the Environment*, Varanasi: Ganga Seva Nidhi, 2002, pp. 53–56.

——, "Feminism, Tradition and Modernity: An Essay in Relation to Manusmrti", in R.C. Tewari (ed.), *Towards Metanoia*, Lucknow: Coomaraswamy Centre, 2002, pp. 193–200.

——, "Gandhi on Women and Liberty", *Gandhi Marg,* Vol. 22, No. 3, 2000, pp. 291–99.

——, "Indigenizing Women's Studies: Focus on Indian Classical Texts", in Malashri Lal and Sukrita Paul Kumar (eds.), *Women's Studies in India: Contours of Change,* Shimla: Indian Institute of Advanced Study, 2002, pp. 91–103.

——, "Mapping the Terrain of Feminist Philosophy in the West", *West Bengal Political Science Review,* Vol. IV, Nos. 1 and 2, 2001, pp. 95–104.

——, "Plato, Aristotle, Rousseau and Hegel on Women: A Critique", *The Indian Journal of Political Science,* Vol. 55, No. 1, 1994, pp. 27–35.

——, "Social Justice: A Conceptual Journey from Plato to Rawls", *Gandhian Perspectives,* Vol. XI, Nos. 1 and 2, 1998, pp. 1–10.

——, "Thinking with and Beyond Human Rights", *Madhya Pradesh Journal of Social Sciences,* Vol. 3, No. 1, 1998, pp. 77–98.

——, "Woman in the Democratization Process: A Conceptual Analysis", in Jag Mohan Singh Verma (ed.), *Gender Justice in India,* Rohtak: Spellbound Publications, 1999, pp. 103–16.

Palriwala, Rajni, "Economics and Patriliny: Consumption and Authority within the Household", *Social Scientist,* Vol. 21, No. 9/11, September-October, 1993, pp. 47–73.

Patel, Vibhuti, "Women's Liberation in India", *New Left Review,* No. 153, September-October, 1985, pp. 75–86.

Phillips, Anne, "From Inequality to Difference: A Severe Case of Displacement", *New Left Review,* No. 224, July-August, 1997, pp. 143–53.

Pinterics, Natasha, "Riding the Feminist Waves: In with the Thirds", *Canadian Woman Studies,* Vol. 20/21, No. 4/1, pp. 15–21.

Rege, Sharmila, "Feminist Pedagogy and Sociology for Emancipation in India", *Sociological Bulletin,* Vol. 44, No. 2, September, 1995, pp. 223–39.

——, "Institutional Alliance between Sociology and Gender Studies", *Economic and Political Weekly,* Vol. 32, No. 32, August 9, 1997, pp. 2023–27.

——, "Sociology and Challenge of Gender Studies", *Economic and Political Weekly,* May 7, 1994, pp. 1155–56.

Ross, Ellen, "New Thoughts on 'The Oldest Vacation': Mothers and Motherhood in Recent Feminist Scholarship", *Signs,* Vol. 20, No. 2, Winter 1995, pp. 397–13.

Rowntree, Mickey and John Rowntree, "More on Political Economy of Women's Liberation", *Monthly Review,* Vol. 21, January, 1970, pp. 26–32.

Roy, Anupama, "Community, Women Citizens and a Women's Politics", *Economic and Political Weekly,* April 28, 2001, pp. 1441–47.

Sabbarwal, Sherry, "The Changing Face of Feminism: Dilemmas of the Feminist Academic", *Sociological Bulletin,* Vol. 49, No. 2, September, 2000, pp. 267–80.

Sangari, Kumkum, "Gender Lines: Personal Laws, Uniform Laws, Conversion", *Social Scientist*, Vol. 27, No. 5/6, May-June, 1999, pp. 17–61.

Sawhill, I.V., "Economic Perspectives on the Family", *Daedalus*, Vol. 106, No. 2, Spring 1977, pp. 115–25.

Schick, I.C., "Representing Middle Eastern Women: Feminism and Colonial Discourse", *Feminist Studies*, Vol. 16, No. 2, 1990, pp. 345–80.

Segal, Lynne, "Only Contradictions on Offer", *Women: A Cultural Review*, Vol. 11, Nos. 1–2, April 2000, pp. 19–36.

Srivastava, S.P., "Feminist Theory: An Overview", *Social Welfare*, Vol. 47, No. 9, December, 2000, pp. 10–14.

Turksma, Riet, "Feminist Classic Philosophers and the Other Women", *Economic and Political Weekly*, Vol. 36, No. 17, April 28, 2001, pp. 1413–24.

Walker, Henry A. and Mary L. Fennell, "Gender Differences in Role Differentiation and Organizational Task Performance", *Annual Review of Sociology*, Vol. 12, 1986, pp. 255–75.

Wolley, Frances, "Degrees of Connection: A Critique of Rawls' Theory of Mutual Disinterest", *Feminist Economics*, Vol. 6, No. 2, 2000, pp. 1–21.

——, "Towards a Feminist Economics of Welfare", *Atlantis*, Vol. 23, No. 2, Spring/Summer 1999, pp. 112–23.

Zerilli, Linda M.G., "Doing without Knowing: Feminism's Politics of the Ordinary", *Political Theory*, Vol. 26, No. 4, August, 1998, pp. 435–58.

Index